AF352641

EPISTOLARY ACTS

Anglo-Saxon Letters and Early English Media

Epistolary Acts

*Anglo-Saxon Letters
and Early English Media*

JORDAN ZWECK

UNIVERSITY OF TORONTO PRESS
Toronto Buffalo London

ISBN 978-1-4875-0100-6

Printed on acid-free, 100% post-consumer recycled paper
with vegetable-based inks.

Library and Archives Canada Cataloguing in Publication

Zweck, Jordan, 1981–, author
Epistolary acts : Anglo-Saxon letters and early English media / Jordan Zweck.

(Toronto Anglo-Saxon series)
Includes bibliographical references and index.
ISBN 978-1-4875-0100-6 (cloth)

1. English literature – Old English, ca. 450–1100 – History and criticism.
2. Letter writing – England – History – Medieval, 500–1500.   3. Letters
in literature.   I. Title.   II. Series: Toronto Anglo-Saxon series

PR275.L47Z84 2018   820.9'353   C2017-903714-5

University of Toronto Press acknowledges the financial assistance to its
publishing program of the Canada Council for the Arts and the Ontario Arts
Council, an agency of the Government of Ontario.

For Colin

Contents

Acknowledgments

It is a great pleasure to acknowledge the many colleagues and friends who helped see this project to completion. Roberta Frank has been an invaluable mentor, whose patience and energetic good humour are matched only by her wit. She has always trusted me to find my way, even when I did not trust myself. Many other faculty and graduate students at Yale University and the community of the Anglo-Saxon Studies Colloquium enriched my life in more ways than I can express. I also could not have asked for more generous and supportive colleagues at the University of Wisconsin–Madison. Lisa H. Cooper and Martin K. Foys offered vital commentary on the book as it developed, and provided sage advice at key moments. I am forever grateful for their unflagging enthusiasm for the project and their keen editorial eyes. The project received crucial support from UW–Madison's Center for the Humanities, which allowed an earlier draft to be read by Sara Guyer, Thomas Dale, Kirsten Wolf, Patricia Rosenmeyer, Tom DuBois, Martin Camargo, and Lisa and Martin. The book is also much richer thanks to the support of the Institute for Research in the Humanities and the feedback of Susan Stanford Friedman and the IRH fellows. I have had several wonderful chairs in the English department at Madison: Theresa Kelley, Caroline Levine, and Russ Castronovo provided skilful guidance.

Many colleagues at UW–Madison and elsewhere have also read chapters or portions of chapters; they include Jessica Brantley, Alistair Minnis, Traugott Lawler, Ian Cornelius, Stephanie Elsky, Christa Olson, Aida Levy-Hussen, Ramzi Fawaz, Joshua Calhoun, Mark Vareschi, Kate Vieira, and Nirvana Tanoukhi. Jonathan Senchyne, Brigitte Fielder, Ellen Samuels, Elizabeth Bearden, Danielle Evans, Timothy Yu, and Ari Friedlander also provided much-needed good cheer and advice. The camaraderie of Irina

Dumitrescu, Denis Ferhatović, and Mary Kate Hurley has sustained me throughout this project; they were willing sounding boards for ideas both serious and silly, and their kindness can never be repaid.

I was fortunate to share earlier stages of this work with members of the Medieval Writing Workshop in Madison, WI and Boulder, CO; the medieval studies communities at UW–Madison and Yale University; and at many conferences. Jill Hamilton Clements and Jonathan Wilcox kindly shared with me works in progress. I must also thank the librarians at the British Library, Lambeth Palace Library, the Parker Library, Durham University Library, and the Beinecke Library for allowing me access to important manuscripts. Olivia Ernst has been an excellent proofreader at a late stage in the process. Thanks also to the members of Beowulf Club and the students in all my courses for inspiring me to think more deeply about letters and media. Suzanne Rancourt believed in this book; she and the anonymous readers at University of Toronto Press have strengthened this project immensely. Barbara Tessman and Barb Porter gracefully shepherded the book through its final stages at the press, and R. Scott Garner provided an excellent index. Support for this research was provided by the University of Wisconsin–Madison Office of the Vice Chancellor for Research and Graduate Education with funding from the Wisconsin Alumni Research Foundation.

My father, uncle, and grandmother were all employed by the United States Postal Service; when my brother took a temporary job with the USPS, we joked that he had fulfilled our generation's obligation to work in the family business. It was nevertheless with some surprise that I found myself following in the family footsteps with this study of medieval letters. Throughout, Jon, Pauline, and Justin Zweck offered unwavering support. Thanks also to everyone at the Madison Circus Space and Cycropia Aerial Dance who kept me grounded while giving me the courage to fly. Finally, thank you to Colin Gillis, without whom none of this would be possible. Thank you for making every day a celebration.

Abbreviations

ASE　　　Anglo-Saxon England
BHL　　　Bibliotheca Hagiographica Latina
BL　　　British Library
BT　　　Bosworth, *An Anglo-Saxon Dictionary*, ed. and rev. Toller
CCCC　　Cambridge, Corpus Christi College
CH I　　*Ælfric's Catholic Homilies: The First Series*, ed. Clemoes
CH II　　*Ælfric's Catholic Homilies: The Second Series*, ed. Godden
DMLBS　*Dictionary of Medieval Latin from British Sources*,
　　　　ed. Latham et al.
DOE　　Cameron et al., *The Dictionary of Old English: A to H Online*
EETS　　Early English Text Society
EHD　　*English Historical Documents, c. 500–1042*, ed. Whitelock
Handlist　Gneuss and Lapidge, *Anglo-Saxon Manuscripts:*
　　　　A Bibliographical Handlist
Ker　　　Ker, *Catalogue of Manuscripts Containing Anglo-Saxon*
LS　　　*Ælfric's Lives of Saints*, ed. Skeat
MGH　　Monumenta Germaniae Historica
OED　　Oxford English Dictionary
OEN　　Old English Newsletter
PL　　　*Patrologia Latina*, ed. Migne

Quotations from the Bible are from *Biblia Sacra, iuxta Vulgatem Versionem*, ed. Fischer et al.; English translations are from *The Vulgate Bible: Douay-Rheims Translation*, ed. Edgar and Kinney.

EPISTOLARY ACTS

Introduction:
Epistolary Acts and *The Husband's Message*

Letters and other documents with epistolary qualities abound in Anglo-Saxon vernacular literature. From the runic message in the poem *The Husband's Message*, to the diplomatic and ecclesiastical documents of the Old English translation of Bede's *Ecclesiastical History*,[1] to the epistolary travelogue of *The Letter of Alexander to Aristotle*, as well as numerous epistolary prefaces, Anglo-Saxon vernacular literature delights in epistolarity. Although letters are embedded in many genres, they are especially well represented in Old English saints' lives and sermons, where miraculous documents appear or are destroyed to communicate God's will to humankind. These letters take many forms: some, like the *Letter of Abgar*, promised healing; others, like those in the *Lives* of Saints Basil and Giles, recorded, displayed, or erased private sins; while still others, such as the *Sunday Letter*, used the pretense of divine authorship to justify or regulate worldly behaviour. Letters also appear in secular prose and poetry, including *The Husband's Message*, as well as the Old English *Apollonius of Tyre* and the Old English *Orosius.* In addition to embedding epistolary communication within other vernacular genres, some Anglo-Saxon authors were also prolific writers of independent public and private letters, primarily in Latin.

Epistolary Acts takes up the question of how Anglo-Saxon authors represented epistolary practice in vernacular literature, including poetry, saints' lives, sermons, and prose romance. Because relatively few "real" Old English

---

1 On the omission and abridgement of letters in the Old English Bede, see Rowley, *The Old English Version of Bede*, 4–5 and Appendix 1. For the Latin text, see Colgrave and Mynors, eds, *Bede's Ecclesiastical History.*

letters survive, and there is no extant formal theory of Anglo-Saxon epistolarity, I seek to recover epistolarity via the representation of letters in other texts.[2] The project focuses not on actual letters intended to be sent from one person to another, but rather on the ways in which authors represented these communicative acts within other longer, sometimes fictional texts, some of which were aimed at audiences who might not have seen or used letters themselves. It may be easy to imagine how an educated cleric or wealthy lay person would have understood a letter (even one from God), but it is much less obvious, given the largely oral culture of the early Middle Ages, why letters would have so captured the imagination of people who might never have produced, sent, or received letters themselves. With chapters on epistolary form and vocabulary, self-replicating letters from heaven, messengers and materiality, and memory and archives, this book moves beyond traditional genre study and traditional binaries (orality/textuality, form/function) to offer a radically new way of conceptualizing Anglo-Saxon epistolarity.

Letters are particularly resistant to definition.[3] While the problem of defining the letter will be taken up in the rest of the book, I would like to propose a working definition of the letter as it appeared in Anglo-Saxon England: a letter is any written message addressed by one or more persons to another person or group of people to whom the message is expected to be delivered, or anything that is written in this form. The distinction

---

2　Many scholars distinguish between "real" and "fictional" letters based on whether or not the letter was meant to be sent to a recipient. See Constable, *Letters and Letter-Collections*, 13. Note that under this definition, a literary letter may be designated "real" rather than "fictional."

3　The problem of identifying what is a letter is not restricted to Old English studies. Giles Constable devotes an entire chapter of *Letters and Letter-Collections* to the definition of the letter, acknowledging that "medieval epistolography … is so broad and varied as to defy any strict definition or classification" (25). He concludes that "for most writers in the Middle Ages a letter was any work which fitted the epistolary situation, was furnished with a salutation and subscription, and paid at least lip-service to the requirements of the *modus epistolaris*," which comprised only two requirements: brevity and unity of topic (18–20, 25). Constable's definition unites form (a letter has salutation and subscription, and is short) and function (a letter is a communication necessitated by the distance between sender and recipient). As he acknowledges, "this concept of the letter as *sermo absentium* opened the way to including within the epistolary genre many works [we would not now consider letters]" (14). See also Camargo, who says that "medieval writers classified a much broader range of writing as epistolary than we customarily do today" (*Ars Dictaminis*, 18).

between written and oral messages is not always clear in Old English, but a letter, as opposed to an oral message, is signalled by the presence of verbs for writing, sealing, or sending, and may or may not include a salutation formula. It often but not always mentions or assumes the presence of an intermediary who will deliver the message. Lexical choices sometimes clarify the nature of a message; it is generally safe to assume that anything labelled an *ærendgewrit* (a written message) or *(e)pistol* is a letter. However, Old English frequently identifies written documents using terms that are so broad that the particular form or genre of the document cannot be ascertained from the label alone. For example, a *gewrit* (something written) can only be identified as a letter if it is treated as such (e.g., if it has a salutation, is sealed, or is delivered by an intermediary). The quality of epistolarity is not restricted to letters. Although this book will focus on documents that are recognizably letters, I argue that epistolarity influenced other genres and textual objects as well.

Careful study of the representation of Anglo-Saxon letters reveals that, far from being a mere preface to the more highly developed documentary culture of the later Middle Ages, Anglo-Saxon epistolarity was widespread, highly sophisticated, and different in kind from later medieval epistolarities. Through what I am calling "epistolary acts," Anglo-Saxon authors explored not just the form and function of letters, but also concepts like memory and the archive, and the preservation and circulation of miracles. This project studies how letters, and especially letters from or associated with the divine, were imagined in early medieval vernacular texts aimed at both educated and/or religious audiences who might have had documentary competency, and less educated lay audiences who might never have seen or used letters themselves. I argue that epistolarity (broadly conceived) was more crucial to Anglo-Saxon literature than we have realized, and that it played a significant role in shaping the development of Anglo-Saxon documentary culture. Second, I theorize that because no account of Anglo-Saxon epistolarity is extant, and because single-sheet documents such as letters were among the least likely to survive, one of the best ways to recover Anglo-Saxon epistolarity is via study of letters embedded in other texts. Finally, I demonstrate that attending to vernacular epistolarity in particular reveals the protocols of Old English epistolary acts.

Epistolary Acts

What makes early medieval English epistolarity unique is that it is not merely about letters but instead about the performance of what I am calling "epistolary acts,"[4] the moments when authors represent or embed letters within vernacular texts, attempting to adapt a Latin epistolary tradition to Germanic or Anglo-Saxon contexts and audiences. In these moments, authors may describe the movement of a message across space and/or time as carried by a messenger or other intermediary; linger over the material object on which the message is written; or imagine how a document's destruction may not guarantee that it has been erased from memory, whether individual or cultural. In this way, Anglo-Saxon epistolary acts involve what are known in media and communication studies as *protocols*. Lisa Gitelman defines protocols as "a vast clutter of normative rules and default conditions," one example of which is that in the United States, one knows that when answering the phone, one should begin by saying "Hello."[5] In contemporary culture, these protocols often go unnoticed, unless one is put into an unfamiliar position (to continue Gitelman's example, trying to use the telephone in a foreign country). But as Gitelman also demonstrates, the defamiliarized context of past forms of media sometimes reveals protocols that might have been second nature to their original audiences (or at least, those educated and/or wealthy enough to participate). While the formal protocols of later medieval letters have received sustained attention, the protocols required of early medieval epistolary communication, including not just composition and rhetorical formulae but also the delivery, performance, and storage of letters, have largely been overlooked. Letters written in the vernacular rather than Latin may have been aimed at audiences who were less familiar with the protocols of letter writing, and as such, it might be expected that these letters describe more explicitly the process of writing, sending, and receiving epistolary documents than epistles written by learned figures such as Boniface do. However, in fact even early English vernacular letters frequently omit reference to salutation formulas, transmission networks, and messengers. This suggests that these protocols may have been familiar to their audiences, and that Anglo-Saxon documentary culture extended deeper into lay society than has previously been believed.[6]

---

4 Many thanks to Martin Foys for suggesting this phrase to me in September 2013.

5 Gitelman, *Always Already New*, 7.

6 As Mary Garrison has demonstrated, what letters survive may not be representative of what letters once existed. While a relatively small set of Latin letters survive because they were carefully copied and preserved, most extant early business and personal letters were thrown away or lost by their original users, and are now known only because

By "epistolary acts," then, I mean all the elements that make up the protocols of letter writing, delivery, reception, and storage. I choose the word "acts" to emphasize that these protocols involved not just the formal qualities of the written message but also the physical activity of the scribes who recorded and sealed messages and the messengers who moved with the letter from the place of composition to the place of delivery, and then often performed the message aloud and in public; the material properties of the letter, whether parchment, wax, or wood, sealed or unsealed, which came into intimate physical contact with scribe, messenger, and potentially recipient; and the content of the message itself, which was often supplemented by the scribe to whom the author dictated the message, then summarized or extemporized orally by the messenger who performed it for its recipient. In all these ways, Anglo-Saxon epistolarity comprised not just the text of a message, but all those who participated in its construction and reception.

Yet, the concept of epistolary acts also offers a new way of thinking about a particular kind of act necessary for *all* authors of Old English texts in which letters were represented or embedded – the act of translation. When a translator encountered a letter embedded in a larger text, he or she had to make decisions about *linguistic* translation (what English vocabulary for letters best matched their Latin counterparts) as well as decisions about *cultural* translation (how to make sense of Latin epistolary culture to an Anglo-Saxon audience). Even when an Old English text had no Latin source, the author who chose to represent epistolary culture within a vernacular text was faced with the question of how to make epistolary culture, which was primarily a Latinate, learned, written culture, legible to Anglo-Saxon audiences. By exploring the kinds of choices, both micro and macro, that Anglo-Saxon authors and translators made when representing epistolarity, we might discover aspects of documentary culture that are specifically Anglo-Saxon; this is one reason why the book focuses on vernacular rather than Latin letters.

This book is not, therefore, a comprehensive history of Anglo-Saxon letters, though such a book is much to be desired.[7] Instead, it is an attempt

---

they were found hundreds of years later by archaeologists. Just because everyday communication was not deliberately stored in the archive does not mean it did not exist. See "Send More Socks."

7 Christine E. Fell had been working on a book on Anglo-Saxon letters before her death, a portion of which was published posthumously as "Introduction to *Anglo-Saxon Letters*."

to reconstruct Anglo-Saxon epistolarity via study of epistolary acts. Because Anglo-Saxon England produced no treatises on letter writing, it is through representations of epistolary acts embedded within other texts that we are best able to recover Anglo-Saxon theories of letter writing, and it is in vernacular rather than Latin texts that we are best able to recover particularly Anglo-Saxon protocols for letter writing. Although some Anglo-Saxons participated in a long, rich tradition of Latin letter writing, and there are many extant Anglo-Latin letters, very few "real" letters (i.e., letters intended to be sent) written in the vernacular survive from Anglo-Saxon England. If we restrict ourselves to "real" letters intended to be sent, then the complete list of items that most scholars would agree are "real" letters written in Old English would number roughly ten, and most were written by well-known Anglo-Saxon churchmen and kings.[8] To these actual letters we might add several epistolary prefaces written by Ælfric and one attributed to King Alfred.[9] Thus it is all the more surprising that

---

8 "Real" Old English letters include the translation of a letter by Boniface to Eadburga (though it is unclear whether the translation itself was meant to be sent anywhere); several pastoral letters by Ælfric (the letters to Sigeweard, Wulfsige, Wulfgeat, Sigefyrth, and the first and second Old English letters to Wulfstan); a handful of letters by Archbishop Wulfstan and King Cnut; the Letter to Brother Edward, sometimes attributed to Ælfric; and the Fonthill Letter (though it is again unclear whether it was sent to its addressee). Anglo-Saxon England produced a large number of vernacular writs that open with a salutation. However, the standard definition of "real" letters excludes writs because, although they were written in epistolary form, they were never intended to be delivered to their addressees. Instead, a writ was given to the beneficiary, whose responsibility it was to display the document to the addressee if the addressee disputed the resolution stated therein. Richard Sharpe argues that Anglo-Saxon writs, which he calls "writ-charters," were often "addressed to – and delivered to – the shire court," though they were still given first to the beneficiary, who brought the document to the court ("The Use of Writs," 251). Writs, therefore, are considered primarily historical or legal documents, though the salutation formulae of writs must have shaped Anglo-Saxon epistolarity. Moreover, most writs are epistolary only in that they contain salutation formulae, which Anglo-Saxon letters embedded in longer texts almost never do. Writs do not invite response, represent the movement of messengers, or linger over the materiality of the message. Writs thus provide little evidence for how epistolarity was conceived in the vernacular imagination. Many of the Anglo-Saxon writs have been collected by F.E. Harmer, in *Anglo-Saxon Writs*. Anglo-Saxon charters were written primarily in Latin and lacked salutation formulae; on the literary qualities of their prose in ninth-century Anglo-Saxon England and beyond, see Snook, *Anglo-Saxon Chancery*.
9 Some scholars might prefer to call these prefaces "fictional" rather than "real" letters. Epistolary prefaces are often excluded from the study of letters because they do not easily fit the parameters of the standard definition of a letter; they were not always sent

letters are so frequently represented in Old English literature. However, because letters were ephemeral documents, relatively unlikely to be preserved, it may be more accurate to say that literary representations of epistolary acts reveal the depths to which letters penetrated Anglo-Saxon culture, which cannot now be recovered via letters themselves. As Simon Keynes writes of a related genre, it is likely that "the surviving writs are but the rump of a long tradition of administrative letters [in Anglo-Saxon England] ... and that people other than the king were also accustomed to convey messages in written form."[10] While authors of "real" letters occasionally mention their difficulty in finding a suitable messenger, their hope that the recipient will keep a copy of the letter nearby for frequent consultation, or their receipt (or lack thereof) of previous letters from their correspondent, it is primarily in the *representation* of letters – in the ways authors frame letters' composition, delivery, performance, reception, and storage – that we can really see how letters were imagined to function in Anglo-Saxon society.

This is, above all, a book about the representation of Anglo-Saxon epistolarity, and especially vernacular epistolarity, though it frequently subverts our expectations about what constituted a "letter" in Anglo-Saxon England. The scope of this project does not include the totality of Anglo-Saxon letters, but instead offers a way to explore, through the lens of Anglo-Saxon epistolarity, cultural and linguistic translation, media, materiality, affect, and the archive. Anglo-Saxon epistolarity operates across a range of genres and forms, from actual letters written and received, to letters embedded or reported within other genres, and to objects understood to function like letters. This is the broad spectrum that is meant by epistolarity in this book.

The project has the following structure: each chapter introduces one aspect of epistolarity, and each subsequent chapter extends, challenges, or complicates the argument of the previous one. Chapter 1 is about literary form and the language of epistolary communication, and comes the closest

---

from one person to another, and they did not invite a response. A related question is whether attaching an epistolary preface to a longer text in order to publish it means that the whole treatise should be understood as a letter. For example, the so-called *Letter to the Monks of Eynsham* written by Ælfric opens with an epistolary preface. The work's most recent editor argues cogently that, as it is based on the *Regularis Concordia*, it should be understood as a customary or consuetudinary, not a letter. See Christopher A. Jones, *Ælfric's Letter to the Monks*, 3–4, 150n1.

10 Keynes, "Royal Government and the Written Word," 248.

to a traditional history of "real" epistolarity. Chapter 2, on the *Sunday Letter*, not only studies a little-known but influential work but also challenges the possibility of a "pure" or "real" epistolary genre by considering the relationship between materiality and communication, examining how the materiality of the miraculous document complicates our expectations regarding the importance of literary and epistolary form. Chapter 3, on messengers and materiality in *Apollonius of Tyre*, the *Letter of Abgar*, and *Mary of Egypt*, moves from the materiality of the message to bodies more generally, and the relationship between bodies and transmission. Finally, chapter 4, on Ælfric's *Life of St Basil* and the anonymous *Legend of the Seven Sleepers*, challenges the idea of material bodies as transmitters by considering other modes of transmission, focusing on storage and temporality.

Epistolarity and Early English Media

Letters are an excellent focal point through which to examine how media theory might intersect with medieval studies, because letters necessarily encompass many of the chief concerns of media theory. In focusing on the representation of epistolarity rather than "real" letters, this study encourages thinking about the ways in which media studies might help us understand Anglo-Saxon epistolary culture as participating in more than the literacy of the elite few. Despite important scholarship on the uses of textuality and orality in Anglo-Saxon England, it is all too easy to fall into the trap of imagining that letter writing and production was the province of the elite, while oral messages might explain the spread of epistolarity to more popular audiences.[11] But in fact all letters and all epistolary acts involve both orality and textuality, though the balance between message and medium varies from work to work. Thinking about letters in terms of *media* offers a simultaneously more capacious and more narrow scope than the content of oral messages versus the textuality of letters. Orality and textuality imply the networks of circulation in which letters participate, both material and non-material, but may not suggest the complex range of media in which letters circulate – oral message, wax tablet, ink on

---

11 One did not need to be literate to have access to textual culture in the early Middle Ages; literacy and textuality are not the same thing. Representative works from the vast bibliography on Anglo-Saxon and early medieval literacy and textuality include Stock, *Implications of Literacy*; Irvine, *Making of Textual Culture*; Kelly, "Anglo-Saxon Lay Society"; O'Brien O'Keeffe, *Visible Song*; Howe, "Cultural Construction of Reading"; and Parkes, "The Literacy of the Laity."

parchment, or messages carved into a wall or scratched in the ground. Media are not limited to the material and aesthetic objects (parchment, stone, metal) on which content is inscribed, or the technology used to produce those inscriptions. As Martin Foys puts it, *"Media are neither the material nor the meaning, but somewhere in-between.* Media: the plural of medium – that which comes in the middle, between things; the means of communication that is also the filter through which that communication must pass."[12] Epistolary acts bring to the fore the inherently mediatory quality of media. Just as media comprise "message, means, and agents," letters unite human agents (both producers and consumers), material supports, and transmission networks.[13] Letters are always already embedded in a social network, and involve the transmission of information on some kind of physical support (wax, parchment, wood) that is moved through a communications system, written by the sender (or an amanuensis), carried via messenger, and received by one or more persons, often in a public, communal setting, and often, at least in the Middle Ages, delivered orally. To these agents we might also add the producers of the parchment or tablet, the makers of the seal matrix, the scribes who later copied the document into a cartulary or register, and the authors who embedded letters into larger narratives. Media are not simply the combination of technology and content, but rather whole systems, rituals, and protocols, as Lisa Gitelman's definition reveals: "I define media as socially realized structures of communication, where structures include both technological forms and their associated protocols, and where communication is a cultural practice, a ritualized collocation of different people on the same mental map, sharing or engaged with popular ontologies of representation."[14] A letter is a material object on which content is inscribed, whereas epistolary acts, like Gitelman's media, are the conjunction of content, object, delivery and storage systems, written (and often Latinate) traditions, and oral culture. Thinking through a media studies lens, then, offers a way to reflect the capaciousness of Anglo-Saxon epistolarity: it offers a way to unite letters' form and function; to analyse their content, their materials, and their circulation; to study senders, transmitters, and receivers; and to reveal the ways Anglo-Saxons imagined the process of recording memory.

---

12 Foys, "Media," 133 (emphasis in original).
13 Peters, "Mass Media," 266.
14 Gitelman, *Always Already New*, 7.

In thinking about medieval letters as and from the perspective of media, I have been influenced not just by the work of media theorists such as Lisa Gitelman, but also by a small group of medievalists who have turned their attention to medieval media. Seeta Chaganti, Martin Foys, and others have proposed that media theorists need to embrace the preprint age, but more importantly, that medievalists must begin conceiving media not just in terms of inscriptional media or the history of the book but in terms of Anglo-Saxon England's rich multi- and hypermediacy. In an article on performance and inscription in the Old English poem *Dream of the Rood*, the Ruthwell monument, and the Brussels Cross, Chaganti reveals the ways in which attention to medieval multimediacy – in this case the differences in the media of stone, metal, and parchment – might help us understand these texts and objects in relation to one another. Using Jay David Bolter and Richard Grusin's concept of remediation, Chaganti demonstrates that Anglo-Saxon multimediacy is always simultaneously transparent and opaque, hypermediate and immediate, present and absent.[15] Likewise, Martin Foys is engaged in revealing Anglo-Saxon and early medieval multimediacy through study of material and aesthetic objects, experiences (such as the ringing of a bell), and other non-inscriptional media.[16] Foys and Chaganti both focus on multimediacy or media ecologies involving multiple media, especially matter and objects such as swords and stone. While I find their work inspiring and provocative, the scope of my project is firmly situated in inscriptional storage media, and it is at its heart a book about Anglo-Saxon literature. Though I consider coins and seals in my last chapter, for example, this remains primarily a project about letters, and the ways in which letters were imagined to circulate, communicate, and make meaning in Anglo-Saxon England.

Letters are both transmission media and storage container, a means of conveying ideas as well as a means of transporting and preserving them. In Anglo-Saxon epistolarity, a letter's content is often less important to the author of a text in which the letter is embedded than its physical form, its travel with and subsequent performance by a messenger, or its storage or erasure. While the author may summarize the general content of the letter's message, the letter is rarely copied word for word into the larger text. The tension between the importance of the materiality of the letter as

---

15 Chaganti, "Vestigial Signs," 51.
16 Foys, *Virtually Anglo-Saxon*, "A Sensual Philology," and "Media."

object and the role of messengers in conveying messages orally reveals how, in Anglo-Saxon England, transmission might be distinct from storage. Media theorists argue that while print had collapsed the difference between transmission and storage, new media create a gap between the two, with storage happening away from users, whether on a hard drive or kept in the Cloud. Like new media, the oral performance of letters in the Middle Ages also separated the letter's transmission from the inscriptional media that stored its message.[17] Some of the Anglo-Saxon texts studied in this project exploit this separation of container and transmission, while others seek to reunite them, if only temporarily, to provide a sense of immediacy, a communication with the divine free from the interference of signal noise or the delay and deferral of transmission by messenger. As I discuss in my second chapter, the Old English *Sunday Letter* foregrounds the orality and thus the transmission of the message, referring only in passing to its storage in a physical document that seems not to have been present when the sermon on the *Letter* was preached. Likewise, representations of letter delivery and performance in the texts I study in my third chapter deliberately draw attention to the physical document and/or to the bodies of messengers. While it might seem that this attention to materiality would unite transmission and storage, in fact these texts transform the messengers' bodies into impossibly perfect conduits for the absent senders. In these fantasies of perfect, real-time communication, there is no need for inscriptional storage media because the content of the message is made legible on and through the body of its messenger. In my final chapter, I turn to the ways in which transmission and storage may seek to be reunited. When letters were copied into cartularies, for example, the intermediary of the messenger was removed entirely, and the copied texts could be accessed only as storage media. In hagiographies such as the Old English *Life of St Basil* and the anonymous *Legend of the Seven Sleepers*, I argue, letters are brought into (or resist being brought into) the archive, and storage media are displayed, concealed, and destroyed as visible textual objects.

---

17 I wish to thank Andrew Higl, along with our fellow panelists and audience members, for suggesting these ideas in a response to a previous version of my third chapter, delivered at the 48th International Congress on Medieval Studies, Kalamazoo, MI in May 2013.

The Husband's Message

Turning to a particular example will illustrate the claims that I am making about Anglo-Saxon epistolary acts. Perhaps the most famous Old English letter is embedded in *The Husband's Message*, a 54-line poem preserved in the mid- to late tenth-century Exeter Book (Exeter, Cathedral Library, 3501).[18] In it, an unnamed man who has been separated from a woman (either his wife or his betrothed) because of a feud writes to tell her that she should join him because he has come into prosperity. The poem has no known source.[19] This means that its author, unconstrained by a Latin or Germanic source text, might have been allowed to make freer choices regarding how to represent Anglo-Saxon epistolarity.

The poem has often been understood as transmitting a message written on a rune stick (a wooden stick on which a message was carved in runes; usually containing a short, pragmatic message) or some other wooden surface. Critical attention to the poem has been devoted primarily to the question of how to interpret the runic message at the end of the poem, the nature of the wooden object on which the message was written, and whether the first-person speaker of the poem is the personified wooden object or a human messenger. If the speaker of the poem ever identified himself clearly, it is likely to have come in the opening lines of the poem, which are heavily damaged by fire.[20] Regarding the nature of the wooden object, one popular solution has been to imagine that the message was

---

18 *Handlist*, item 257; Ker no. 116. Patrick W. Conner dates the Exeter Book c. 950 x 968, though this has not been accepted by all scholars, many of whom date the manuscript later in the tenth century. Conner, *Anglo-Saxon Exeter*. The date of composition of the poem itself is unknown, as is the provenance of the manuscript before 1072, by which time it had arrived in Exeter.

19 There is one analogous line in the Paris Psalter, Psalm 100 (Paris, Bibliothèque Nationale, MS lat. 8824; *Handlist*, item 891; Ker no. 367). See Muir, *Exeter Anthology of Old English Poetry*, 698.

20 Those who believe that the speaker is a human messenger point to lines early in the poem stating that the speaker has made multiple trips, which may preclude the possibility of its being a rune stick: "Ful oft ic on bates bosme ..... gesohte,/þær mec mondryhten min onsende/ofer heah hafu" (Very often I sought [word missing] in the hold of a boat, where my lord of men sent me over the high seas) (6–8a). All quotations from *The Husband's Message* are from Muir's edition. Unless otherwise noted, all translations are my own. For the argument that only a human speaker could make multiple trips, see Leslie, *Three Old English Elegies*, 13–14. However, archaeological evidence has shown that rune sticks could be used repeatedly, so it would be perfectly reasonable for one to have made multiple trips. See Ericksen, "Runesticks and Reading *The Husband's Message*."

inscribed on a rune stick. However, no Anglo-Saxon rune sticks have been found, and the surviving Norwegian rune sticks are from a later period.[21] Another issue is the word *beam* in the expression "se þisne beam agrof" (he who inscribed this wood) (13b). Because *beam* usually implies something larger than a rune stick, several scholars have suggested that we are dealing not with a rune stick, but with a ship's mast or walking stick.[22] More recently, Martin Foys has provocatively argued that the problematic *beam*, like any good Anglo-Saxon riddle, revels in its polysemy, resisting being made to mean any single type of wood. Instead, the poem asks that we understand "*beam* as media."[23] Regardless of what kind of wooden object the message is imagined to have been inscribed on, most scholars now agree that the speaker of the poem is likely to be the wooden object itself. Readers of the Exeter Book manuscript would have been prepared to find such a personified speaker; many of the riddles in this section of the manuscript are spoken by inanimate objects such as horns, ice, and even books.

The Husband's Message is a rare example of interpersonal communication in the vernacular between secular people on non-religious subjects, but in some ways what is so remarkable about it is how unremarkable it is – it is a runic message on some kind of wood, known elsewhere, if not in Anglo-Saxon England, to be used for everything from business letters to secret messages and love letters.[24] The existence of this vernacular message

---

21 The Bergen rune sticks date to 1150–1350. Knirk, "Learning to Write with Runes," 171–2. For Scandinavian rune sticks, see also Aslak Liestøl, "Correspondence in Runes." For an overview of medieval communication written on wood and potsherds (the Vindolanda tablets, Bergen rune sticks, and letters written on birchbark found at Novgorod), along with a defence of the view that the *Husband's Message* could be a rune stick, see Garrison, "Send More Socks."

22 Bragg, "Runes and Readers" and Niles, "Trick of the Runes," 202–4. Niles argues that "the speaker is *the wooden ship itself*; or to be precise … it is *the ship's personified mast*" (204; emphasis in original).

23 As Foys describes it, "in this poem, the engraved *beam* exists within an expressive ecology of these other manifestations of *beam*, a transmedia continuum concerned with the traversing of distance and to varying degrees with the qualities of communication and reception across that distance" ("Media" 142).

24 The messages on the Bergen rune sticks include everyday correspondence, including news about trade. Unlike most extant Anglo-Saxon letters, these letters are not carefully crafted, but instead represent ordinary communication in ordinary speech, written (or at least dictated) by businessmen, not just royals and elite churchmen. A tantalizing analogue to *The Husband's Message* is a secret message written in the wood base of a wax tablet, then covered by wax in which was written a more innocuous message. For examples of both, see Liestøl, "Correspondence in Runes."

implies that the laity – or at least the elite, since the woman is *sinchroden* (adorned with treasure) (14) and a *þeodnes dohtor* (ruler's daughter) (48) and the man has an abundance of horses and treasure, which he hopes to distribute to retainers (33–6, 45b–47) – had the means to send and receive letters, and that the audience of the poem would not have been shocked by this representation of epistolary communication among the laity. It is true that the letter is written on a potentially unfamiliar material, but the content of the message and its mode of delivery must have been perfectly comprehensible to the audience within the context of Anglo-Saxon documentary culture, or the poem would have done more to explain it. Even the runic message, so puzzling to modern audiences, supports this claim. Whether intended as riddle or not, the fact that the poem leaves all the work of interpreting the runes to the audience suggests to me that the author thought it *was* possible for the runes to be comprehended in an Anglo-Saxon context. This is true even if that comprehension went no further than recognizing that this added an archaizing flavour to the text, without any ability to interpret the message.[25] The allusiveness of the runes, so frustrating to modern readers, is what implies that an Anglo-Saxon audience sufficiently familiar with runic practice might have comprehended them, just as Cynewulf expected audiences to recognize (and possibly also read) his runic signatures. After all, no one likes an impossible puzzle.[26]

Whether the poem is spoken by the human messenger or the personified wooden object (as I believe), it is *not* spoken by the absent man who wrote the message, who has for some reason (perhaps the original feud) been unable to travel to the woman himself. The man's absence is characteristic both of the letter as a genre and of love letters in particular, where the plot is often kept in motion only because some obstacle prevents the lovers from meeting except through letters. Emphasis on the messenger or intermediary who delivers the letter in the *Husband's Message* has the effect of heightening the sense of physical distance between the man and his

---

25 For the argument that runes archaize the poem, like adding artificial weathering to new furniture, see Niles, "Trick of the Runes."

26 But see Foys, who argues that the difficulty of understanding the runes, like the difficulty of identifying the *beam*, is intentional. In his reading, the poem resists interpretation as a way of modelling the unfulfilled desire of the poem's subjects: "In effect, this poem uses a richly convergent sense of media history to reinforce the 'real' message of the poem: the difficulty of unresolved separation as amplified through the difficulty of readers' struggles with the runic message" ("Media," 145).

beloved. While the speaker of the poem uses the first person from the opening lines – "Nu *ic* onsundran þe secgan wille" (Now privately *I* wish to say to you)[27] – the man's affection for the woman is presented as indirect speech by the speaker of the poem and defamiliarized by use of the third person. Despite the fact that most Anglo-Saxon letters are written in the first person (other than the salutation), the man is not allowed to speak for himself. This use of the third person to describe the man's feelings for the woman both subdues his expressions of love and emphasizes that the feud that drove him from her still prevents him from returning to her now. For example, in lines 30–5a, the speaker produces this somewhat tortured declaration of the man's affection:

Ne mæg him on worulde   willa gelimpan
mara on gemyndum,   þæs þe he me sægde,
þonne inc geunne   alwaldend god
þæt git ætsomne   siþþan motan
secgum ond gesiþum   sinc brytnian
næglede beagas.

Nor can a greater worldly pleasure befall him in his mind, as he said to me, than that almighty God might grant you two that you two together afterward might distribute treasure, nailed rings, to men and companions.[28]

While the use of the dual pronoun (*inc, git*) meaning "you two" subtly reminds the woman of the intimate relationship she and the man once enjoyed, the man's message, as reported by the speaker, is presented at a distance.[29] Denied the use of the first person, the husband has his declaration of love mediated through the messenger, who can only report to the woman what the man has told him about the deepest desires of his mind. The messenger's interjection "as he said to me" jolts the audience into

---

27 Line 1 (emphasis added).

28 Another example of the poem's tendency to foreground the intermediary role of the messenger or speaking object addresses the difficulty the man might have accessing the woman's feelings: "eom nu her cumen / on ceolþele, ond nu cunnan scealt / hu þu ymb modlufun mines frean / on hyge hycge" (I have now come here on a ship-plank, and now you must know how you think in your mind about the heart's love of my lord) (8b–11a).

29 One of the two duals (*git*) is supplied by editors because the manuscript is damaged here, but *inc* is legible in the manuscript.

remembering that this letter does not offer direct, unmediated communication between two individuals, but the messenger's *interpretation* of the man's feelings and intent, introducing the possibility of signal noise and corruption of the message. Even this fantasy of intimate reunion comes freighted with the presence of others, the loyal retainers (*secgum ond gesiþum*) that the man imagines the woman will join him in rewarding in the hall. Although the speaker of the poem declares he must speak his message "privately" to the woman, the desired reunion, like the message as performed by the speaker, can exist only in the public, social realm, not in private, one-to-one communication between two individuals. The presence of the messenger or personified wooden object reminds the woman (and the audience) of the physical, temporal, and perhaps even emotional distance between the man and woman, which is both constructed and erased by the conceit of the letter. As Janet Gurkin Altman writes of eighteenth-century epistolary fiction, "the letter is both a reflection of the gap [between suitor and lady] and an instrument for gap closing."[30]

If the presence and interventions of the messenger remind the woman of the sender's absence, the unusual material support on which the message is written increases both the sense of intimacy and the sense of the object's hypermediacy. In media theory, hypermediacy is a condition in which an object forces a viewer to confront its nature as medium rather than looking through or past the medium to its content. This is often achieved by including gestures to other media; for example, a painting might represent objects like windows and mirrors, or a website might include text, photographs, and video and audio clips that require the viewer to interact with and navigate between them. Hypermediacy is associated with "opacity," or being unable to ignore the physical medium. By contrast, immediacy is associated with "transparency" because it encourages the audience to forget the medium entirely, as when readers feel they are looking through printed words in a codex to "see" the imagined worlds described therein.[31] In the words of Jay David Bolter and Richard Grusin, "in all its various forms, the logic of hypermediacy expresses the tension between regarding a visual space as mediated and as a 'real' space that lies beyond mediation … A viewer confronting a collage, for example, oscillates between looking at the patches of paper and paint on the surface of the work and looking

---

30 Altman, *Epistolarity*, 189.
31 Bolter and Grusin, *Remediation*, 19.

through to the depicted objects as if they occupied a real space beyond the surface."[32] The wooden surface represented in *The Husband's Message* is not a "transparent" or immediate object, like a parchment letter whose materiality disappears in favour of the document's content, but an "opaque" or hypermediate one that problematizes our access to its content at every turn. Recall that, although wood seems to have been a common medium for Scandinavian business letters, we have no evidence of wooden rune sticks from Anglo-Saxon England so, to the audience of the poem, the wood was potentially an unusual medium. Moreover, the speaker of the poem frequently draws attention to the materiality of the message, asking the audience to confront that the message is on wood rather than the expected parchment or wax, explicitly demanding that they look at, rather than through, its medium. This defamiliarizes the physical form in which letters appear, inviting the woman and the audience of the poem to contemplate the letter as physical object rather than spoken message. On the one hand, this focus heightens the sense of distance between sender and recipient by reminding us that the wooden object substitutes for the man's human body, which, unlike the letter, is not in the presence of the woman. At the same time, the focus on the materiality of the message invites a reminder of their former intimacy, as the woman looks at, lingers over, and perhaps even touches the wooden object her beloved has marked with his hand and his thoughts.

The poem's attention to the unusual material on which the letter is written, and the ambiguity regarding whether the messenger is a human being or the personified letter itself, painfully reminds the woman (and the poem's audience) that the messenger and the letter are necessary only because the man cannot come himself. The poem's message is both a promise of reunion and a reminder of the distance between lover and beloved, a fantasy of direct access to the man's feelings and a reminder that his hopes have been and must continue to be deferred, at least for as long as it has taken the messenger to reach the woman and will take the woman to travel to the man, assuming she accepts his offer, or perhaps eternally, if she refuses him.[33] The poem reminds the woman that even if she does accept, she

---

32 Ibid., 41.

33 Because the poem ends without giving any indication of the woman's response, we can only say that within the world of the poem, his wishes are suspended indefinitely. Foys makes a similar argument about the difficulty of understanding the nature of the *beam* and the meaning of the runes: "this work resounds with a desire to communicate, cut with the fear and frustration at the mediated difficulty of doing so" ("Media" 140).

too must wait a bit longer (at least until the cuckoo sings a sad song) before setting sail. In this way, the letter, rather than uniting man and woman, suspends them in a state of permanent separation, instability, and deferral of desire. The poem wants to imagine the woman closing the gap between them by taking the same journey the man once did, reversing the path so recently taken by his message, which stands before her (or perhaps in her hand) in all its wooden glory. During the anticipated journey, she will be in a transitory state, a state of movement and contingency, of becoming rather than being. The speaker of the poem frequently invokes this movement across the water, first describing his own repeated travel in the hold of a boat (6–9), then telling the woman he has been ordered to ask her that she travel the sea (21), specifying that she must take a sea journey south after she hears the cuckoo's song (23), and reminding her of the more difficult, lonely journey the man took to escape the feud (41–4). In recalling the man's initial journey, the letter encourages the woman to follow in his footsteps, to be metaphorically or partially reunited with him by placing her body in the same path his body once travelled, an asynchronous reunion in which their two bodies might occupy the same space, but at different times. (With the hope, of course, of a more permanent, less metaphorical reunion at the end of her journey.)

The poem also moves frequently between temporal positions, oscillating between the present in which the letter is delivered to the woman, the happier days when the couple were together, the man's exile, and the imagined future in which they might be reunited. The poem's resistance to a linear chronological account of their relationship foregrounds the asynchronicity of all epistolary communication – the letter writer's present will always be the recipient's past, and, despite the speaker's repeated use of the word "now," what that "now" is will never be the same for sender and addressee. Even the "now" of the poem's first use of *nu* ("Nu ic onsundran þe secgan wille" [Now privately I wish to say to you]) does not refer to the same temporal moment as its later uses of *nu* ("heht nu sylfa þe / lustum læram" [he himself now commanded me joyfully advise you]).[34] At the same time, these rapid temporal shifts introduce a note of doubt into the proceedings by resisting certainty, fixity, and closure. Epistolary fiction always resists closure by offering the possibility of more letters to be sent in reply,[35] but

---

34 Lines 1 and 20b–21a. *Nu* also occurs in lines 8, 9, and 44.
35 Altman, *Epistolarity*, 148.

in the case of *The Husband's Message*, this closure is forever denied us, as we are never shown the woman's response. The characters of the poem remain fixed in a permanent deferral of desire and narrative closure.

In all these ways, the poem anticipates how the woman might embody the letter itself. If she accepts her suitor's invitation, she will repeat the letter's journey to be joined not just with the man's physical stand-in (the letter), but with his body itself. If there is any hope of reunion, it may be located in the fact that there may be something especially intimate in engraving the message in wood rather than writing it with ink. Choosing such an unusual medium, and having the poem begin by calling attention to its wooden nature, defamiliarizes the epistolary process and invites the audience to linger over the message's shape, making intimate contact with its surprising form, imagining the moment when her suitor placed his hand on it, and the moment when the woman, too, might touch the wood, and one day, the man for whom it speaks.

In many ways, this poem, enigmatic though it may seem, is typical of literary representations of letters in Old English. The letter lacks salutation, valediction, and date ("real" letters were rarely dated at this time). It can be difficult to determine which parts of the poem are meant to represent the text of the letter itself and which parts are paraphrases of the message produced by the speaker or poet. Old English literary representations of letters are rarely concerned with formal features like salutations, and often, as in this example, take little care to distinguish the textual content of the letter itself from the rest of the text. Instead, Anglo-Saxon epistolary acts privilege attention to the letter's status as physical object; the messenger's delivery of the message, which rarely involves presenting the text of the letter exactly as written by the scribe; and other epistolary characteristics such as the distance, both physical and temporal, between sender and addressee.

Like *The Husband's Message*, Anglo-Saxon epistolarity has a broad scope, encompassing the letter's content and status as material object, its delivery and performance by a messenger, and its storage as embedded in another text (as in *The Husband's Message*, in which the letter is incorporated in a poem) or in another medium. These key features of Anglo-Saxon epistolarity provide thematic structure for the rest of this book. This study takes its structure from the primary protocols of epistolary acts – writing or composition (chapter 1), delivery and reception (chapters 2 and 3), and storage (chapter 4). Throughout, it expands and challenges the characteristics of Anglo-Saxon epistolarity as exemplified by *The Husband's Message*.

Epistolary Acts proceeds by a series of linked studies exploring epistolary form, communication networks, messengers and materiality, and memory and archives. Because there are no extant Anglo-Saxon treatises on epistolarity, chapter 1 excavates Anglo-Saxon vernacular epistolary theory by studying salutation forms and vocabulary, including both Latin and vernacular examples. While the rest of the project focuses on the representation of letters, this chapter examines letters actually intended to be sent, and offers a brief history of "real" or independent letters in Anglo-Saxon England. Through study of the formal characteristics of these letters, I propose ways in which epistolarity could be both immediate and hypermediate, and I explore the ways in which epistolary forms control audiences' access to and experiences of the texts that follow. The chapter also surveys Old English lexical choices for letters, focusing on the mysterious appearance of the writing on the wall in the Old English poetic *Daniel*, arguing that the polysemy of Old English vocabulary for written media originates in a careful consideration of Latin source material, along with a capacious sense of what constituted a letter. The rest of the book turns from rhetorical theory and "real" letters to the intersections of message and medium in fictional letters or letters embedded within hagiographies, sermons, and literary texts. While chapter 1 considers the production of letters, chapters 2 and 3 focus on their delivery and reception. Chapter 2 examines a work known as the *Sunday Letter*, a potentially apotropaic document (designed to protect the bearer from harm) that purports to have been written by God or Jesus Christ in heaven and transmitted to earth by an angelic messenger to enforce proper Sunday observance. Much like modern chain letters, nearly all the Old English versions of the *Sunday Letter* demand that their audiences continue to circulate the letter's message or face terrible retribution. The *Sunday Letter*'s adaptability allowed Anglo-Saxon authors to emphasize its content rather than the material object on which the message was written, in order to create a hybrid community of disseminators of its message who were able to participate in its circulation no matter their level of literacy or access to technologies of manuscript production. By contrast, in chapter 3, I address the importance of materiality in epistolary transmission, arguing that rather than highlighting the letter as object, Old English epistolarity often celebrates the physical body of the messenger. Chapter 3 takes as its focus the importance of messengers in conveying messages as well as transporting documents, and the ways in which messages are read in and through the bodies of messengers. The Old English prose romance *Apollonius of Tyre*; Ælfric's *Letter of Abgar*, in which an ailing king exchanges letters with Jesus of

Nazareth; and the anonymous Old English *Life of St Mary of Egypt*, in which Mary's death is miraculously recorded in a message written on the ground, all imagine ways in which contact with the container of the letter can make messages legible in and through the bodies of those who carry them, even as the movement of messengers' bodies through space and time reminds us that letters are always mediated and deferred. Turning from letters that travel across distance to letters that travel across time, chapter 4 considers the epistolarity of the archive and of objects that behave like letters, opening up new ways of thinking about how Anglo-Saxons negotiated complex questions of belief and memory. How did Anglo-Saxons memorialize and circulate a miracle in cases where they did not have access to the use of relics, or where saints' stories advocated resistance to being made relics, and how could they transform the miraculous into publishable, iterable form? My analysis of the anonymous Old English *Legend of the Seven Sleepers* and Ælfric's *Life of St Basil* demonstrates that Anglo-Saxon letters and documents do not just make miracles material, or even record miracles – they also offer a way to bring what are often intangible miracles into the archive. Drawing on the work of Mary Carruthers, this chapter proposes that erasure or destruction of epistolary documents does not remove them from memory. Instead it allows them to be overwritten, transformed from record of sin to record of miracle, and inscribed in new archives. The book ends, then, with what is typically the final step in the transmission of a letter: its preservation, whether as embedded in other texts (as in chapters 1–3), or in archives, whether traditional or metaphorical.

1 Reconstructing the Anglo-Saxon *ars dictaminis*: Form, Vocabulary, and Immediacy

To study epistolarity in the later Middle Ages, one can begin by consulting handbooks on proper letter writing, model letter formularies, and other rhetorical treatises on the subject, which together provide a clear articulation of the ideal formal qualities of the genre: salutation, closing formula, length, acceptable topics, and so on. Even if these materials represent ideals rather than the realities of epistolary communication, they offer a wealth of information about the formal protocols of the genre. But Anglo-Saxon England produced no extant epistolary theory and, as I will discuss later in this chapter, deployed a broad range of lexical terms for letter writing. This raises a difficult question: how did Anglo-Saxons conceive of epistolarity? Because we lack a sufficient archive of Anglo-Saxon vernacular letters or manuals for epistolary communication, the only way that Anglo-Saxon vernacular epistolarity can be recovered is through study of how epistolarity in all its aspects – real and imagined, written and oral – penetrated Anglo-Saxon textual culture. This chapter begins to answer how Anglo-Saxons conceived of epistolarity, by examining the history of "real" Anglo-Saxon letter writing, concentrating especially on recovering the literary forms and language of epistolary communication. I do not seek to offer a comprehensive catalogue of extant Anglo-Latin and Old English letters, but instead focus on a representative selection of "real" independent letters, both Latin and vernacular. Whereas the rest of the book examines the representation of letters within other texts, this chapter examines the production of "real" letters in order to establish the formal protocols of Anglo-Saxon letter writing, which enabled the epistolary acts necessary to translate Latinate epistolarity to Anglo-Saxon audiences. In this chapter, I will first briefly survey the variety of epistolary forms available to Anglo-Saxons, primarily those writing in the vernacular. I will then use this historical background to inform a discussion of what I call the "double immediacy" of letters in Anglo-Saxon England. As a whole, this chapter lays both the historical and theoretical groundwork on which the rest of my considerations in this book will rely.

One of the chief arguments of this chapter is that Anglo-Saxon authors did know something of the formal structures associated with letters, and that they deliberately set out to imitate them. This suggests that Anglo-Saxon authors believed that epistolary formulae would mean something to their audiences as well. At the same time, I argue that Anglo-Saxon epistolary acts were different in kind from the Latin epistolary tradition. Translating Latin protocols and vocabulary into Old English necessitated that Anglo-Saxon authors think explicitly about these forms, which were defamiliarized by their transfer to a new culture and new contexts. Like Lisa Gitelman's example of placing a phone call in a foreign country (discussed in the introduction), transferring epistolary formulae to English would have made these forms suddenly unfamiliar, strange, and susceptible to transformation. While the Latin epistolary tradition receives some attention in this chapter, it is only to demonstrate that some Anglo-Saxon authors were aware of it, even as they deliberately, sometimes playfully, transformed it. Recent scholarly attention to the relationship between the vernacular and Latin in Anglo-Saxon England has caused us to overlook the many ways in which the vernacular necessarily fulfilled different functions and revealed different aspects of the culture. Anglo-Latin letters have received more attention, but the presence of Latin epistolary communication in Anglo-Saxon England is relatively unremarkable (despite generally low Latin literacy among the general population). It is epistolary communication as represented in the vernacular that is truly surprising and deserving of sustained study. When Anglo-Saxon authors adapted epistolary formulae by omitting or altering them, it was not because they lacked understanding of the genre. On the contrary, some of them were keenly aware of the requirements of the form, and their skilful treatment of epistolary forms suggests they were cognizant of the strengths and limitations of the genre. They knew the rules, and when they broke them, they did so thoughtfully, with an intense awareness of the web of connections between a variety of media forms, including genres such as treatises, documents, and letters, as well as mediums such as single-sheet parchment, codex, and tablet.

In addition to surveying representative examples of epistolary formulae, another way to recover Anglo-Saxon letter-writing protocols is through examination of Old English and Anglo-Latin vocabulary for letters. This vocabulary is incredibly porous, and reflects a much broader conception of epistolarity than we might anticipate. This terminological slippage, however, does not mean that the Anglo-Saxons had no conceptual idea of the variety of forms of written media. In the second part of the chapter, I survey Old English and Latin epistolary vocabulary, focusing on the writing on the wall in the Old English *Daniel*. I argue that, while translators often chose vernacular equivalents for Latin sources very deliberately, they were not limited to vocabulary we would now associated with letters, because Anglo-Saxons conceived of letters in terms of genre, writing supports, and the movement of documents from one place to another. Ultimately, I argue that the polysemy of Old English vocabulary for written media originates in a careful consideration of Latin source material, and that Anglo-Saxons may have had a relatively capacious sense of what constituted a letter.

This chapter therefore excavates Anglo-Saxon epistolary theory by surveying the form of letters (including their structure and literary formulae); examining the early history of letters in Anglo-Saxon England, including how they were produced and what their sources and influences may have been; and studying their vocabulary. These steps allow me to recreate an Anglo-Saxon theory of epistolarity vis-à-vis "real" letters, but the chapter is still primarily about epistolary acts and their intersection with media theory. Riffing on media theorists Jay David Bolter and Richard Grusin's theory of "the double logic of remediation," I introduce the concept of the double immediacy of epistolarity, which involves both the fantasy of immediate communication between sender and recipient as well as the idea, more familiar from media studies, of the immediacy of media forms, in which the medium of an object desires to become invisible to the audience. In this way, I am able to join theories from media studies and epistolary theory in order to unite a more historicist overview of Anglo-Saxon practices of letter production with the more theoretical framework of the rest of this project. While this chapter is about form and protocols, it is also about beginning at the beginnings, by which I mean the origins and sources of Anglo-Saxon epistolarity, as well as the epistolary features most likely to appear at the beginnings of texts: salutation formulae.

The History of Anglo-Saxon Letters: Earliest Origins and Influences

Even before the Angles, Saxons, and Jutes arrived in England, Roman Britain was producing pragmatic messages written in ink on small thin pieces of wood. Hundreds of these tablets, most roughly the size of a postcard, have been found at Vindolanda, in northern England, most dating from CE 92–104.[1] Single tablets could be strung together to form a longer message, then folded to protect and conceal the written text. Produced by and for Roman soldiers, the content of these letters ranged from military business to personal messages. Some letters were literary, even quoting lines from Virgil.[2] However, there is no evidence that Anglo-Saxons wrote on leaf tablets such as these. Instead, most Anglo-Saxon letters were written in ink on parchment or inscribed in the wax of wax tablets, using the Latin alphabet.

The first letters produced in Anglo-Saxon England were written in Latin by the Christian missionaries; as Christine Fell puts it, these letters "were assuredly not by Anglo-Saxons," in that they were written by missionaries who brought their knowledge of letter writing with them from the Continent.[3] Extant Anglo-Saxon letters of the seventh and eighth centuries were written in Latin; letters in Old English were not produced until later in the period.[4] Early Anglo-Saxon England has produced a wealth of epistolary material; the Bonifatian correspondence (late seventh–late eighth century), which included letters to and from Anglo-Saxon England, features Latin letters by such luminaries as Boniface, Aldhelm, and Alcuin.[5] Alcuin was an incredibly prolific letter writer, and his letters were also remarkably well preserved, with nearly 300 extant (though mostly copied in much later manuscripts), "more than the surviving correspondence of Augustine and considerably more than that of Jerome."[6] For Boniface, fewer than fifty letters are extant.[7] Thirteen letters to or from Aldhelm survive, one of doubtful authorship, along with the *Epistola*

---

1 Bowman, *Life and Letters*, 7–8. See also the Vindolanda Tablets Online at http:// vindolanda.csad.ox.ac.uk/. Not all the Vindolanda documents were written on wood; wax tablets have also been found, though they must have been imported (Bowman, *Life and Letters*, 80–1).

2 Bowman, *Life and Letters*, 10–11.

3 Fell, "Introduction," 278.

4 Fell, "Introduction," 286. Fell attributes the shift to vernacular to the Alfredian educational reforms. In Fell's view, Anglo-Saxons in the early period would have naturally written letters in Latin rather than Old English, even when writing to other Anglo-Saxons (280–1).

5 Fell, "Some Implications of the Boniface Correspondence."

6 Bullough, *Alcuin*, 35–7. It is not until Anselm of Bec and Canterbury (1033–1109) that we get another English letter writer whose work is so well preserved, with almost 400 extant letters (37–8).

7 Ibid., 37.

ad Acircium (which Michael Lapidge and Michael Herren describe as "neither a letter nor a unified treatise, but rather a composite work," though it does begin with a salutation),[8] and the prose *De Virginitate*, which is addressed to Hildelith and the nuns of Barking.[9]

Several single-sheet letters survive from early Anglo-Saxon England. In the early eighth century, Bishop Wealdhere wrote a letter seeking advice regarding or permission to attend a meeting meant to establish peace between the West Saxons and East Saxons. It is said to be the earliest extant letter "written by one Englishman to another."[10] The manuscript measures 363 mm x 145 mm. Although both sender and addressee are English, the letter is written in Latin, not the vernacular. There is no date, and very little formatting to help visually identify separate sections of the letter. After its composition, the letter was folded several times, the names of sender and addressee were written on what became the outside of the letter, and it was then tied shut with a strip of parchment. A similar example of a surviving single-sheet letter from Anglo-Saxon England is the Fonthill Letter, written in the early tenth century. Unlike the Wealdhere letter, it was written in the vernacular, not Latin. Written by Ealdorman Ordlaf to King Edward the Elder, the Fonthill Letter explains how various people came to have rights to local estates that were involved in a dispute over the control of Fonthill. It opens with a very simple but formulaic address ("Leof, ic ðe cyðe …" [Sir, I make known to you …]), and it ends with a short plea to the king that land rights remain as they are and have been.[11] After it was written, the letter was folded and likely tied shut with a strip

---

8 Lapidge and Herren, trans., *Aldhelm*, 31.

9 Ehwald, ed., *Aldhelmi Opera Omnia*. For translations of the *epistolae*, as well as the *Epistola ad Acircium* and prose *De Virginitate*, see Lapidge and Herren, trans., *Aldhelm*.

10 Stenton, *Anglo-Saxon England*, 142. Pierre Chaplais' work on the early eighth-century Latin letter of Bishop Wealdhere provides an excellent introduction to the production of early Anglo-Saxon letters, including how they were physically prepared to be sent, folded, sealed, and addressed. See "Letter from Bishop Wealdhere."

11 This may be intended to echo the phrase "and ic cyðe eow," which appears after the address formula in Old English writs, and "corresponds to the Latin 'sciatis' or 'notum sit'" (Bishop and Chaplais, eds, *Facsimiles of English Royal Writs*, x). Ælfric's Old English Preface to the *Lives of Saints*, addressed to Æthelweard, includes a similar phrase (*ic secge þe leof*), as does Wulfstan's letter to Cnut and Ælfgifu on the appointment of Æthelnoth as archbishop of Canterbury (*7 ic cyþe inc leof*) (Harmer, *Anglo-Saxon Writs*, no. 27). For an edition of the Fonthill Letter, see Keynes, "The Fonthill Letter." It is possible that the Fonthill Letter, unlike most writs, was actually given to its addressee King Edward the Elder, though it was in Christ Church, Canterbury, in the twelfth century (Keynes, "Fonthill Letter" 62–3, 95).

of parchment. A later scribe, not the one who wrote the letter, added to the dorse a record of the result of the letter's petition.[12] The Wealdhere and Fonthill letters were both deliberately preserved in archives, and the note added to the Fonthill Letter regarding the outcome of the case suggests that someone at the archive was actively updating these files. There is also evidence that these files were being accessed and catalogued as late as the twelfth century, when someone wrote *inutile* (useless) on the dorse. This notation was probably not because the letter was in a much earlier form of English, but rather because the case it described was no longer relevant for the status of that estate.[13]

Very few letters were preserved as single-sheet originals, in part because single-sheet documents were easily lost, but also because most letters considered worth preserving were copied into cartularies. When letters were copied into cartularies or other codices, scribes made no attempt to imitate the letters' original physical format.[14] In Anglo-Saxon manuscripts that include both letters and texts of other genres, the layout of the letters is not distinguished in any way from the other texts in the manuscript. When letters were copied into cartularies, scribes also felt free to make minor emendations to the text itself, often omitting the letter's salutation formula.[15]

While a brief note on a wax tablet could conceivably have been written anywhere that afforded the writer a way to balance the tablet on a flat surface,[16] many Anglo-Saxon letters and legal documents were produced at ecclesiastical scriptoria that actively shaped documentary form. It is clear that charters, for example, had certain standard formulae and may even in later Anglo-Saxon England have been written by scribes trained at or imitating a hand associated with a particular scriptorium. Although it

---

12 Keynes, "Fonthill Letter," 61.

13 Ibid., 63.

14 By contrast, some manuscripts of the later medieval *Charters of Christ* poems, including the fifteenth-century London, BL Additional 37049, f. 23r, draw a charter (complete with seal) on the manuscript page.

15 On the posthumous preservation and transmission of Alcuin's letters, see Bullough, *Alcuin*, 43–102. He demonstrates that these letter collections were edited by later compilers. Changes included adaptations to fit context (55) as well as removing addressees and other names (64). Even after the major Tours collection was produced, the letters continued to be edited (70).

16 Brown, "Role of the Wax Tablet." Richard H. and Mary A. Rouse believe that most tablets were "balanced on the right thigh while one wrote" ("Vocabulary of Wax Tablets," 221). For tablets through the Early Modern period, see Stallybrass et al., "Hamlet's Tables," esp. 383–5.

seems likely that early Anglo-Saxon documents were produced at ecclesiastical scriptoria, the question of whether there was ever a royal chancery in Anglo-Saxon England has been a matter of some debate. Pierre Chaplais has argued that there was no royal chancery in Anglo-Saxon England, or at least that there was no well-organized royal chancery by the end of the period.[17] *Contra* Chaplais, Simon Keynes is adamant that charters must have been produced outside of ecclesiastical scriptoria by at least the tenth century, because they involve secular concerns and because kings might have wanted to produce documents without the involvement of churches, with whom they did not share interests.[18] He believes there was a secretariat that travelled with the king in the 930s and 940s,[19] and, although production of charters was not static, he argues that this central royal agency existed at least through the end of the Anglo-Saxon period. Keynes concludes that this agency was also responsible for producing royal letters to be sent to the English people.[20]

While there is no evidence for a fully articulated Anglo-Saxon epistolary theory, several scholars have argued that the epistolary tradition must have continued uninterrupted from antiquity through to the birth of the *ars dictaminis* in the late eleventh or twelfth century.[21] The *ars dictaminis* dictated that letters follow a five-part structure, comprising:

1 *salutatio* (greeting)
2 *exordium* (also known as the proem, *arenga*, or *captatio benevolentiae*)
3 *narratio*
4 *petitio*
5 *conclusio*

---

17 Chaplais, "Origin and Authenticity" and "Anglo-Saxon Chancery."
18 Keynes, *Diplomas of King Æthelred*, 38–9.
19 Ibid., 39–46.
20 Ibid., 229.
21 The production of the first *ars dictaminis* is generally attributed to Alberic of Monte Cassino (late eleventh century) or to Adalberto Samaritano (early twelfth century). C. Julius Victor's *Ars rhetorica* (fourth century) is often cited as an early epistolary theory, and Donald Bullough argues that Alcuin was familiar with it even though he does not quote the chapter on letters (*Alcuin*, 298–9). However, Martin Camargo calls Victor's work an "anomaly" that did not influence later theorists (*Ars Dictaminis*, 29–31). For evidence of epistolary theory in Anglo-Saxon England and the early Middle Ages, see Patt, "The Early 'ars dictaminis'" and Lanham, "Freshman Composition." For more on the *ars dictaminis* of the twelfth to fifteenth centuries, see Camargo, *Ars Dictaminis* and Murphy, *Rhetoric in the Middle Ages*.

The *salutatio* identified both the writer and addressee; which name came first was usually determined by social protocol. The *exordium* was aimed at persuading the reader to be sympathetic to the letter writer's cause. It might take the form of proverbial material, scriptural quotation, or personal anecdote. The *Rationes dictandi* (1135) recommends the sender humbly state the cause or experience, praise the recipient, and remind the recipient of their relationship.[22] The *narratio* presented the main subject of the letter, including the history or current state of the situation. The *petitio* made a request, and the *conclusio* could restate the letter's main subject or offer a formulaic farewell address.

In the view of some scholars of early medieval epistolarity, the *ars dictaminis* merely codified a practice that had been developing for centuries, evidence for which can be found in classroom texts and patristic letter writers. Letter writing was taught in early medieval classrooms.[23] Alcuin refers to teaching students *epistolas*, and the collection of Alcuin's Latin letters found in London, BL Cotton Vespasian A.xiv pt iii, an early eleventh-century manuscript produced for or by Wulfstan, may have formed a model letter collection for the use of students.[24] There is no equivalent to the *ars dictaminis* from the early Middle Ages, but there are at least two references to epistolary theory (one a paragraph, the other a short phrase) from the late eighth to early ninth centuries.[25] As possible evidence for a continuous practice of epistolary theory between antiquity and the *ars dictaminis*, Martin Camargo cites Carolingian formularies as well as tenth-century letters that seem to follow the five-part structure of later letters.[26] Some Anglo-Latin formularies may have been available to Anglo-Saxon letter writers; for example, Donald Bullough argues that the eleventh-century collection of Alcuin's letters in folios 2–66v of BL Cotton Tiberius A.xv was "a modest-sized 'formulary'" organized around letters associated with Canterbury.[27] Likewise, Andy Orchard suggests that the Bonifatian

---

22 Anonymous of Bologna, "Principles of Letter-Writing," 17.

23 Lanham, "Freshman Composition," 124–7.

24 Ibid., 125; Chase, ed., *Two Alcuin Letter-Books*, 3. However, Donald Bullough counters that this manuscript was "for portability and personal use rather than for the schoolroom or scriptorium" (*Alcuin*, 97). The manuscript is *Handlist*, item 383; Ker no. 204.

25 The paragraph is in Paris, Bibliothèque nationale lat. 7530, and the phrase appears in "at least nine grammars or commentaries on Donatus" (Lanham, "Freshman Composition," 120).

26 Camargo, *Ars Dictaminis*, 29–30.

27 Bullough, *Alcuin*, 86.

correspondence may have been "intended to offer a kind of epistolary pattern-book for a range of occasions."[28] Moreover, it seems that Anglo-Saxon authors were aware of and producing letters that conformed to a four- or five-part structure.[29] As Mark Griffith has shown, Ælfric's *Preface to Genesis* (no later than 998) follows the five-part epistolary structure. Although the *Preface to Genesis* predates the formal *ars dictaminis*, Griffith cites evidence of tenth- and eleventh-century authors who used a five-part structure before it was explicitly codified.[30] Likewise, Bernard Huppé has demonstrated that the vernacular prose preface to the Alfredian translation of Gregory's *Regula Pastoralis* follows the five-part structure commonly associated with the *ars dictaminis*.[31] It seems that early medieval letters owe their form not to the great Classical letter writers like Cicero, Pliny, and Horace, but to the patristic writers of the fourth to sixth centuries. Griffith demonstrates that Ælfric was influenced by Jerome's prefaces to the Bible and could have been influenced by prefaces by Augustine, Gregory, and Bede as well.[32] Alcuin's sources and influences included Augustine and Jerome, papal letters and other patristic authors, and the Psalter and lectionary.[33] Anglo-Saxon letter writers were also influenced by their predecessors and contemporaries; Andy Orchard demonstrates the use of Aldhelmian style and shared literary formulae among the Boniface circle.[34] Anglo-Saxons may also have been exposed to epistolarity via the salutation formulae that opened writs, and by the reading of the Epistles as part of the liturgy.[35]

---

28 Orchard, "Old Sources," 18.

29 Early medieval Anglo-Latin letters used a four-part structure that lacked a separate *petitio* (Griffith, "Ælfric's Preface to Genesis," 233).

30 Ibid., 227–8.

31 Huppé, "Alfred and Aelfric," divides the prose preface into five sections based primarily on repeated words and phrases found at transitional moments. Although some of the evidence he marshals in support of this structure seems tenuous, the overall claim holds.

32 Griffith, "Ælfric's Preface to Genesis," 220.

33 Bullough, *Alcuin*, 171–8, 263–6, 296–9.

34 Orchard, "Old Sources."

35 For an introduction to manuscript evidence relating to the Anglo-Saxon liturgy, see Lenker, "The *West Saxon Gospels*." We know that there were two readings (a first reading, which could be from Epistles, and a second reading from the gospel), but there are no extant Anglo-Saxon books for just the first reading. However, Lenker finds evidence for their existence in Anglo-Saxon booklists, including a reference to a *pistolboc* (epistolary), which was probably a full lectionary (157–9).

Salutations and Forms of Accessibility

Having surveyed the history of Anglo-Saxon letters and their sources and influences, the rest of the chapter turns to the theory of letters we can derive from letters themselves, and especially the ways in which Anglo-Saxon authors manipulated salutations and other formal protocols to increase access to epistolary content. Given the number of legal documents with epistolary salutations, the broad range of lexical choices used to describe letters, and the ambiguity of words like *ærende*, which could designate an oral or written message, a task, or even intercession, the concept of the letter in Anglo-Saxon England seems capacious indeed. Instead of seeking to define it, I urge that we follow the Anglo-Saxons' lead, conceiving of epistolarity not in terms of formal classification of letter types, but in terms of epistolary acts. These acts include all the protocols of letter writing, as well as the acts of translation necessary to represent epistolarity in the vernacular, sometimes to audiences who were less familiar with epistolary practices. In what follows, I attempt to define what "form" means in an epistolary context. Next, I turn to salutation formulae, arguing that Anglo-Saxon authors writing in Latin and the vernacular made use of standardized salutation forms, though as the next section of the chapter will demonstrate, they were equally comfortable omitting these formulae in order to create a sense of transparent access to the letter's content at the same time as they made visible the mediating role of a letter's editor.

The "form" of a letter comprises several meanings, ranging from salutation forms, to literary and generic structures, and to the layout of the message on a physical support. The rest of this chapter focuses on structural form – the formulae of the message's content. Form is crucial to letters because it is typically their special form (whether epistolary formulae or physical shape) that identifies them as letters and not some other kind of document. It should be said from the outset that it is difficult to reconstruct the formal (or rather, formulaic) qualities expected of an Anglo-Saxon letter, not only because rules were often broken, but also because letters copied into cartularies or excerpted within literary works often lost their salutation formulae. While I concentrate on form in this chapter, subsequent chapters will unsettle this focus, revealing that epistolary form is not the only feature that might identify something as a letter. Indeed, even this chapter, which focuses on salutations, vocabulary, and other formal characteristics, suggests the crucial role that materiality, style, and function play in Anglo-Saxon conceptions of epistolarity.

Because of the importance of the highly formulaic set of letter-writing conventions known as the *ars dictaminis*, scholars who study later medieval letters have tended to frame epistolarity primarily in terms of letters' formal characteristics. However, many representations of Old English letters seem to disregard form almost entirely, frequently omitting even the salutation and valediction, and there is no evidence of a similar drive to formally classify and categorize letter types in Anglo-Saxon England. Even when such classifications were formalized, letters were resistant to these categories. As John van Engen warns, historians of medieval letters "have … inherited an unresolved tension between contents and form" that comes not just from qualities inherent to the letters themselves, but also from trends in twentieth-century scholarship, which focused on categorizing letters by content and by whether they were real or fictional.[36] It is tempting but problematic to place too much emphasis on the letter's formal qualities; according to Martin Camargo, medieval genres were defined more by function than by form.[37] Still, an awareness of form and genre helps us conceptualize how readers of letters and epistolary prefaces might have understood such documents. The familiar protocols of a genre help audiences recognize and interpret a text, placing it in the context of similar texts and judging it based on this comparison.[38] For example, if a reader had previously been exposed to epistolary prefaces, he or she would have recognized an epistolary preface as such from its opening lines, and would also have expected that preface to provide certain kinds of information – an account of how the work was translated or composed, the major themes of the work, and so on. Genres prepare audiences to encounter a text, and they also allow authors a container in which to play, a set of rules to follow or break. A sophisticated reader would have been sensitive to any deviations from the norm.

Salutation formulae are among the most obviously recognizable letter-writing protocols, with rules governing whose name was placed first, the number and kind of honorifics involved, and the nature of the greetings offered. According to Carol Dana Lanham, by the twelfth century Latin salutation formulae had developed from the relatively simple forms used in antiquity (*salutem*) to much more elaborate forms, gradually adding

---

36 van Engen, "Letters, Schools, and Written Culture," 109.
37 Camargo, *Middle English Verse*, 8.
38 For a survey of approaches to and definitions of genre applied to a medieval context, see Mullett, "Madness of Genre," esp. 233–5.

more complicated honorifics and titles, as well as greetings.[39] Aldhelm and other early Anglo-Saxon letter writers wrote salutations that were unusually elaborate for the time; Lanham describes Aldhelm's salutations as "precocious."[40] To take an example nearly at random, Boniface's early eighth-century letter to Nithard begins with this flourish: "To his dearest companion and friend Nithard, to whom he has recently been drawn, not by the passing gift of gold nor the smoothness of flattering words, but by the affinity of spiritual sympathy and the bonds of unfailing love, Wynfrith [Boniface] sends greeting and wishes for eternal welfare in Christ Jesus."[41]

It is difficult to identify a corpus of vernacular salutations from the period because so few remain except in writs. Nevertheless, there are a few conclusions we can draw about Old English salutation formulae, though the relatively small number of surviving letters written in Old English means these conclusions must be tentative. Ælfric often uses an expression on the model of "Ælfric [rank] gret [name, rank] [adverb]," as in the *Preface to Genesis* ("Ælfric munuc gret Æthelwærd ealdormann eadmodlice" [Ælfric, a monk, humbly greets ealdorman Æthelweard]) or the *Old English Letter to Sigeweard* ("Ælfric abbod gret freondlice Sigwerd æt Eastheolon" [Abbot Ælfric greets Sigeweard at Asthall in a friendly manner]).[42] A similarly spare form was used for most Old English writs as well. By contrast, the preface to the Old English *Prose Life of Guthlac*, itself a translation of Felix's preface to his Latin version of the text, begins "Urum wealdende rihtgelyfendum a worulda woruld, minum þam leofestan hlaforde ofer ealle oðre men, eorðlice kyningas, Alfwold Eastengla kyning, mid rihte and mid gerisenum rice healdend, Felix þone rihtan geleafan gesette eallum geleafullum godes folcum, and ecere gesundfulnysse hælo and gretingce gesend" (To our faithful ruler world without end, my most beloved lord above all other people, earthly kings, Ælfwald king of the East Angles, ruling the kingdom justly and properly, Felix decrees the true faith to all faithful people of God, and sends the salvation of eternal soundness

---

39 Lanham, *Salutatio Formulas.*

40 Ibid., 29.

41 "Carissimo sodali et amico dilectissimo, quem mihi non temporalis caducum auri munus nec mellitate per blandimenta adolantium verborum facetię urbanitas adscivit, sed spiritalis necessitudinis famosa adfinitas inmarcescibilis catena caritatis nuper copulavit, Nithardo Uuynfredus supplex in Christo Iesu perpetuae sospitatis salutem." Translation slightly modified from Emerton, *Letters of Saint Boniface*, Letter 1 [Tangl 9]. Latin from Tangl, *Die Briefe des Heiligen Bonifatius*, 4.

42 Wilcox, ed., *Ælfric's Prefaces.*

and greeting).[43] This suggests that Old English could adapt to elaborate Latinate formulae, but authors generally chose not to unless translating a Latin source.

Legal documents such as writs provide the largest quantity of evidence for Old English salutation formulae. The typical formula seems to have been "[King] greets [names, titles] in a friendly manner (*freondlice*)," but documents written on behalf of lower-ranking officials and women show more variation. The change may be as simple as substituting "humbly" for "in a friendly manner" when addressing a superior, as in Wulfstan's writ of c. 1020: "Wulfstan arcebiscop gret Cnut cyning his hlaford 7 Ælfgyfe þa hlæfdian eadmodlice"[44] (Archbishop Wulfstan humbly greets his lord King Cnut and the lady Ælfgifu). Another popular modification of the adverb is to add "wel," as in Edwin's message to Bishop Ælfsige of Winchester regarding his recent vision of St Cuthbert: "Ic Eadwine munuk cilda mæstere an Niwan mynstre grete þe wel Ælfsige biscop"[45] (I, monk Edwin, childmaster at Newminster, greet you Bishop Ælfsige well). Notice that, even when the sender is lower ranking than the addressee, the sender's name almost always comes first (as in the two writs just cited). This means that salutation formulae in Old English do not necessarily conform to Latin standards for indicating social rank, which had strict rules regarding where to place the name of the highest-ranking party.[46]

Salutation formulae are typically written in the third person, though some are in the first person. For example, Harmer 113 (cited above) opens "Ic Eadwine" (I, Edwin). Likewise, Ælfric, who generally uses the third person to refer to himself in salutations, opens his letter to Wulfgeat "Ic Ælfric abbod on ðisum Engliscum gewrite / freondlice grete mid godes gretinge / Wulfget æt Ylmandune"[47] (I, abbot Ælfric, in this English writing greet Wulfgeat at Ylmandun in a friendly manner with God's greeting). The use of first person also appears in some letters embedded in saints' lives, as in Gregory's letter to Apollo in Ælfric's sermon *De Falsis Diis*

---

43 Gonser, ed., *Das angelsächsische Prosa-Leben*, 1.1–6.

44 Harmer no. 27.

45 Harmer no. 113.

46 In Alcuin's private letters, the addressee was usually named first (Bullough, *Alcuin*, 465). This does not follow the Latin protocol for selecting position of names based on rank, nor does it conform to the Old English standard of placing the sender's name first. Aldhelm's Latin letters generally place the addressee's name first.

47 Assmann, ed., *Angelsächsische Homilien*, p. 1, ll. 1–3.

("Ða awrat Gregorius þis gewrit to þam gode: / Ic grete þe, Apollo, and ic þe leafe sylle / eft to farenne into þinre stowe, / and þa þing to donne þe þu ær dydest"[48] [Then Gregory wrote this letter to the god: I greet you, Apollo, and I give you leave to travel again into your place, and to do those things which you previously did]) and in the preface to the Old English translation of Bede's *Ecclesiastical History* ("Ic Beda Cristes þeow and mæssepreost sende gretan ðone leofastan cyning Ceolwulf"[49] [I, Bede, servant of Christ and masspriest, send greetings to the most beloved king Ceolwulf]). Unlike formulae written in the third person, use of the first person immediately turns the letter into a speaking object, presenting itself from the beginning as though it offers unmediated access to the mind of the sender. This immediacy is a fictive, if common, suggestion. For example, Ælfric wrote several letters on behalf of his fellow religious, which he expected them to deliver as though written by them. The Latin preface to his letter for Wulfsige concludes "Nos vero scriptitamus hanc epistolam, quę Anglice sequitur, quasi ex tuo ore dictata sit et locutus esses ad clericos tibi subditos, hoc modo incipiens" (Indeed, we have written this letter, which follows in English, as if it were dictated from your mouth and you had spoken to the clerics under your charge, beginning in this way).[50]

In conclusion, there was some standardization in Old English salutation formulae, though slight variations were allowed in the choice of adverb, and some authors used first person as well as or instead of third person, even in the salutation formula. Moreover, there seems to be no major difference in salutation formulae between Old English independent letters, embedded letters, and epistolary prefaces. The fact that many epistolary legal documents were written in the vernacular rather than Latin suggests that the laity did have some awareness of epistolary form, and the standardization of salutation formulae also implies that letters in the vernacular were not an entirely new concept. However, the fact that Old English salutation formulae are rather succinct as compared to their Latin counterparts suggests that salutations were considered more utilitarian and less necessary for communicating social status.[51] Even if Anglo-Saxons did not

---

48 Pope, ed., *Homilies of Ælfric*, 21, 615–18.

49 Miller, ed., *Old English Version of Bede*, preface, 1–2.

50 Wilcox, ed., *Ælfric's Prefaces* 8a, lines 10–12. Wilcox's translation.

51 By contrast, van Engen places a great deal of weight on the function of the salutation in eleventh- and twelfth-century letters: "When such letters were read out to their intended recipients, the *salutatio* was crucial … All that one intended to communicate, either for one's self or for one's patron, would achieve little effect if one did not enter

use Latinate formal conventions, they were still interested in the theoretical underpinnings of the protocols of epistolary acts, such as accessibility, transmission, and immediacy, as the next section will demonstrate.

Remediation: Editorial Prefaces and Interventions

When letters were represented within other texts or recopied into cartularies, epistolary formulae were often removed and, in some cases, the content of the message was abridged or omitted. Rather than seeing this as evidence that Old English audiences were unfamiliar with epistolarity, I argue that this suggests the breadth of what letters could be and do. Old English salutation formulae suggest that Anglo-Saxons had a rigorous epistolary theory, which adapted Latin formulae and something like the five-part structure of the later *ars dictaminis* even in the absence of formal epistolary rhetoric as such. That Anglo-Saxon epistolarity *could* participate in formal strategies known on the Continent makes it all the more significant that representations of epistolarity did not always do so. In this section, I examine how editors adapted salutation formulae and other epistolary forms to heighten the letter's sense of immediacy when storing or retransmitting letters. Sometimes the omission of a salutation was a deliberate choice meant to create a more universal audience for the message. When salutation formulae were preserved, they were often used to remind audiences of the larger Christian communities within which the Anglo-Saxons sought to participate. In both cases, editorial choices regarding epistolary formulae were intended to shape the accessibility of the letter's content, and editors were willing to manipulate the formal protocols of independent letters. In other words, the Anglo-Saxons could play with form, which suggests they knew the standard formulae, and they knew them well.

When Anglo-Saxon editors omitted salutations, added new prefatory material, or otherwise modified a letter's original context in the act of recopying it for new audiences, they participated in what new media theorists Jay David Bolter and Richard Grusin call the "double logic of *remediation.*"[52] According to Bolter and Grusin, remediation, which always involves "oscillat[ion] between immediacy and hypermediacy,

---

properly into the presence of the person for whom it was intended. It was the literary equivalent of bodily etiquette at court" ("Letters, Schools, and Written Culture," 114).
52 Bolter and Grusin, *Remediation*, 5; emphasis in original.

between transparency and opacity," explains why new media often represent older media forms, as when early printed books were hand illustrated or set in type meant to imitate the look of medieval manuscripts.[53] In this context, "immediacy" refers to a lack of mediation, the fantasy that the medium disappears before the viewer's eyes. For example, literate people reading a standard bound codex (i.e., one without special illustrations or formatting) in the twenty-first century may feel as though they are in the world of the story, forgetting that the text is printed on paper and enclosed between boards. "Hypermediacy" refers to an excessive mediacy or mediacies, something that deliberately draws the audience's attention to the medium, often by combining old and new media. For example, a website might include text (mimicking the codex), but also embedded video and audio clips. I argue that epistolary prefaces and letters copied into other manuscripts embody this "double logic" of remediation, one made possible by the special characteristics of epistolarity. Encountering a letter as copied in a manuscript or as explained by someone who knows the text, rather than encountering a letter as mediated by a salutation or by a messenger (or the representation of a messenger embedded within a longer narrative), may devalue or even seem to make transparent the vessel that transmits the message, creating a sense of immediacy. Simultaneously, such editorial interventions draw attention to the letter as letter, making audiences sensitive to epistolary protocols and media.

Although Anglo-Saxons who were well trained in Latin were more than capable of supplying appropriate salutations, letters embedded within other texts, or "real" letters copied into other manuscripts, often omit the salutation and/or subscription, sometimes replacing the salutation with an editorial preface, a kind of extended rubric that announces the subject of text. Substituting editorial voice for epistolary salutation reshapes the audience of the letter as well as the temporal fixity of the message. The message is thus made simultaneously more and less accessible to its new audience. On the one hand, without a formal salutation, there is no list of named addressees from which the reader or listener might be excluded. On the other hand, in drafting a preface, the editor of the letter adds a layer of separation between the audience and the letter itself, reminding them that their access to the letter is only ever as mediated through or framed by the editor. The preface exhibits hypermediacy, making the

---

53 Ibid., 19.

audience aware of the medium as medium, or of the letter as letter, even as it strips away one of the formulae most likely to identify a document as epistolary. To take one example, here is the beginning of the Old English *Letter of Alexander to Aristotle*:

> Her is seo gesetenis Alexandres epistoles þæs miclan kyninges 7 þæs mæran Macedoniscan, þone he wrat 7 sende to Aristotile his magistre be gesetenisse Indie þære miclan þeode, 7 be þære widgalnisse his siðfato 7 his fora, þe he geond middangeard ferde. Cwæþ he þus sona ærest in fruman þæs epistoles ...[54]

> Here is the composition of the letter of Alexander the great king and famous Macedonian, which he wrote and sent to his teacher Aristotle about the extent of the great nation of India, and about the vastness of his expeditions and journeys, which he travelled throughout the world. He said thus first of all in the beginning of the letter ...

No salutation formula follows this editorial preface, though Alexander's letter continues in the first person, saying that he keeps Aristotle and his mother and sisters in mind always. The letter proper opens "Simle ic beo gemindig þin ..." (I am always mindful of you).[55] The preface mediates our access to the letter, framing it as the composition or written account of the letter, as summarized by the editor, rather than the original letter as such.

Likewise, when Boniface's letter to Eadburga about the vision of the monk of Much Wenlock was translated into Old English, an editorial preface was substituted for the original salutation formula:

> Her sagað on þissum bocum þæt domne Wynfrið sende þis gewrit ærost to þissum leodum, bi sumum preoste se wæs þrage forðfered and gehwyrfde þa eft to his lichaman. He sæde þæt he bicome to þisse þeode, and þæt he spæce wið ðone preost, "and he me þa rehte þa wundorlican gesihðe þa þe he geseah þa he wæs buton lichaman, and þis he me rehte eall his agene worde.
>
> "He cwæð þæt him geeode þurh nedbade þæt his lichama wære seoc geworden, and he was semninga þy gaste benæmed. And him þuhte þæt it wære

---

54 The *Letter of Alexander* has been edited and translated by Andy Orchard in *Pride and Prodigies*, §1. (Translation my own.)
55 Ibid., §2.

on þære onlicnysse þe him man þa eagan weccende mid þicce hrægle for-
brugde ..."[56]

It says here in these books that lord Wynfrith [Boniface] sent this letter first
to these people, about a certain priest who had died for a time and then returned to his body. He said that he came to this people, and that he spoke
with the priest, "and he told me the wonderful vision which he saw when he
was without body, and he told me all this in his own words.

"He said that it happened to him through bodily torment that his body
became sick, and it was immediately deprived of the soul. And it seemed to
him that it was in appearance as if someone covered his waking eyes with a
thick cloth ..."

The omission of the salutation transforms the letter from Boniface's direct address to his reported speech, itself reporting the account of the
priest who had the vision. The framework of the letter, which in Latin included a subscription and salutation to a beloved sister named Eadburga,
has been removed. By removing the salutation, the Old English translator
eliminates the potential for the new, more general audience to feel excluded from the letter or unidentified with the original addressee (who was,
after all, a woman who lived hundreds of years earlier). At the same time,
the Old English translator creates a series of barriers to access to the original story by layering this preface with references to the letter's transmission history: the account Boniface heard from the monk himself, retold in
Boniface's letter, which was then found by the translator *on þissum bocum*.
By both removing the potential barrier of the address to Eadburga and
imposing the barriers of the editorial preface, the Old English translator
creates a simultaneous sense of immediacy and hypermediacy. Just as
Boniface's original letter remediates the oral account of the priest's vision,
the Old English editor remediates Boniface. On the one hand, the translation of Boniface's letter seeks immediacy, the erasure of our awareness of
the medium. The translator attempts to remove some of the potential mediation between the monk's experience and the audience's reception of his
account by eliminating reminders that this letter was originally addressed

---

56 Sisam, ed., *Studies in the History of Old English Literature*, 212–13, §1–2. Sisam also
   prints the Latin source. Boniface's original letter is c. 717, while the Old English
   translation is eleventh century.

to someone who lived hundreds of years earlier. The intervening textual medium is obscured by presenting the bulk of the message as the reported speech of the monk himself. At the same time, when the translator carefully cites his chain of sources, he makes explicit to the audience the layers of mediation that separate them from the monk's experience: it is an English translation of a written Latin letter describing an oral account of a personal vision. In this way, the translation might be said to be hypermediate, making opaque and visible its own media instantiation. As Bolter and Grusin put it, "our culture wants both to multiply its media and to erase all traces of mediation: ideally, it wants to erase its media in the very act of multiplying them."[57] In the same way, the Old English translator multiplies the layers of prefatory materials (hypermediacy) while simultaneously erasing the salutation formula (immediacy). The illusion of immediacy is achieved via several techniques. By modifying the salutation, the Old English translator removes the roles of Boniface and Eadburga, allowing the audience to forget what they have just been told (that this is an account found in a book and written in a letter by Boniface). This makes it possible for the audience to imagine that they are hearing a report of the vision directly from the priest who experienced it. Without the epistolary framework, the letter offers the illusion of transparency and direct access to the priest, as though the letter records perfectly the message the priest spoke, without human intervention or mediation. Omitting salutation formulae does not take letters out of circulation. They continue to speak to their audiences, potentially circulating on a broader scale than they might have if the original address were preserved.

The Double Immediacy of Letters

Immediacy is not only a concern of editors who transmit letters in cartularies. Immediacy is an inherent desire of salutations as well, because they offer the fiction of direct access to the mind of the sender. Immediacy as a driving concern of letters is reflected in the Biblical Epistles, which represented to medieval audiences concerns of the present, as opposed to the Gospels, which were seen as messages about the more distant past and/or sent from the distance of heaven. Alain Boureau, describing the rise of letter-writing norms in the eleventh century and beyond, argues that medieval Christians' understanding of letters was directly influenced by the

---

57 Bolter and Grusin, *Remediation*, 5.

presentation of the Epistles in the liturgy. For medieval audiences, he claims, the Epistles were associated with the present moment, ordinariness, and "immediacy," while the Gospels always looked backward, to the past.[58] In this section, I introduce the concept of the "double immediacy" of letters, then turn to a selection of illustrative examples for how Anglo-Saxon authors may have conceived of proper epistolary style and function, including the use of overtly personal and emotional content to evoke immediacy.

Anglo-Saxon epistolarity reflects what I call the double immediacy of the letter.[59] Letters intend immediacy in two senses. The first draws on epistolary theory, in which "immediacy" refers both to the fiction of face-to-face communication between letter writer and recipient, as though the distances of time and space that separate them have fallen away, and the recipient has unfettered access to the writer's thoughts, as well as to the fantasy that the letter is written spontaneously and represents unimpeded access to the thoughts and feelings of the writer as they occurred to him or her. Eighteenth-century letters are commonly associated with "epistolary tropes of immediacy, intimacy, and authenticity."[60] Second, the immediacy of the letter reflects "immediacy" as it is understood in media studies. This concept is also related to the immediacy of epistolary theory, but with a difference. In media studies, "immediacy" refers to the desire to create a strong a sense of unimpeded communication between sender and addressee (despite the fact that the two are separated by distance and/or time, and that the message is delivered not by the author but by a third-party messenger) by making the materiality of the message as unremarkable and therefore invisible as possible. If one can look past, or look through, the fact of words written on parchment or incised on wax, one might begin to imagine that there is no medium at all dividing sender and recipient. In this way, the immediacy of epistolarity is already bound up with some of the driving concerns of media studies. As I will demonstrate, the basic tenets of epistolary theory in Anglo-Saxon England *do* strive for a range of expressions of this double immediacy. One way the letter contributes to this is by mimicking spontaneous personal communication via the use of first

---

58 Boureau, "Letter-Writing Norm," 28–30.

59 This term, and the idea behind it, is influenced by Bolton and Grusin's "double logic" of remediation.

60 Cook, *Epistolary Bodies*, vii.

person, elaborate salutation forms, persuasive *exordia*, and other formal techniques. Paradoxically, the vernacular letter also sometimes achieves this immediacy by omitting these same forms in order to translate a letter to a new context.

One characteristic of epistolary theories of many periods is that they often emphasize the separation of sender and receiver as crucial to the ways letters are imagined to create meaning. Anglo-Saxon authors repeated this familiar anxiety about the distance between sender and recipient, but it was reflected differently in Anglo-Latin and vernacular letters. In both, the double immediacy of letters (i.e., the desire to make letters "immediate" in a media studies sense as well as an epistolary one) informs concerns about the sender's absence. Anglo-Saxon authors did care about how letters could make the absent sender present to the recipient, and they conceived this in affective terms. Some Latin authors, at least, were confident in expressing intimate emotions as a way of imagining how a letter's immediacy could both make the absent writer present, erasing the intervening medium of the document and the presence of the messenger, and also create the fiction of conducting the writer's spontaneous, most private ideas and thoughts as they occurred to him or her. For example, Alcuin writes of how letters and messengers make the faces and voices of absent friends seem almost unmediated and present before him: "I received your loving and religious letter from the priest Eanbald, who strongly endorsed its peaceful message with an affectionate greeting, conveying your never-ceasing brotherly love towards me, so that I wept as we talked, for I thought I heard your voices in every word. This came to me most clearly in your letter too, for, as I read, I seemed to see your faces."[61] This passage also highlights how both the spoken word of the messenger (Eanbald) and the written artefact of the document worked together to make the absent sender more present. The messenger produces one effect by some extra-textual extemporizing, but the letter (which he reads) has a similar but not

---

61 "Venerabiles vestrae dilectionis ab Eanbaldo presbitero accepi litteras, quarum pacificam inscriptionis seriem idem ipse, qui portavit, mellifluis vestrae salutationis verbis valde amplificavit, referens a vobis fraterni amoris perseverantiam in nos; ita ut inter lacrimas allocutionis nostrae vestras per singula verba voces me audire aestimarem. Quod et in litteris aperissime agnovi. In quibus legens vestras visum est mihi facies cernere." Dümmler, MGH, *Epistolae*, no. 43. Translation from Allott, *Alcuin of York*, Letter 2, pp. 3–4. Donald Bullough argues that Alcuin's personal and private correspondence is more emotionally expressive than scholars assume most medieval letters are (*Alcuin*, 110).

identical effect: conversation between messenger and recipient reproduces the sender's voice; reading reproduces his face.

Despite this fiction of immediacy, Anglo-Saxon letters were, in actuality, carefully crafted documents; even personal letters were generally not hastily composed. Moreover, the majority of extant Old English letters are public or practical rather than personal, especially if we include writs. One key difference between Anglo-Latin and Old English letters is in their treatment of the separation between letter writer and addressee. While distance between sender and recipient is sometimes foregrounded in Anglo-Latin letters, as it is in the Alcuin example discussed above, concerns about this distance appear much less frequently in the letters embedded within vernacular texts (outside more pragmatic letters alluded to only briefly in the Old English version of Bede's *Ecclesiastical History* or the Old English *Orosius*), and certainly much less often in miraculous letters than we might expect, given the religious desire to know God. While Anglo-Latin letters explain how they might bridge the distance between sender and receiver so that the sender becomes present via the letter, Old English embedded letters often eliminate the temporal and/or physical distance entirely, moving immediately from the desire to send a letter to its reception, without any attention to the process of writing, sending, or delivering it.

John van Engen's study of the culture of letter instruction in schools in the eleventh and twelfth century is predicated on the idea that what defines a letter is not salutation and subscription formulae, but the persuasive representation of the self: "The key trait distinguishing letters from treatises, documents, or books was therefore *the intention to represent one self to another*; or, following an antique image, to write as if two *personae* were speaking face to face, one voice personally addressing the other."[62] Van Engen's argument is that letters were *the* major genres taught in the schools, so theoretically they might have shaped literary expression and thought. But by excluding epistolary legal texts and other more documentary or bureaucratic texts, van Engen creates a false sense of continuity between medieval and post-medieval epistolary theory. His definition also does not take sufficient account of the fact that messengers were often authorized to elaborate on the written message of a letter, which complicates the idea of a letter as the self-expression of a single self. Van Engen argues that when messages were delivered by a messenger, the *salutatio*

62　van Engen, "Letters, Schools, and Written Culture," 107; emphasis added.

became even more important as a way for the author to represent his or her self despite physical absence, but as we will see, Old English letters did not place so much rhetorical weight on the *salutatio*. The idea that letters were intended to "represent one self to another" is the result of imagining the letter as a document whose primary purpose was to persuade the recipient, rather than to record events (as in the case of legal documents like writs). Although it is certainly true that some medieval letters sought to cultivate friendship or to express private feelings, this definition unfairly ignores the epistolary documents that sought to transact business, establish relationships between king and country, introduce travellers, or simply offer thanks.

At the same time, Old English letters were fully capable of exploiting the idea of representing one self to another in order to persuade the recipient to act as the sender prefers. The case of the so-called *Letter to Brother Edward* neatly illustrates this point. This fragmentary letter expresses anxiety at the behaviour and hairstyles of those in the Danelaw or "up-country." The author (possibly Ælfric) is appalled to learn that his rural compatriots wear their hair as the Danes do, long in the front and short in the back, in a reverse mullet. Even worse, the women eat and drink at the toilet. Ælfric is so overcome by the horror of the women's conduct that he stutters before he describes it, telling Edward that he has difficulty addressing the issue at all: "Ic bidde eac þe, broðor, forþam ðe þu byst uppan lande mid wimmannum oftor þonne ic beo, þæt þu him an þing secge, gif ðu for sceame swaþeah hit him secgan mæge; me sceamað þearle þæt ic hit secge ðe"[63] (I bid you also, brother, because you are up-country among women more often than I am, that you tell them one thing, if you might say it to them despite fear of shame; it shames me severely that I say it to you). Ælfric's letter of instruction creates a persona for the letter writer, whose own personal shame would ideally be absorbed by Brother Edward in the service of re-establishing proper conduct in the Danelaw. That is, the letter writer creates this persona to try to induce the recipient to feel what the persona (real or fictionalized for greater effect) claims to feel. But this is not a personal appeal to an individual; it is about community policy. The emotions expressed do not necessarily represent Ælfric's true self so much as they are intended to communicate the severity of the infraction and Ælfric's superior sense of

---

63 Clayton, ed., *Letter to Brother Edward*, ll. 21–3.

decorum. While the letter to Edward attempts to represent the writing self, many other Old English letters are equally or even more reserved, or seek to represent a stereotype or function (a good king, a good abbot, etc.) rather than the self of a unique individual.

Finally, theories of epistolary novels might inspire our understanding of Old English epistolarity, but they cannot account for many of the special conditions under which Anglo-Saxon letters were produced, transmitted, and received. Theories of epistolarity based on other periods or even "real" medieval Latin letters can be of only limited use to this project, not just because the circumstances of letter production and reception are so fundamentally altered by the creation of the public post office, but also because extant Old English letters do not seem to conform to some of the major themes and concerns identified by scholars studying both classical letters and letters influenced by the *ars dictaminis*. Anglo-Saxon epistolary style allowed emotional expression, but did not necessarily seek to communicate the feelings of an individual so much as those of a persona. Moreover, while personal letters were more expressive, we must not overlook the epistolary legal documents and business documents that represent the bulk of Anglo-Saxon vernacular epistolarity, many of which conformed to different stylistic rules. Still, Anglo-Saxon letters are more emotional than some have believed early medieval letters are, and it is through exploiting the distance between sender and addressee, and the double immediacy of the letter, that these affective styles are achieved.

Porous Vocabulary and the Writing on the Wall

The first part of this chapter has examined ways in which we might recover Anglo-Saxon epistolarity via study of salutations and the creation of immediacy. Another method of recovering the protocols and theories behind Anglo-Saxon epistolarity is through study of the vocabulary with which Anglo-Saxon authors named what letters were, and of how they transferred Latinate concepts of epistolarity to English vocabulary. Anglo-Saxon authors' porous sense of what a letter was, and their more capacious understanding of inscriptional media, is reflected in the wide range of words that Old English used to denote letters. In what follows, I survey the lexical choices, both Latin and vernacular, that Anglo-Saxon authors applied to epistolary acts, ending with an extended consideration of the relatively rare Old English word *ærendboc* (letter), used in the poetic *Daniel* to describe the writing on the wall. The semantic flexibility of this word perfectly captures the ways in which Anglo-Saxon understandings of epistolarity and inscriptional media were broader and more metaphorical than a staid consideration of epistolary categories and forms might suggest. Ultimately, Old English vocabulary for letters and other written media suggests not that Anglo-Saxons had a weak idea of the letter, but rather that some Anglo-Saxons were aware of Latin epistolary traditions and were translating them, sometimes in playful or surprising ways, into vernacular contexts for new audiences.

The word "letter" (in the sense of epistle) did not enter the English language until the early thirteenth century. The Latinate *(e)pistol* was used in Old English only in limited contexts, and, according to the *OED*, the Latin *breve* "entered at an early period into all the Germanic languages" except Old English.[64] Anglo-Saxon authors writing in the vernacular had to make choices about how to present letters to their audiences without using terms that were potentially unfamiliar because they were considered too Latinate or because they were not yet available in English. Latin vocabulary for letters also reflected the broader range of genres that were considered epistolary in the Middle Ages. Latin *epistola* most obviously meant "letter," but could also mean a "literary composition in epistolary form … [or] preface."[65] Vernacular authors had recourse to terms whose semantic range seems to have been restricted to letters, written messages, and short documents, such as *ærendgewrit* (written message or letter), but frequently referred to letters by the more generic *(ge)writ* (any written document).[66] A *carte* could be a letter, but it could also refer to a charter or legal document or to the parchment on which such documents were

---

64   *OED*, *s.v.* "letter, n. 1"; *OED*, *s.v.* "brief, n. 1." *DMLBS*, *s.v.* "brevis, n. 4" offers several examples of the Latin word meaning "short letter or document, note," as does "brevis, n. 9," meaning "papal brief," all of which are from the twelfth century or later. The term is also used with reference to writs. For *epistol*, see *DOE*, *s.v.* "epistol, epistola" ("a letter, written message; written decree") and "epistol, epistola, 1a": "specifically: one of the apostolic Epistles forming part of the canon of Scripture." BT, *s.v.* "epistol," "a letter"; *s.v.* "pistol," "an epistle, letter."

65   *DMLBS*, *s.v.* "epistola, n. 1 and n. 2."

66   *Ærendwrit* appears only twice in the corpus, while *ærendgewrit* appears c. 85 times. Both have the primary meaning "written message, letter" (*DOE*, *s.v.* "ærend-writ"; *s.v.* "ærend-gewrit"). See also BT, *s.v.* "ærend-gewrit," "a message or report in writing, a letter, an epistle, letters mandatory, a brief writing, short notes, a summary." BT defines the more general *gewrit* "something written, writing, scripture, inscription, a writing, letter, treatise, writ, charter, book" and *writ* as "a writing" or "holy writ, scripture." The Old English Thesaurus entries for "writing materials" are under 09.03 .07.06; for "a letter," see 475. Roberts and Kay, with Grundy, *Thesaurus of Old English*.

written.[67] Sometimes the use of verbs for sending or nouns for messengers (*ærendraca, ar, boda, hleapere*) helps distinguish letters from other documents, but the presence of messengers could also signal the delivery of a purely oral message. In general, Old English vocabulary for letters tends to centre around three main concepts: materiality, textuality, and movement. Words like *carte* could indicate genre (letter, charter, diploma) or the material on which such a document was written (a small piece of parchment).[68] Other words for letters emphasized the fact that letters, unlike oral messages, required the practice of writing (*ærendgewrit, gewrit*). For example, in a story about a document miraculously saved from a greedy bird, the Old English prose *Guthlac* restricts *gewrit* to contexts referring to the genre or writtenness of the document, while *carte* refers only to the material on which the message is written: "Mid þy he þær unmanige dagas wunode, þa gelamp hit, þæt he sum *gewrit* awrat on *cartan*. Þa he þa hæfde þæt *gewrit* awriten, þa eode he ut." (When he had stayed there a few days, then it happened that he wrote a certain *document* on *vellum*. When he had written that *document*, then he went out.)[69] Finally, compound words beginning in *ærend-*, such as *ærendgewrit* (letter), *ærendboc* (letter), and *ærendraca* (messenger),[70] distinguish letters from other written genres by emphasizing the movement of the message (*ærende*) across space and the absence of the sender, on whose behalf the messenger has been authorized to act.

Though fluid, Old English vocabulary for letters was not interchangeable.[71] *Ærendgewrit, epistol, pistol,* and *carte* appear only in prose, while

---

67   *Carte* appears c. 35 times in the corpus. *DOE, s.v.* "carte," offers a range of definitions, including medium as well as genre: "(leaf or sheet of) writing material (usually vellum)," but also "charter, diploma, document." See also BT, *s.v.* "carte," "paper, a piece of paper, a deed."

68   The related Latin *c(h)arta* also refers to the material on which a message is written, as well as a message of sufficient brevity to fit on that material. *DMLBS, s.v.* "charta, n. 1" "a. papyrus, b. paper, c. (sheet of) writing material (usu. parchment)," but also "literary work, letter or informal note" (n. 2) or "charter" (n. 3). Likewise, Lewis and Short, *s.v.* "charta," includes both "a leaf of the Egyptian papyrus, paper" and "that which is written upon paper, a writing, letter, poem, etc." (*A Latin Dictionary*). Niermeyer, *s.v.* "charta," gives "any written document ... 1. letter." Other definitions include "mandate," and "charter" (*Mediae Latinitatis Lexicon Minus*).

69   Gonser, ed., *Das angelsächsische Prosa-Leben*, 9.2–4. For the phrase "awrat on cartan," see *DOE, s.v.* "carte."

70   *DOE, s.v.* "ærend-wreca, ærend-raca," "one who is sent on an errand or mission" (c. 200 occurrences).

71   Research for this paragraph was facilitated by use of the Dictionary of Old English Corpus.

ærende appears in both prose and poetry. *Ærendgewrit*, which Nicole Guenther Discenza calls a "learned term and a prose word much more than a poetic one," sometimes refers to Pauline and apostolic letters, and appears in works by Ælfric, in the Old English translation of Bede's *Ecclesiastical History*, in religious and legal texts, and in glosses, where it translates or glosses words like *epistola*, *pittacium*, and *legationes*.[72] Likewise, *pistol* and *epistol* are used in learned contexts and to refer to apostolic letters, the letters of Jerome, and others. Ælfric uses the word *pistol* frequently, and other learned authors such as Byrhtferth use it, but it also appears in perhaps less learned contexts such as *Lacnunga*. Ælfric did not trust all his audiences to recognize this Latinate word; in *On Auguries* he explains that a letter of Paul is written in "anum pistole, þæt is ærendgewrit" (a *pistol*, that is a letter).[73] The closely related *epistol*, while also applied to apostolic letters, is used in a broader context than *pistol*, though most often when translating from Latin sources such as Gregory's *Dialogues*, Bede's *Ecclesiastical History*, and the *Orosius*. While some Old English authors translate Latin *epistola* with *(e)pistol*, others choose more Germanic vocabulary. For example, in the Old English *Gospel of Nicodemus* XV.3, Latin *epistole* becomes the more generic (but likely more familiar) Old English *gewryt*, while the Old English translation of Gregory the Great's *Dialogues* uses forms of *epistol* as well as forms of *ærendgewrit*.[74] Significantly, even when

---

72 Discenza, "Alfred's Verse Preface," 627. Discenza demonstrates how the blend of Latinate prose and English poetic forms and vocabulary in the Alfredian verse preface "enacts the cultural translation it describes" (629).

73 *LS* XVII, 2–3.

74 In Book 4, the Old English translator uses forms of *ærendgewrit* where the Latin has *epistolas*: "Ac he þa Mellitus him andwyrde þissara worda 7 þus cwæð, þæt þa tida his lifes wæron gefyllede 7 agane, 7 eac he sæde þam biscope, þæt him wære sum geong man ætywed, 7 se him brohte *ærendgewritu* 7 cwæde to him: 'untyn nu 7 ræd.' Þa sæde he, þæt he hi untynde, 7 þa funde he þær 7 geseah awritene mid gyldenum stafum in þam ylcan *ærendgewritum* ealle, þa þe wæron gefulwode in þa tide þære easterlican symbelnesse fram þam forecwedenan biscope Felice." Hecht, ed. *Bischofs Waerferth von Worcester*, 27.299.5–12 (emphasis added). (But Mellitus then answered him in these words and said thus, that the times of his life had been fulfilled and were gone, and likewise he said to the bishop that a certain young man had been revealed to him, and he brought him *letters* and said to him: "open now and read [them]." Then he said that he opened them and found there and saw written with golden letters in that same *letter* all those who had been baptized in the time of the Easter feast by the foresaid bishop Felix.) The Latin has "Sed ad haec ille respondit, cursus sui tempora esse completa, dicens apparuisse sibi juvenem, atque *epistolas* detulisse, dicentem: Aperi, et lege. Quibus apertis, asseruit quia se et omnes qui eodem tempore a praedicto episcopo in Paschali

an Anglo-Saxon author refers to a document using a range of terms we would not associate with a single genre in Modern English, the author is generally consistent in translation choices. What at first appears to be inconsistency or undertheorized translation choices may actually reflect the fluidity of the Latin original. Latin vocabulary for letters also affirms the Middle Ages' more capacious sense of what constituted a letter; for example, in a single poem, Baudri of Bourgueil (1046–1130) calls a letter *carta*, *volumen*, *liber*, and *pagina*; Peter the Venerable (c.1092–1156) used *libellus* and *tractatus* to mean "letter," and, according to Charles B. Faulhaber, Guido Faba's early thirteenth-century *Summa dictaminis* does the same: "He defines the letter in similar fashion: It is a *libellus* – technically a legal petition – sent to one who is absent (II.ii)."[75]

To illustrate the polysemy of Old English vocabulary for written documents, and the difficulty of determining the genre of a text solely from the vocabulary used to describe it, I want to turn to the appearance of the writing on the wall in the Old English poem *Daniel*. The word *ærendboc* appears three times in the Old English corpus: once in a prose sermon describing the *Sunday Letter* (a letter dictating proper Sunday behaviour, which claims to have been sent by Christ from heaven to earth), once glossing the Latin word *pittacium* (a short message or the material support for such a message), and once describing the writing on the wall in *Daniel* (line 734). A compound formed by the combination of *ærende* (message or

---

festivitate fuerant baptizati scriptos in eisdem *epistolis* litteris aureis invenisset" (*PL* vol. 77, Dialogi, XXVI col 361A, emphasis added). But in Book 1, Latin *epistolas* is rendered as English *epistol*: "Þa þe æfterfylgendan dæge sona on dægred com ærendraca to Iuliane mid *epistolan* 7 mid swiðe geswenctan horse for ærninge. In þam *epistolan* wæs beboden, þæt he ne gedyrstlæhte to þon, þæt he aht grette þone Godes þeowan, oþþe hine of ðam mynstre styrede" (4.38.27–4.39.1, emphasis added). (Then the next day a messenger came to Julian immediately at dawn with a *letter* and with a horse very fatigued from running. In that *letter* was commanded, that he dare not approach God's servant or direct him from the minster.) This translates the Latin "Cum ecce sequenti die sub ipso lucis crepusculo vehementer equo in cursu fatigato ad Julianum puer cum *epistola* pervenit, in qua praeceptum est ei ne servum Dei contingere vel movere de monasterio auderet" (*PL* vol. 77, Dialogi, IV col. 173C, emphasis added). But in the comparable passage from this text in Oxford, Bodleian Library, Hatton 76 (*Handlist*, item 632; Ker no. 328A), the translation calls the document *ærendgewrite* and *write*.

75 For Baudri, see Chartier, *Inscription and Erasure*, 8. For Peter the Venerable, see Constable, *Letters and Letter-Collections*, 25. For Guido Faba, see Faulhaber, "The *Summa dictaminis*," 94. Donald Bullough's study of Alcuin assumes that *libellus* refers to a letter on a bifolium or multiple folios (*Alcuin*, 42).

mission) and *boc* (any written document, not restricted in form or content), *ærendboc* is typically translated as "letter" or "written message."[76] This translation makes a certain amount of sense for the first two texts in which it appears, but it seems inappropriate to describe the writing on the wall in *Daniel* as a letter, not least because letters are usually *portable* documents that are transmitted across distances in time and/or space. Why, then, might *ærendboc* appear in the Old English *Daniel*, along with the two other contexts? Also at stake in the definition of *ærendboc* is the question of whether there is any significant difference between translating the word as "letter" or as "written document." And if the two are equivalent, what could that tell us about how Anglo-Saxons conceived of inscriptional media?

One use of *ærendboc* describes the *Sunday Letter*, a document that claims to have been sent from heaven to earth via an angelic messenger. There are five extant manuscripts of the *Letter* in Old English, representing at least two separate recensions.[77] In one subtype of the *Letter*, when people fail to believe the message, an Irish deacon named Niall is reincarnated to establish the *Letter*'s authenticity. The two extant witnesses of this version of the *Sunday Letter* in Old English are quite similar, but only one of them describes the letter from heaven as an *ærendboc* (the comparable passage in the other witness, Haines E, has *boc*). In what may be a moment of heightened or formal rhetoric, Pope Florentius and Bishop Peter swear an oath averring the letter's authenticity:

> Soþlice hie þæs wæran gewitan, þæt þis halige *gewrit* of heofonum com, and hio hit fundan anufan Sancte Petres altare. And hie þa forþan þus cwædan and miclum cyþdan: wit swerigaþ þurh þane micelan anwald ures dryhtenes and þurh þa halgan Cristes rode, þe he for manna helo aþrowade, þæt hit is eal soþ, þæt wit sæcgaþ, þæt fram nanum eorþlicum men þios dryhtnes *ærendboc* awriten ne wæs, ne mid bocblece, ne mid nenigum eorþlicum andweorce, ac hit wæs on Sancte Petres heahaltare funden þis gewrit þus awriten mid geldnum stafum.[78]

---

76 "written message, letter, document" (*DOE, s.v.* "ærend-boc"); "A letter, message; *epistola, litteræ*" (BT, *s.v.* "ærend-boc").

77 For the *Sunday Letter*, see chapter 2.

78 Haines F 215–22 (emphasis added; translation mine); Haines, ed. and trans., *Sunday Observance*. Haines notes that the oaths in non–Old English witnesses of this recension are more "elaborate" (196n58). The Latin version of the text found in the eleventh-century Munich, Bayerische Staatsbibliothek, clm 9550, which belongs to the same recension as the Old English Niall *Letter*, uses "epistola" here. Delehaye, "Note sur

Truly they [Peter and Florentius] were witnesses of this, that the holy *letter* came from heaven, and they found it on Saint Peter's altar. And they therefore spoke thus and made it much known: "we swear by the great power of our Lord and by the holy cross of Christ, on which he suffered for the salvation of men, that it is all true, that we say, that this *letter* [?] of the Lord was not written by any earthly man, nor with ink, nor with any earthly material, but this letter was found on Saint Peter's high altar thus written with golden letters."

At the beginning of this passage, the document is called a *gewrit*, which denotes any kind of written document. The use of *gewrit* here is deliberately ambiguous and multiple in its connotations. The phrase *halige gewrit* is obviously intended to suggest the document's affinity with holy scripture. At the same time, because the document has clearly been described as a letter earlier in the sermon, and because it is described here as having been transmitted from heaven to the altar, audiences would have been prepared to understand this document as a letter.[79] The use of the generic *gewrit*, followed by the more specific *ærendboc*, I argue, is meant to reflect how mysterious the letter had been to its recipients before it was successfully interpreted. Whereas it first seemed to be any kind of holy writing, once it was interpreted, and then attested by Peter and Florentius, it could be understood more precisely as an *ærendboc* (letter). A similar desire to replicate for the audience the initial process of assessing what this miraculous document is may have motivated the use of the generic *boc* at the equivalent moment in Haines E. While *boc* could mean any kind of written document, the term sometimes glosses Latin words for "letter, document." More significantly, *boc* could mean "charter" (as in *bocland*); its use here therefore conveys the legal authority of the letter from heaven.[80] Taken together, *ærendboc* might mean not just a letter, but "a legal or authoritative message transmitted via an intermediary."

---

la légende," 180. However, Munich 9550 is not a direct source for the Old English and, as Haines acknowledges, "few of the elements contained in both [Munich 9550 and Haines E and F] are verbally close to each other" (48). Haines F appears in the eleventh-century London, BL, Cotton Tiberius A.iii (*Handlist*, item 363; Ker no. 186).

79 The document is described elsewhere in the sermon as an *ærendgewrit* (written message, letter) and as God's *handgewrit* (handwriting or manuscript).

80 *DOE, s.v.* "boc[1]" and "boc-land."

A second use of *ærendboc* in the Old English corpus glosses the word *pittacium* in the Cleopatra Glossaries.[81] There are three glossaries in the Cleopatra Glossary (London, BL Cotton Cleopatra A.iii);[82] this word is found in the third, which provides glosses to Aldhelm's *De Virginitate*. In the passage from which the gloss is taken, Anatolia and Victoria have just upset their suitors by giving away all their possessions:

> Tunc Eugenius et Aurelius, qui sponsi earum futuri fore credebantur, fraudulento consilio et dissimulato negotio imperatoris *pittacia* impetrant, ut ab urbe Roma ad propria praedia ducerentur, ne forte, si christianae religionis titulo eas accusantes publica insimulatione propalarent, possessiones earum et agrorum fundi fiscali iure proscriberentur.[83]

> Then Eugenius and Aurelius, who were considered to be their [Anatolia and Victoria's] future spouses, by means of a fraudulent plan and dissembling procedure wangled out of the emperor a *note* (to the effect that) their fiancees would be taken away from the city of Rome to their own estates, because they wanted to avoid branding them with the name of the Christian religion by accusing them with a public charge, in case the virgins' possessions and their landed property would be confiscated by fiscal law.[84]

While Michael Lapidge and Michael Herren translate *pittacia* as "note," it is another capacious term, meaning "short letter or document," or a small leaf of parchment on which a short text could be written.[85] From the larger context of this passage, the *pittacium* is a document intended to be

---

81 The chronological relationship of these two examples is difficult to assess: the Haines F version of the *Sunday Letter* is found in an eleventh-century manuscript, but may have been composed in the ninth or tenth century (Haines, *Sunday Observance*, 86); the Cleopatra Glossaries have been dated to the 930s by Philip Guthrie Rusche in his unpublished PhD dissertation "The Cleopatra Glossaries," 3–4.

82 *Handlist*, item 319; Ker no. 143.

83 Ehwald, ed., *Aldhelmi Opera*, 308 (emphasis added).

84 Lapidge and Herren, *Aldhelm*, 120 (emphasis added).

85 Niermeyer, *Mediae Latinitatis Lexicon Minus*, s.v. "pittacium." *DMLBS*, s.v. "pittacium," gives as the first meaning "small piece, strip, or scrap of cloth or leather, patch, clout," which partly suggests how it also means, in its second definition, "small piece or scrap of parchment (w. ref. to writing thereon), short letter, brief text." Lewis and Short, *Latin Dictionary*, s.v. "pittacium," offers "a little leaf or slip of parchment, etc.; a ticket, label, on wine-bottles, etc."

shown to others, bearing the imprimatur of the emperor. Like the *Sunday Letter*, it is a legal document issued by a high ruler that is intended to be shown to multiple people in order to display that ruler's will and to legislate proper behaviour. It is entirely possible that an Anglo-Saxon author, thinking of the epistolary formulae that open Anglo-Saxon writs, would imagine the emperor's *pittacium* opened with a similar salutation.

Aldhelm's *De Virginitate* has been called "the most heavily glossed work from Anglo-Saxon England."[86] By examining the Latin and Old English glosses of *pittacium* in other glossed manuscripts of Aldhelm's *De Virginitate*, we can see that the word was frequently associated with letters, and that the use of *ærendbec* in the Cleopatra Glossary is not an aberration. The glosses for *pittacia* these manuscripts provide are the following:

ærendgewritu (three manuscripts)
i[d est] legationes, æryndgewritu (one manuscript)
i[d est] legationes (two manuscripts)
epistolas (one manuscript)
i[d est] legationes, ærendgewritu (one manuscript)
i[d est] sigillum (one manuscript)[87]

Five manuscripts give a form of *ærendgewrit* (one of the clearest designators of a letter in Old English), and one gives the Latin *epistolas*. What strikes me about this is not the overwhelming evidence that *pittacia* could be understood to mean "letter," but that the Cleopatra Glossary gives *ærendbec* when *ærendgewrit* was available as a gloss to so many other scribes, especially because *ærendgewrit* is used elsewhere in the Anglo-Saxon corpus to denote edicts and papal letters.

At this point, we could probably agree that the first two uses of *ærendboc* could be translated as "letter" or as "a written document taking a particular form and transmitting a particular kind of content, often legal or authoritative." The third use of the word complicates this picture. How can the writing on the wall in *Daniel* be a letter? Let us consider the appearance of the

---

86 Lendinara, *Anglo-Saxon Glosses*, 21.
87 Gwara, ed., *Aldhelmi Malmesbiriensis Prosa De Virginitate*, 688. These glosses have a complicated transmission history. Many survive in manuscripts associated with Canterbury, where the manuscript containing Haines F was produced, but the extant manuscripts mostly postdate the Cleopatra Glossaries (though they were copied from earlier source texts).

writing on the wall in the Old English poem, found in Oxford, Bodleian Library, Junius 11:

> Him þæt tacen wearð   þær he to starude,
> egeslic for eorlum   innan healle,
> þæt he for leodum   ligeword gecwæð.
>   Þa þær in egesan   engel drihtnes
> let his hand cuman   in þæt hea seld,
> wrat þa in wage   worda gerynu,
> baswe bocstafas,   burhsittendum.
>   Þa wearð folctoga   forht on mode,
> acul for þam egesan.   Geseah he engles hand
> in sele writan   Sennera wite.
>   Þæt gyddedon   gumena mænigeo,
> hæleð in healle,   hwæt seo hand write
> to þam beacne   burhsittendum.
> Werede comon   on þæt wundor seon,
> sohton þa swiðe   in sefan gehydum,
> hwæt seo hand write   haliges gastes.
>   Ne mihton arædan   runcræftige men
> engles *ærendbec*,   æðelinga cyn,
> oðþæt Daniel com,   drihtne gecoren,
> snotor and soðfæst,   in þæt seld gangan.[88]

To him [Baltassar] there appeared a sign where he looked, terrible for the men in the hall, that he had spoken a falsehood before the people. Then horribly the angel of the Lord allowed his hand to come into that high hall, wrote on the wall mysterious words, red/purple letters, for the city dwellers. Then the leader became frightened in his mind, dismayed because of the horror. He saw

---

88 Farrell, ed., *Daniel and Azarias*, ll. 717–36 (emphasis added). *Handlist*, item 640; Ker no. 334. On the Junius manuscript and its illustrations, see Karkov, *Text and Picture*. The provenance of the manuscript is unknown before the seventeenth century, but it is generally dated c. 1000. For a date of c. 960–c. 990, see Lockett, "Integrated Re-examination." On the poem's relation to its possible sources and the poet's treatment of the Song of the Three Youths, see Remley, *Old English Biblical Verse*, 231–434. After a period of sustained interest in the unity of the poem, much of the scholarship on the Old English *Daniel* has focused on the Nebuchadnezzar portion of the story (and the poet's modifications to it) rather than the Baltassar section. See, for example, Harbus, "Nebuchadnezzar's Dreams."

the angel's hand write the punishment of the Shinarites in the hall. The multitude of men, men in the hall, discussed what the hand had written as a sign for the city dwellers. Multitudes came to look on the wonder, they sought fiercely in the thoughts of their minds [for understanding of] what the hand of the holy spirit had written. Nor could the people skilled in mysteries, the group of nobles, interpret the angel's *letter/written message* [?], until Daniel, the one chosen by the Lord, wise and truthful, came walking into the hall.

The writing is described as a *tacen* (sign or portent), a *beacen* (sign or portent), and *wundor* (wonder, miracle).[89] Unlike the biblical account, the poet does not present us with the text of the message (Mane Thecel Phares), describing it allusively as "the punishment of the Shinarites" and "mysterious words" written in red or purple letters.[90] Like the *Sunday Letter*, the writing on the wall cannot be understood by its initial audience, and requires a mediating figure to explain it to them. The words of the message are not even revealed when Daniel comes to interpret them at the end of the poem, so the audience of the poem has access to the message only via the mediating figure of Daniel, as well as the mediating figure of the poet. The poet emphasizes not the message's content, but its appearance, both its physical characteristics and its enigmatic nature, as well as the fact that it is addressed to the *burhsittend* (city dwellers) (723, 729), who gather to stare uncomprehending at it until Daniel arrives to explain it to them. As many scholars have noted, Daniel is presented in the poem as an interpreter or scholar, and his ability to understand the writing on the wall stands in direct opposition to the oral boasts made by Baltassar that prompted the appearance of the writing.[91]

---

89 Karkov argues that in the Junius manuscript, "*beacen* and its compounds are used to describe striking spectacles, miracles, or signs witnessed by large groups of people," while in *Genesis*, "*tacen* is used only for marks made on the body" (*Text and Picture*, 130).

90 On the colour of the letters, see Farrell, *Daniel and Azarias*, 134–5; Remley, *Old English Biblical Verse*, 323n239; Lucas, "A Daniel Come to Judgement?" 88; and Anderson, "Style and Theme," 12–13. Anderson argues that Daniel 1–5 is the "*locus classicus*" for *translatio imperii*, and the writing on the wall has often been read in that context (18). Samantha Zacher argues that the Old English poet downplays *translatio imperii*, instead favouring what she calls *translatio electionis* – "transmission and expansion of the *status of election* from the nation of Israel to a more heterogeneous community of believers" (*Rewriting the Old Testament in Anglo-Saxon Verse*, 91; emphasis in original).

91 For Daniel as exegete, see Irvine, *Making of Textual Culture*, 449–51, and Lerer, *Literacy and Power*, 126–57.

Can we say more about the use of *ærendboc* here than that it designates some kind of written message whose nature is as mysterious as the words used to describe it? In trying to answer this question, I have looked at multiple illustrations of the writing on the wall in medieval manuscripts, including ones thought to best represent the illustrations that were intended for this portion of Junius 11.[92] No medieval examples that I have found help to clarify the medium of the message. Likewise, no comparable word describes the writing on the wall in the Vulgate:

in eadem hora apparuerunt digiti quasi manus hominis scribentes contra candelabrum *in superficie parietis* aulae regiae et rex aspiciebat articulos manus scribentis ... Et proloquens rex ait sapientibus Babylonis quicumque legerit *scripturam* hanc et interpretationem eius manifestam mihi fecerit purpura vestietur et torquem auream habebit in collo et tertius in regno meo erit. Tunc ingressi omnes sapientes regis non potuerunt nec *scripturam* legere nec interpretationem indicare regi ... Et nunc introgressi sunt in conspectu meo sapientes magi ut *scripturam* hanc legerent et interpretationem eius indicarent mihi et nequiverunt sensum sermonis huius edicere.[93]

In the same hour there appeared fingers as it were of the hand of a man writing over against the candlestick *upon the surface of the wall* of the king's palace, and the king beheld the joints of the hand that wrote ... And the king spoke and said to the wise men of Babylon, "Whosoever shall read this *writing* and shall make known to me the interpretation thereof shall be clothed with purple and shall have a golden chain on his neck and shall be the third man in my kingdom." Then came in all the king's wise men, but they could neither read the *writing* nor declare the interpretation to the king ... [who said] "And now the wise men, the magicians, have come in before me to read this *writing* and shew me the interpretation thereof, and they could not declare to me the meaning of this writing."

---

92 Though, as Karkov cautions, "comparison with other early medieval pictorial cycles is of limited value, as the completed Junius 11 drawings are as dissimilar as they are similar to the comparative material" (*Text and Picture*, 45).

93 Daniel 5:5–15 (emphasis added). There is some debate as to whether the Vulgate or an Old Latin text is the source for the Old English *Daniel*. I have consulted the Vetus Latina database and found no major differences between it and the Vulgate in this portion of Daniel – certainly nothing that justifies the use of *ærendboc*.

If the biblical source is not particularly illuminating, Middle English presentations of the writing on the wall are. In the *Gawain* poet's late fourteenth-century *Cleanness*, the writing is described in elaborate terms, referring to the appearance of not just a hand, but a *poyntel* (stylus) in its fingers: "Þer apered a paume, with poyntel in fyngres, / Þat watz grysly and gret, and grymly he wrytes; / Non oþer forme bot a fust faylande þe wryste / Pared [cut] on þe parget [plaster], purtrayed [formed] lettres."[94] After this description of the horrible appearance of the hand holding the stylus, the poet turns to the wall itself, expanding on the Vulgate's description of the writing as appearing on the surface or plaster of the wall. The poet emphasizes the wall's roughness, comparing the act of writing to plowing furrows in a field. The horrified onlookers stare as the hand continues to carve, "til hit hade al grauen / And rasped [scratched] on þe roȝ woȝ [wall] runisch sauez [saws]. / When hit þe scrypture hade scraped wyth a scrof [rough] penne, / As a coltour in clay cerues þe forȝes [furrows], / Þenne hit vanist verayly."[95] The *Cleanness* poet delights in the strangeness of the medium, as well as of the message. The hand's appearance is wondrous, but so is the labour it conducts in order to leave its message on such an uninviting surface. One can almost hear the stylus scraping, with great effort, against the rough wall. The poet borrows from a long tradition associating the comparatively easier and more familiar act of inscribing in wax with plowing the fields.[96] It is partly for this reason that I might be willing to agree with those who translate Old English *ærendboc* as "inscription."[97] In fact, in Chaucer's account of the writing on the wall in *The Monk's Tale*, the writing *is* described as an inscription. After the armless hand writes its message on the wall, Baltassar seeks an interpretation of the three words, but "In all that land magicien was noon / That koude expoune [explain] what this *lettre* mente."[98] The *Middle English*

---

94 *Cleanness*, 1533–6, in Andrew and Waldron, eds, *Poems of the Pearl Manuscript*. On the *Cleanness* poet's expansion of this scene from the Vulgate as compared to the *Daniel* poet's omissions, see Lucas, "A Daniel Come to Judgement?"

95 *Cleanness*, 1544–8.

96 Curtius, *European Literature*, 313–14.

97 Irvine, *Textual Culture*, 450. Lerer translates *ærendboc* as "message," but compares this passage to Aldhelm's analysis of Daniel in *De Virginitate*. Lerer draws suggestive connections between Aldhelm's analysis of Daniel and Aldhelm's *Enigma* 32 (writing tablets): "The curving forms of the divine handwriting, like the forms cut into schoolboy wax, are both acts of incision" (*Literacy and Power*, 136–8). However, Aldhelm's *De Virginitate* does not explicitly call the writing on the wall incisions in wax.

98 Chaucer, *The Riverside Chaucer*, 2207–8 (emphasis added).

Dictionary cites this text under definition 3(d) of *lettre*, "an inscription." Old English *ærendboc* cannot be an inscription in the *Sunday Letter* or the Cleopatra Glossary, but what if it were an inscription in *Daniel*? While there is no clear etymological reason for translating the word as such, if the writing were conceived in general terms as an inscription, then that sense must come not only from the *Daniel* poet's references to runic characters and mysterious writing, but also from the idea of carving words into the surface of a wall suggested by the Vulgate, and this would suggest that Anglo-Saxons understood that epistolary communication could take place in a wide variety of media forms, including messages carved in a wall.[99]

What conclusions can we draw from this survey of *ærendboc* and the writing on the wall? I believe that while the writing on the wall may not literally be a letter, it is meant to be understood metaphorically as one. The writing on the wall is a written message transmitted by God or his angelic messenger to the people of earth to warn them about their behaviour. In this sense, it is certainly like the *Sunday Letter*. Like letters, the writing on the wall is a written message sent from someone (God) to another person or group of people (the Babylonians or *burhsittend*), and Daniel can be understood as the intermediary who will perform and elaborate on the written message. Indeed, the *Daniel* poet frequently refers to him as a messenger of God, or *spelboda*. Metaphorically, then, the writing on the wall *is* a letter, with God as the author, the angel as the scribe, and Daniel as the messenger who delivers understanding of the message's contents to its intended audience. A letter, unlike an inscription, carries the sense of conveyance, of transmission over time and/or distance, both of which are implied by the first two uses of *ærendboc* discussed above. An inscription made by an angelic hand is remarkable to be sure, but why call attention to a mere inscription with such a rare word as *ærendboc*, unless one wants also to draw on the particular resonances of that word? An *ærendboc*, unlike the more general "inscription," is not just transmitted from sender to recipient; it is also affiliated with a special authority (legal or otherwise) not granted to all letters or *gewritu*. Moreover, if the writing on the wall is a letter rather than an inscription, then it needs a messenger to deliver it. Like a messenger who reads a letter aloud to its recipient, Daniel publicly interprets the message for its audience, who could not access the message

---

99 See also the discussion of Mary of Egypt's message written in the ground as a letter in chapter 3.

without his aid, and he bears the legal authorization of the sender (God), who designates him as messenger and vests him with the authority to interpret or expand on the written message, just as many messengers were expected to extemporize on the written text they conveyed.

As this excursus on Old English *ærendboc* demonstrates, terms for written media could be quite porous in Anglo-Saxon England. But that does not mean that the Anglo-Saxons had no conceptual idea of the variety of forms of written media, or of the letter. It is worth noting that *ærendboc* most clearly describes a letter in the *Sunday Letter* sermon, a text designed to be preached to a lay audience who may or may not have produced or received letters, while the most ambiguous use is in Junius 11, a manuscript designed for a more educated audience. I argue that the writing on the wall in the Old English *Daniel* is meant to be understood metaphorically as a letter from God. In order to have a metaphorical conception of something, one must first have a relatively advanced literal conception of it, and the act of imagining the writing on the wall (normally understood as a message or inscription) as a letter implies a sophisticated understanding of the ways in which written media could be remediated in new forms, asking audiences to attend to the letter's medium, portability, and protocols. Although there may be little evidence for an Anglo-Saxon *ars dictaminis*, and although Anglo-Saxon authors sometimes felt free to describe a single document using a wide variety of seemingly contradictory terms, it is clear that the Anglo-Saxons had a rich conception of written media in general and of letters in particular.

This chapter has surveyed the evidence for "real" Latin and vernacular epistolarity in Anglo-Saxon England, arguing that Anglo-Saxon epistolary acts involve thoughtful, deliberate translation of Latin epistolary culture and vocabulary for a vernacular context. I have attempted to recover Anglo-Saxon epistolary theory via study of epistolary practice, especially in "real" letters. This revealed two sets of protocols for letter writing: in the first section of the chapter, I traced the protocols of form, production, and preservation of letters via the history of the genre's structure and forms (especially salutations), sources for Anglo-Saxon epistolarity, and the early production of single-sheet letters versus cartularies. The second part of the chapter examined protocols for letters' style, content, and vocabulary. Old English letters' manipulation of form represents a desire to be doubly immediate, in both a media studies and epistolary theory framework. In the epistolary sense, letters strive to create immediate communication not impeded by temporal or geographic distance, representing the spontaneous thoughts of the sender. In a media sense, immediacy implies the disappearance of the letter as physical medium, such that the recipient imagines there is no medium separating him or her from sender. At the same time, letters may strive to be hypermediate – that is, to make the recipient all too aware of the touch of the material object once held by the sender, now held by messenger or recipient. Throughout, I have demonstrated that Anglo-Saxon letters, whether "real" or not, borrowed from Latin conventions in thoughtful and sometimes unexpected ways. Their use of salutation formulae was standardized, if less elaborate than some of their earlier Anglo-Latin counterparts, and they could manipulate the features and conventions of epistolarity to suit their purposes. Although no serious Anglo-Saxon *ars dictaminis* survives, Anglo-Saxons were far from being cut off from epistolary culture. Manipulating salutation formulas to make letters accessible to new audiences, thinking of inscriptional media as *metaphorically* epistolary, as in the Old English *Daniel*, or using the idea of the letter as a means to enter a Christian communications and cultural network, suggests that Anglo-Saxon epistolarity could be very sophisticated indeed.

2 Spreading the Word: The *Sunday Letter*, Mass Communication, and the Self-Replicating Document

In the previous chapter, I discussed the protocols of epistolary acts that are associated with the composition of letters, especially salutation formulae, exploring the ways in which letters' formulaic language controls access to their texts, shaping and preparing audiences for the message to come. In this chapter, I turn from formulaic and literary language to the ways in which Anglo-Saxon authors manipulated and understood a different kind of epistolary form: the physical, material format of letters. This chapter focuses on a work known as the *Sunday Letter*, a document that claims to be a letter sent from Christ in heaven to one of a number of holy sites on earth, mandating proper Sunday behaviour and threatening punishment for those who misbehave. In its post-medieval incarnations, the *Sunday Letter* becomes apotropaic, promising healing or protection for those who have it in their home or wear it on their bodies. In Anglo-Saxon England, by contrast, the Old English *Sunday Letters* devote minimal attention to their material qualities, and they do not claim to be apotropaic, although related Old English charms that claim to be based on letters delivered from heaven to earth do.[1] The Old English *Sunday Letters'* disavowal of the importance of the materiality of the original document subverts the expectations we might have for the genre, even as it reveals how broadly epistolary messages could appeal to Anglo-Saxon society and the ways in which authors of letters might encourage their continued transmission. By attending to materiality as an aspect of the *Letter's* provenance, but not making materiality the primary focus of the *Letter*, the authors of the

---

1 For letters as documents worn on the body for healing or protective purposes, see Skemer, *Binding Words*.

Letters are able to encourage the creation of textual communities of trans-mitters and enforcers of the *Letter*'s message.

The fact that the Old English *Letters* do not make more use of the dis-tinctive physical appearance of a letter can be explained by the form's adaptability. The Old English *Letters'* focus on the content of the docu-ment's message rather than its materiality frees them to be circulated in new and different ways, thus affording them more power to be what Emily Steiner calls "performative ... outside the literary fiction."[2] It might be most useful to think of these Old English *Letters* as early examples of the chain letter: by a combination of threats and promises, the chain letter in-spires its recipient not just to make a single copy, but to make multiple copies (or, in the twenty-first century, to forward the chain email to a pre-determined and often dismayingly large number of recipients).[3] Like the modern chain email, the medium in which the *Letter* circulates is important insofar as it is recognizable and replicable, but the written letter is only one of the media in which the *Sunday Letter* circulates, and ultimately it is its *content* that has the performative force.

The *Sunday Letter*[4] is an apocryphal document that purports to have been written by Jesus Christ while in heaven and sent by an angel to Rome or another holy site. In it, Christ admonishes the people to keep Sunday free from work or face terrible retribution, such as burning rain, sulfurous fire, poisons, flying adders, and gnats. The *Letter* comprises a series of catalogues of events said to have happened on Sunday along with lists of acceptable and forbidden behaviour, testimonials to the *Letter*'s authentic-ity, and accounts of its circulation. In Old English, the *Letter* never exists as an independent text, but is always found as part of a sermon. Many of

---

2 Steiner, *Documentary Culture*, 35.

3 This has been independently noted by many scholars of the *Sunday Letter*.

4 Also known as the *Carta Dominica*, the "Lettre du Christ tombée du ciel," and the "Heavenly Letter." The latter has fallen out of favour because it confuses the distinction between the *Sunday Letter* and other letters that claim to have come from heaven. Few Latin *Sunday Letters* survive before the Anglo-Saxon period. The best surveys of the Latin manuscripts are in Delehaye, "Note sur la légende"; Lees, "Sunday Letter"; and Haines, ed. and trans., *Sunday Observance*, 36–62. While many scholars believe that the *Letter* originated in fifth- or sixth-century Gaul and was originally composed in Latin, there are some advocates for an eastern origin, perhaps written in Coptic and later translated into Latin. As far as I have been able to tell, after Robert Priebsch published a series of articles advocating for a western origin, most later readers have been content to accept his argument. One of the few exceptions is Clare Lees, who merely cites in a footnote E. Renoir's entry in the *Dictionnaire d'archéologie chrétienne et de liturgie*

these *Letters*, or more properly, the sermons in which they appear, were once attributed to Archbishop Wulfstan, but their authorship is now considered anonymous.

In this chapter, I argue that the *Sunday Letter* imagines one way in which mass communication, or at least communication to (and by) the masses, might have been achieved via a combination of manuscript production and oral circulation. The Old English *Sunday Letter* sermons were catechetical *ad populum* or *quando uolveris* sermons meant to be preached to mixed and multiple audiences of lay people and clerics. Much like modern chain email, these sermons always contain injunctions to their audiences to continue to circulate the message whenever possible. I show that the Old English *Letter* seeks to create a community of believers, not by promising protection or healing attributed to the *Letter*'s special form, as post-medieval *Sunday Letters* do, but by encouraging neighbours to become informants (through the extension of the punishment for improper Sunday behaviour to those who witness it but do not report it). This community bears some similarity to Brian Stock's concept of textual communities. By blurring the distinctions between elite and popular culture; preacher, writer, and reader; and written and oral transmission, I argue, the *Sunday Letter* enforced and demanded its own continued circulation, creating an almost self-replicating document. Finally, I argue that, by blurring the distinction between preacher and audience, and by deputizing all audiences (lay, learned, or otherwise) to continue to circulate the message, the *Sunday Letter* created a hybrid community of disseminators of its message who were able to participate in its circulation no matter their level of literacy or access to technologies of manuscript production.

---

suggesting the possibility of an eastern origin ("Sunday Letter," 131n13). Priebsch connected the *Letter* to events in Gaul and Spain in 585 in his "Quelle und Abfassungszeit," 138. For eastern versions of the letter, see Dennis Deletant (who nevertheless thinks that the origin of the letter was Latin, in the fourth or fifth century, in Rome), "Sunday Legend," 449–51. For a fuller edition of early eastern *Letters*, see Bittner, *Der vom Himmel gefallene Brief Christi*. For other possible origins of the *Letter*, see Borsje, "The *Bruch*," 84n9. For attitudes towards Sunday in Byzantium from the ninth to twelfth centuries, see Baun, "Taboo or Gift?" Accounts of other letters from heaven, including some whose descriptions are so vague that we cannot know whether they are the *Sunday Letter* or not, may be found in W.R. Jones, "Heavenly Letter," 172, and Priebsch, *Letter from Heaven*, esp. pp. 30–1. This survey includes a fish being sent from heaven to a Cistercian abbot. For letters from heaven from ancient Egypt to 1900, see Bevan, *Sibyls and Seers*. For the Russian tradition, see Ryan, *The Bathhouse at Midnight*, 300.

Ultimately, I argue, the *Letter*'s brief popularity in Anglo-Saxon England and the later British Middle Ages derived not from a claim to have a single, fixed function such as apotropaism, but because the flexibility of the *Letter*'s form and content made it endlessly adaptable.

The History of the *Sunday Letter* in Early Medieval Insular Culture

From as early as the days of Moses to as recently as the present century, people have claimed to have received letters from God. Although the *Sunday Letter* is part of this larger tradition of heavenly letters, some of which, including the *Letter of Abgar*[5] and the *Charters of Christ*,[6] became popular in later medieval England, it has its own unique transmission history and content. There are six extant vernacular witnesses of the *Sunday Letter* from Anglo-Saxon England in five manuscripts, representing at least two different recensions.[7] The incipit of a seventh witness, now destroyed

---

5 More properly an exchange of letters between the ailing king Abgar and Jesus of Nazareth, the *Letter of Christ to Abgar* is represented in Old English by *De abgaro rege*, part of Ælfric's *Lives of Saints*. There are also glosses to the Abgar letter in two Anglo-Saxon manuscripts. I discuss the Abgar letter in the next chapter.

6 Most scholars believe that the *Charters of Christ* are unrelated to the *Sunday Letter*. Nevertheless there are some similarities between them, including the basic fact that both emphasize the use of Christ's body for the construction of a written document addressed to a wide audience. For an edition of the *Charters of Christ*, see Spalding, *Middle English Charters*. See also Steiner, *Documentary Culture*.

7 Both Recension I and Recension II are represented. Old English also has a special subtype of Recension II featuring a reincarnated Irish deacon named Niall. The most recent editor of the Old English *Sunday Letters*, Dorothy Haines, has called for "a new and more comprehensive study" of the relationships between the recensions (44). Throughout this essay, I will refer to the six Old English *Letters* using the designations of the new edition, calling them Haines A–F. The correspondence between Haines's designations for the letters and those used in earlier editions is as follows:
Haines A: Priebsch CCCC 140
Haines B: Napier XLV
Haines C: Napier LVII
Haines D: Napier CCCC 162
Haines E: Napier XLIII
Haines F: Napier XLIV
    For previous editions of the sermons formerly referred to as Napier XLIII, XLIV, XLV, and LVII, see Napier, *Wulfstan*. For Napier CCCC 162, see Napier, "Contributions to Old English Literature." For Priebsch CCCC 140, see Priebsch, "The Chief Sources."

by fire, was recorded in Wanley's catalogue.[8] Although there are accounts of the *Letter* in England dating to the ninth century, all five extant manuscripts can be dated to the eleventh century.[9] The popularity of the *Letter* in England seems to have been intense but sporadic. After the Anglo-Saxon period, vernacular versions of the *Letter* appear in medieval England only a handful of times, and with considerable gaps between appearances.[10] A Middle English sermon on the *Letter* and one independent Middle English text of the *Letter* are both found in a single manuscript from 1477, Durham University Library MS Cosin V.IV.2,[11] and John Audelay wrote a devotional poem on the subject in the first quarter of the fifteenth century.[12]

The *Letter* was also known in early medieval Ireland as part of a legal text called *Cáin Domnaig*. The *Cáin Domnaig* comprises three parts: the *Epistil of Jesus* (based on the *Sunday Letter*), a Sunday List, and the *Cáin Domnaig* proper.[13] According to the Irish tradition, an abbot named

---

8 In London, BL Cotton Otho B.x. *Handlist*, item 356; Ker no. 178.

9 The manuscripts are CCCC MS 162 [s.xi[in]] (Haines D) *Handlist*, item 50, Ker no. 38; CCCC MS 419 [s. xi[1]] (Haines B and E) *Handlist*, item 108, Ker no. 68; London, BL Cotton Tiberius A.iii [s. xi[med]] (Haines F) *Handlist*, item 363, Ker no. 186; London, Lambeth Palace MS 489 [s.xi 3rd quarter] (Haines C) *Handlist*, item 520, Ker no. 283; and CCCC MS 140 [s.xi[2]] (Haines A) *Handlist*, item 44, Ker no. 35.

10 Later Latin versions also appear in England, including in several chronicles that describe Eustace of Flay's visits to England in 1200 and 1201, during which he preached the *Letter* with varying degrees of success as part of his program of preaching the Fourth Crusade. Accounts of his preaching were preserved in Roger of Hovedon's chronicle, which was the source for other later English chroniclers, including Matthew of Paris and Roger of Wendover (Jones, "Heavenly Letter," 166). Jones believes that Eustace did not have the *Sunday Letter* with him the first time he was in England but brought it with him when he returned in order "to heighten his appeal and dramatize his message," and that the letter "seemed to serve as his warrant" (168). Beverly Mayne Kienzle seems to support Jones's opinion that Eustace did not have the letter with him the first time he was in England ("Medieval Sermons," 112–13). Frustratingly, neither of them considers what this letter might have looked like and how he might have used it. Eustace was not seen as a heretic, and his "difficulties in England were political, not theological" (Jones, "Heavenly Letter," 171).

11 For an edition, see O'Mara, *Study and Edition of Selected Middle English Sermons*.

12 *Our Lord's Epistle on Sunday*, in Fein, ed., *John the Blind Audelay*. For an older edition of the poem, presented alongside a possible Latin source, see Priebsch, "John Audelay's Poem." On the *Letter*'s burgeoning popularity as apotropaic document in early western print culture, see the epilogue.

13 An edition and modern English translation of the *Epistil* section of *Cáin Domnaig* may be found in O'Keeffe, "Cáin Domnaig." An edition and translation of the *Cáin Domnaig* may be found in Hull, "Cáin Domnaig."

Conall mac Coelmaine brought the *Epistil* to Ireland after making a copy of the letter in his own hand.[14] The real Conall mac Coelmaine died c. 590, but there is no evidence for the presence of the *Sunday Letter* in Ireland at that time.[15] Furthermore, the *Epistil* makes no claim to have been known in Ireland as early as the sixth century. The *Epistil* specifies that Conall's copy of the *Letter* lay with him in his shrine for many years before he appeared to a cleric in a vision to reveal the *Letter*'s location. It is not until the ninth century that we find a spate of records in the chronicles and annals describing the arrival of the *Epistil* in Ireland.[16] Unlike the Old English *Letters*, which feature no local saint, the Irish *Epistil* is motivated by a desire to establish or strengthen the cult of Conall mac Coelmaine. Conall is already a personage of some value when he appears to the cleric – he has a shrine, and the fact that he copied the letter in his own hand is clearly meant to increase the document's value.[17] Other Celtic versions of the *Letter* also survive, with several variants. One seventeenth-century Welsh version of the *Letter* claims to have been delivered to earth in 390.[18]

Most early references to the *Sunday Letter* condemn it as heretical, so it is particularly surprising that there is so little evidence for such an opinion of the *Letter* in Anglo-Saxon England, and that it found its way into the manuscript collections of people such as Bishop Leofric of Exeter.[19] The

---

14 O'Keeffe, "Cáin Domnaig," §21.

15 Ibid., 212.

16 Whitelock, "Bishop Ecgred," 65. There is no critical consensus about the date of the Irish *Epistil*. Whitelock's own belief is that there was a Latin source known in Ireland that predates the *Epistil* (57–8, 65–6).

17 "But the account [of the cleric's vision] is probably only an attempt to exalt the honour of a church connected with Conall" (ibid., 65).

18 Jones, "A Welsh 'Sunday Epistle.'" Jones also prints the end of the "Ebostol y Sul," which is one of the earliest Welsh versions of the letter. An Old Norse poem on the *Sunday Letter*, the *Leiðarvísan*, was composed in the twelfth century and is preserved in two manuscripts from the fifteenth century. The poem is based more closely on the Sunday List than the *Sunday Letter*, and is a personal, devotional poem in praise of God. For an edition and translation, see Attwood, "Anonymous, *Leiðarvísan*."

19 Concerns about the authenticity of the *Letter* are not restricted to the medieval period. After one Mr Bilous published a *Sunday Letter* in Ukraine in 1877, a group of nationalist clergymen responded with the following very practical objection: "We must say: (1) that no one in heaven wrote or writes letters; (2) that neither the patriarch of Jerusalem [to whom the letter was imagined to have been sent] nor Mr Bilous ever received any such letters from heaven because all letters are delivered by the postal service which does not extend to heaven." Andriy Zayarnyuk, "Letters from Heaven," 165.

first mention of the *Sunday Letter* in England is in a letter written c. 835 by Egred, bishop of Lindisfarne (831–846) to Wulfsige, archbishop of York.[20] Wulfsige, whose letter unfortunately has not survived, had informed Egred that the *Letter* was being circulated in his district in a book attributed to a monk named Pehtred.[21] Egred's response to Wulfsige is measured but firm. He asks, quite logically, "and if such letters written in gold by the hand of God had arrived upon the tomb of the blessed Peter in the days of Pope Florentius, why was not such a message divulged throughout the Christian peoples by the apostolic see? Or what should be done about it, if it were true? For in our documents where we have the names of the pontiffs of the apostolic see, we have not found the name of Pope Florentius."[22] Egred further advises that messengers or letters be sent to Pehtred's diocese to teach Pehtred his error; if Pehtred will not repent, Egred says, "let him be as a despiser of the Church."[23] Egred's letter is written after the heyday of Bonifatian correspondence in England, but it reflects how comfortable Egred was with the available systems of epistolary communication. He expects that if such a letter had fallen from the sky and landed on St Peter's altar, then the pope would have spread the news of this by sending out papal legates bearing letters describing the arrival of the *Sunday Letter* and its message. Furthermore, he expects that the problem of the circulation of the apocryphal letter may be resolved by issuing a combination of more letters and threats, the same technique, as we shall see, employed by some of the Old English *Sunday Letters*.

---

20 The full text is printed by Whitelock in "Bishop Egred," 48–9, and is translated in Whitelock, ed. and trans., *EHD*, 875–6.

21 Whitelock believes that Pehtred was a monk "living in a diocese under the authority of the metropolitan church of York, but not in the diocese of York or Lindisfarne. Hexham and Whithorn, but also the English church of Mayo in Ireland are possible" ("Bishop Egred," 49–50). In Whitelock's view, Pehtred could not have belonged to a large monastery because if he had, "Egred would have suggested an approach to his abbot" (50). Katrina Attwood, though she cites Whitelock, assigns Pehtred to Mayo ("Leiðarvísan and the 'Sunday Letter' Tradition," 63).

22 *EHD* no. 214, p. 876 (Whitelock's translation). "Et si tales litterę manu Dei auro scriptę super sepulchrum beati Petri in diebus Florentii pape uenerunt, quare non ab apostolica sede per populos christianos diuulgata est talis legatio? uel quid de illa agendum fore, si uera esset? In nostris enim scriptis ubi nomina pontificum apostolice sedis habemus, nomen Florentii pape non inuenimus" (Whitelock, "Bishop Egred," 48–9).

23 *EHD* no. 214, p. 876 (Whitelock's translation). "sit sicut contemptor ęcclesię" (Whitelock, "Bishop Egred," 49).

The *Letter*'s veracity was questioned on the Continent as well. In the first confirmed appearance of the *Sunday Letter* (c. 580), Licinianus, Bishop of Cartagena, strongly rebukes Bishop Vincentius of Ibiza for having believed in the authenticity of the *Letter*. Licinianus does not record any of the text of the *Letter*, which apparently upset him so much that he tore it to pieces and threw it on the ground.[24] Licinianus's strong negative reaction to the *Letter* is typical of the responses to the *Letter* in the early Middle Ages. One of its most famous detractors was the Anglo-Saxon Boniface, who twice had a Frankish priest named Adelbert condemned for, among other things, preaching the *Letter*.[25] Adelbert was condemned at Soissons on 3 March 744 and at a Roman synod on 25 October 745. The synod advised that Adelbert's letter be burned, but Pope Zacharias intervened, preferring to preserve Adelbert's heretical texts in the archive "for his perpetual condemnation."[26] A few years later, Charlemagne's *Admonitio Generalis* (789) says that the *Letter* should be burned wherever it is found.[27] Licinianus's and Charlemagne's destruction of heretical documents stands in contrast to Pope Zacharias's desire to preserve it as a caution for posterity. Those who destroy it recognize that there is a power in the letter as material object, and a symbolic value to publicly destroying it – they imagine that getting rid of the object itself will prevent further spread of its content. But the later history of the *Sunday Letter* belies their attempts to destroy it, and the *Letter*'s continued popularity in the Middle Ages and beyond in fact confirms that sometimes attempting to erase something only makes it more memorable.[28]

Scholarship on the Old English *Sunday Letter* is sparse and focuses nearly exclusively on transmission and sources, although the *Letter* has also been studied in the context of apocrypha and the history of laws on

---

24 "At once I tore it up, and threw [the pieces of the letter] onto the ground" (*statim scidi, et eas in terram projeci*). *PL* vol. 72: 699B. The letter is also printed in full in Priebsch, *Letter from Heaven*, 1–2.

25 For a translation of Boniface's letters about Adelbert, as well as the record of the sessions of the councils, see Emerton, ed. and trans., *Letters of Saint Boniface*, 98–111. Boniface and the synod are more concerned with other aspects of Adelbert's heresy than with his use of the *Sunday Letter*.

26 Ibid., 105 (Emerton's translation). Despite the pope's desire that the *Letter* be recorded, all that survives of Adelbert's *Letter* is the preface.

27 Boretius, ed., MGH, *Capitularia regum Francorum*, no. 22, p. 160, ch. 78.

28 On this point, see chapter 4.

Sunday.[29] Early work by Delehaye and Priebsch sought to bring together all extant versions of the *Sunday Letter*, both in Latin and in the vernacular, and to categorize them by method of transmission or other characteristic details.[30] Since then, the primary debate about the *Letter* in medieval Britain has been whether the Irish brought the apocryphal letter to England or whether the English brought it to Ireland, with most scholars placing the blame on Ireland.[31] Jonathan Wilcox has recently moved the conversation on this issue forward by addressing what the two Old English *Letters* associated with the Irish deacon Niall can tell us about Anglo-Saxon attitudes towards Ireland.[32] Many of the *Sunday Letters* also incorporate the so-called Sunday List,[33] a catalogue of important events that happened on Sunday. Although the Sunday List is present in all of the

---

29 For apocrypha, see Deletant, "Sunday Legend." His focus is on the east, and begins with the later Middle Ages. Although he begins with a history of the *Letter* as apocrypha, he concludes that "the epistle was not, however, a popular form among the writers of apocrypha, probably because, as M.R. James suggests, it was more liable to be proved spurious and therefore unlikely to gain popularity" (431). Rudolph Willard connects the *Letter* to Sabbatarianism in his "Address of the Soul." The 2010 publication of Dorothy Haines's edition of the Old English versions of the *Letter* has already garnered more interest for the work; I hope this scholarly attention to the *Letter* will continue.

30 Delehaye, "Note sur la légende." Delehaye's purpose was to give enough information about each Latin version that the reader would know to which type it belongs. Priebsch's "Chief Sources" surveys the sources and divides the Old English *Sunday Letter* into three groups. Priebsch later divided the *Letter* into four redactions, but died before he could publish his full explanation. His *Letter from Heaven*, published posthumously, is about the first redaction, and seeks to demonstrate how popular it was in medieval Europe with evidence from the history of Sunday laws, Latin sources, and other types of heavenly letters. On the recensions of the *Letter*, see also Haines, *Sunday Observance*.

31 Priebsch thought that Pehtred had a Latin source that he got from Ireland ("Chief Sources," 142), and that he incorporated into it the story of the reincarnated deacon Niall after hearing it from an Irish cleric who visited him in England ("Quelle und Abfassungszeit," 148–9). Priebsch's imagined encounter between Pehtred and this unnamed Irish cleric is quite improbable. Whitelock agrees that Pehtred got his Latin source from Ireland, but believes that the "Pehtred homilies," as we have them in their eleventh-century forms, had a vernacular source, now lost, for their direct source ("Bishop Ecgred," 58 and 62). Therefore, while the primary direction of transmission was from Ireland to England, "later copies [of the *Letter*] probably came from elsewhere, so that Pehtred and the Irish need not alone bear the blame for the spread of an unorthodox document" (Whitelock, "Bishop Ecgred," 68).

32 Wilcox, "A Voice of the Irish." I wish to thank Jonathan Wilcox for generously sharing with me a prepublication version of this essay.

33 Also known as the *dignatio diei dominici* or "Benedictions of Sunday."

Old English *Letters* save one, Clare Lees has shown that it was not originally a part of the *Sunday Letter* tradition, and arose from the observance of Sunday, not the *Sunday Letter*.[34]

Perhaps the most interesting work on the *Sunday Letter* has been done by folklorists studying the *Letter* in other periods and places. Their methodology generally involves putting the *Letter* into the context of popular religion, a field of study that, while it has attracted the attention of Anglo-Saxonists, has not yet, to my knowledge, been applied to the Old English *Sunday Letters*. The work of Andriy Zayarnyuk on the *Letter* in nineteenth-century Ukraine goes a long way towards explaining why a communication from God that is specifically in written form would have been so well embraced by Anglo-Saxon peasants.[35] According to Zayarnyuk, the Ukrainian *Letter*'s appeal stems primarily from the fact that it is extremely accessible, written in a plain language and style. More importantly, peasants are given to understand that they may own or wear a copy of the same letter that has been delivered to the pope. This creates the appearance of equal access to a powerful religious symbol by people of every level of society.[36] The difficulty with applying Zayarnyuk's reading to the Old English *Sunday Letter* is that his analysis depends on the belief that nineteenth-century peasants could conceive of letters as quite commonplace, everyday forms of communication. This was not the case in Anglo-Saxon England, and Anglo-Saxon peasants certainly could not have thought of a letter from God as ordinary communication. Furthermore, while it is tempting to use the concept of popular religion to help understand apocrypha, sermons are not strictly popular works, because they are produced by church elite. Rather, they display "the popularity of an elite form."[37] Even with these reservations about applying Zayarnyuk's

---

34 Lees, "Sunday Letter." The exception is Haines A.

35 Remarkably, the *Sunday Letter* tradition has been so continuous that these nineteenth-century Ukrainian letters have much the same content as those letters from eleventh-century England.

36 Galician peasants, like many other users of the *Letter*, believed that it had apotropaic powers (Zayarnyuk, "Letters from Heaven"). There is little to no evidence that Anglo-Saxons conceived of the *Letter* as a protective amuletic text, but Old English *Letters* do address themselves to many layers of society.

37 Lees, *Tradition and Belief*, 32. Richard Landes proposes the term "demotic religiosity" as a contrast to popular religion. In his formulation, "demotic elevates while popular condescends" (107). Although Landes specifically mentions heavenly letters as an example of demotic religiosity (108), his reading is too optimistic. He believes that the conditions of demotic religiosity lead people to try to treat each other well and that this improves economic conditions ("Economic Development").

argument to Anglo-Saxon England and about using the term "popular religion," I believe that his essay can draw our attention to important features of the Old English *Sunday Letter*, namely, that it suggests that everyone can (and in fact must) have access to the *message* of the *Letter*, even though not everyone would have access to the written *Letter* itself, nor would they have imagined, as Zayarnyuk's nineteenth-century peasants did, that everyone had equal access to the *Letter*. Evidence suggests that some medieval lay people might have had copies of the *Letter*, and, as we reach the Middle English period, we find more and more evidence of the appeal of the *Letter* arising from its properties as a written document.

The Audiences of the Old English *Sunday Letter*

All the Old English *Sunday Letters* are found in sermon texts, so to address the potential audiences of the *Letter*, it is important to consider the problem of sermon audiences.[38] Several of the Old English *Letters* were contained in manuscripts designed for use by an archbishop or bishop. While the manuscript in which a sermon is written might be intended for preachers, the sermon itself might be intended for delivery to a lay audience, and a single sermon could have been delivered on separate occasions to different audiences. Conversely, a sermon written in a manuscript may never have been preached, but simply read privately. I want to stress that when I argue that the *Sunday Letter* sermons were designed for a mixed or lay audience, I do not mean to claim that the same is true of the manuscripts in which they were preserved. Rather, the archbishop or bishop is the proximate audience of the *Letter*, while the congregation to whom he may preach the *Letter* are the ultimate audience.[39] When the subject of the sermon is the *Sunday Letter*, there is a further complication: the framework of the sermon may address one kind of audience, while the *Letter*

---

38 The genre of the Old English *Sunday Letters* is complex. The message purports to have been a letter, but it appears only as embedded in sermons. Moreover, the message of the *Sunday Letter* is often legalistic in tone and vocabulary, offering proscriptions, threats, and commands. The letter adopts some features of legal genres, and it experiments with what one might do with the combination of legal text and letter. Regardless of the genre into which the letter is embedded, or the genres from which the letter borrows stylistic devices, it is clearly an epistolary document, and while Anglo-Saxons may not have venerated the original document as an apotropaic object, they did exploit the epistolary qualities of the letter in numerous ways.

39 I borrow the terms "proximate" and "ultimate" from d'Avray, *Preaching of the Friars*, 105.

proper, embedded within the sermon, may preserve its own epistolary forms of address.

It is often assumed that most audiences for early medieval sermons were monastic or clerical, and that popular preaching was rare before 1200.[40] However, the intended audiences of the Old English *Sunday Letters* often comprised lay people from different levels of society, not just the elite, as well as the more expected ecclesiastical audience. Archaeological evidence supports the possibility that sermon audiences were changing and growing in late Anglo-Saxon England. According to John Blair, the new English churches built during the eleventh century "were conceived more clearly as community buildings, planned to accommodate the whole mass-hearing population as a primary rather than incidental function."[41] At Raunds, for example, the tenth-century church could have held 29 people, whereas the eleventh-century church could hold 104.[42] This suggests that many people were expected to gather within the church and, although it does not reveal whether the laity heard sermons there or not, the new building plan implies that there was now an expectation of participation in church events by more members of the community. We know that the Anglo-Saxon laity were required to attend church at "Lent, Rogationtide, Easter Day, Pentecost, and the Ember Days";[43] furthermore, we know that

---

40 Phyliss B. Roberts argues that "the distinguishing mark of most early medieval preaching was that it was essentially preaching by clerics for audiences of clerics," although "popular audiences" did exist ("*Ars Praedicandi*," 44). Roberts believes that the rise of the popular audience came in the late twelfth to thirteenth centuries (44). Cf. Thomas N. Hall, who cautions against generalizations such as the "tendency [in recent scholarship] to assume that the audience of most early medieval sermons was predominantly clerical and monastic" ("Early Medieval Sermon," 228). Twenty years earlier, Milton McC. Gatch had felt confident that most scholars would probably assume that Old English sermons "were to be read by the clergy to the people on Sundays or Feasts in a liturgical setting, most probably at the Mass" (*Preaching and Theology*, 25). He shows how sermons (or more specifically, catechetical sermons) were probably given during the office of Prone, due in part to Carolingian influence. It is worth noting that this office could be "separable from the Mass" (37–8). Mary Clayton, responding to Gatch, argued that there were three kinds of Anglo-Saxon homiliaries: those for monks, those for private devotional reading, and those for preaching to the laity. She demonstrates that Ælfric's innovation was to produce sermons for "a mixed audience" of laity and religious (Clayton, "Homiliaries and Preaching," 189). On Old English sermons, see also Corradini, "Preaching in Old English," and Kleist, ed., *The Old English Homily*.

41 Blair, *Church in Anglo-Saxon Society*, 457.

42 Ibid., 457.

43 Lees, *Tradition and Belief*, 56.

catechetical sermons were delivered to the laity at Rogationtide. The *Regularis Concordia*, a late tenth-century monastic rule preserved in one of the Old English *Sunday Letter* manuscripts, also "assumes a regular presence of lay people at mass."[44]

Like the Rogation sermons, the Old English *Sunday Letters* are all catechetical sermons.[45] As their name implies, catechetical sermons were intended to instruct the laity in basic matters of Christian faith, such as the Ten Commandments; as such, they were delivered in many different contexts, including extra-liturgical settings.[46] In fact, none of the Old English *Sunday Letters* are attached to a particular date in the church calendar, so it is quite likely that they were intended for extra-liturgical use.[47] Therefore, while evidence indicates that more people were expected to attend mass in the eleventh century, the laity would not necessarily even have had to attend mass in order to have heard catechetical sermons, like the *Sunday Letter* sermons, preached. Moreover, at least two of the manuscripts in which *Sunday Letter* sermons are contained (CCCC 419 and Lambeth 489) were intended for a bishop or archbishop, who might have needed sermons appropriate for many occasions, including preaching to both clerical and lay audiences.

By inviting all members of society to form its audience, the *Sunday Letter* created not just a body of potential believers in and disseminators of the message, but hybrid textual communities that spanned the divide between elite and popular culture. The concept of textual communities was introduced by Brian Stock to describe the formation of heretical and reform groups in the eleventh and twelfth centuries. Stock argued that each community was bound together by a charismatic leader who interpreted a text for his followers, whether they were literate or not. What mattered was not the presence of a written document but the individual

---

44 Tinti, "Introduction," 7.

45 Anglo-Saxon sermons could be one of three types: "exegetical, catechetical, or hagiographic" (Lees, *Tradition and Belief,* 30). These categories are modified from Gatch's "missionary, catechetical, and liturgical-exegetical" (*Preaching and Theology,* 31).

46 Preaching could take place within a church, though it did not have to – it could be done outdoors, and Rogationtide ceremonies involved outdoor procession. Wulfstan sometimes preached in extra-liturgical contexts, including to the *witan* (Gatch, *Preaching and Theology,* 19). On the likelihood that sermons in Old English were intended for private reading or extra-liturgical preaching, see Clayton, "Homiliaries," 188. For other places preaching could take place, see Kienzle, "Medieval Sermons," 91.

47 Haines, *Sunday Observance,* 73.

who "educated" his audience about its message in a way that could "supersede the differing economic and social backgrounds of the participants, welding them, for a time at least, into a unit."[48] My reading of the textual communities formed by the *Sunday Letter* differs from Stock in two important ways: first, I do not share Stock's idealized view of a Habermasian public sphere formed by these communities. The *Sunday Letter* may wish to imagine that it brings together members of different social classes, but it nevertheless preserves the hierarchy inherent in Anglo-Saxon social structure. More importantly, I argue that the Old English *Sunday Letters* deputize each member of the audience to become disseminators of the message, thus eliminating the need for Stock's charismatic leader.

Four of the six Old English *Sunday Letter* sermons were directed at mixed lay audiences. One representative example, Haines C, the most emblematic of the *Letters* addressed to a lay audience, contains a version that claims that the letter was originally sent to Peter of Antioch. This sermon was ultimately intended for a mixed lay audience, though it was to be delivered by a bishop. The manuscript in which it is contained, Lambeth 489, was part of Bishop Leofric of Exeter's own library[49] and formed part of his homiliary.[50] The sermon opens with a phrase identifying the speaker as a bishop, and naming the audience as laity: "Leofan men, us bisceopum and eallum mæssepreostum is swiðe deope beboden þæt we æfre sculon mynegian and tyhtan eow, læwede menn ..."[51] (Dear men, it is very solemnly commanded to us bishops and all mass-priests that we must always remind and teach you, lay people ...) Although the sermon opens with an acknowledgment that the speaker is a bishop, it is clear that his intended audience is a lay audience (among other things, the speaker addresses the audience as *læwede men* [lay people]). The rubric also designates it an "ad populum" sermon,[52] which indicates a lay audience and suggests that this sermon might have been delivered at a cathedral or on some special

---

48 Stock, *Listening for the Text*, 150. Stock originally formulated the idea of textual communities in *Implications of Literacy*. The concept has been taken up and redefined many times, including by Martin Irvine, *Making of Textual Culture*, 15, and Richard Firth Green, "Textual Production."

49 Treharne, "Producing a Library."

50 Treharne, "Bishops and Their Texts." Lambeth 489 and London, BL Cotton Cleopatra B.xiii were originally a single manuscript.

51 Haines C, 1–3.

52 "Sermo ad populum de dominicis diebus" (Sermon to the people on the days of the Lord).

occasion – that is, as a *quando uolveris* sermon rather than a sermon for a particular day.

When the sermon addresses its audience directly elsewhere, it names them as belonging to a variety of groups that encompass all members of lay society. Sometimes it identifies them as elite members of the laity, calling them *ægðer ge cyningas ge eorlas and gerefan* (both kings and earls and reeves)[53] or *ge rican men* (you rich/powerful men).[54] The community formed by this audience was not egalitarian, even if its members represented many levels of society. Rather, hierarchy is respected and maintained in the order in which the audience is named, with kings coming first, then earls, and finally reeves. At other times, the audience is described as comprising members of the lower levels of society, *ægðer ge freoh ge þeow* (both free and slave).[55] Even if the reference to "free and slave" is merely a rhetorical device, the lists of activities forbidden on Sundays give us a clue to the occupations and status of the intended audience. For example, it is stipulated that on Sundays no craftsmen may work and there may be no trade. Domestic labour is also forbidden, including baking bread and washing clothes.[56] Moreover, there is no other Old English sermon in which the *Letter* is so clearly presented as a letter – the preacher is very attentive to the need for oral cues marking the divisions between his comments and the letter itself, and one might suspect from this fact that this sermon was intended for a less educated audience that might have needed more help understanding written documents.[57] Therefore all indications suggest that this is a sermon that is directed, at least rhetorically, at a mixed and multiple lay audience, one that ranges the spectrum of society, from kings to slaves.

---

53 C 21.

54 C 132.

55 C 115.

56 "Swa hwa swa ænige cypinge on þam dæge begæð oððe oðre þing, þæt man claðas waxe, oððe ænig cræftig man him on his cræfte tylige, oððe man efesige oðerne man oððe bread bace ... he scel beon utlaga wið me" (C 97–100).

57 For example, after prefatory comments on the need for bishops and priests to preach to the people, the homilist summarizes the letter's delivery and content, then precedes the supposed message performed by the angelic messenger with "Nu is þis þæt angin þæs engles spræce, þa þa he þæt gewrit þam bisceope on hand sealde. He cwæð ..." (Now this is the beginning of that angel's message, when he gave that letter into the hand of the bishop. He said ...) (C 19–20). Likewise, after the letter proper concludes, the homilist announces "Nu we habbað eow gesæd be þæs halgan sunnandæges freolse, swa swa ge habbað gehyred" (Now we have told you about the feast of holy Sunday, just as you have heard) (C 128–9).

To briefly survey two representative sermons from the two other major recensions of the Old English *Letter,* Haines A, a sermon of the Effrem Gate type, names its audience as a mixed lay audience, is short enough to have been performed, and is rhetorically aimed at sinners who seem to know little of the specifics of the Bible. However, this sermon was likely intended for a mixed lay and ecclesiastical audience, because the sermon ends by commanding bishops and mass-priests to send the letter throughout their districts.[58] Haines E, the most technical sermon and least likely to have been performed before a mixed lay audience, is one of the Pehtred/Niall homilies. It includes an intensely technical interpolated passage on tithes, and employs Latin names for times of the liturgical calendar without translating them into the vernacular.[59] Yet, the narrative interest of the reincarnated deacon Niall, the use of rhetorical fireworks such as alliterating pairs, internal rhyme, and linguistic play, and the sermon's prohibition on basic tasks like baking bread, shaving, or cleaning the house[60] also suggest that the preacher sought to make his content memorable, perhaps even to lay audiences, who would have had no access to its message outside the context of the oral sermon.

Circulation, Community, and Audience

The Old English *Sunday Letter* asks three things of its audience: 1) to observe Sunday properly, pay tithes, and behave rightly; 2) to enforce correct behaviour among neighbours and fellow Christians; and 3) to circulate the message further. The first task is laid out quite explicitly in all the sermons. The *Letter*'s flexibility as oral and written document allowed it to be adapted to the specific anxieties of late Anglo-Saxon England involving tithe payment in a new age of smaller manorial churches. All six extant Old English *Letters* include at least some mention of tithe payment, and

---

58 "Ge bisceopas and mæssepreostas kyðaþ þis gelomlice eallum folce and sendað þis gewrit geond ealle scira." (You bishops and masspriests make this known frequently to all people and send this letter throughout all districts.) A 83–4.

59 "And we forbeodað ordal and aðas freolsdagum and ymbrendagum and lenctendagum and rihtfæstendagum and from aduentum domini oð octabas epiphanie and fram septuagesima, oð fiftene niht beon geeastrode." (And we forbid ordeal and oaths on feast days and Emberdays and Lent and duly appointed fast days and from *aduentum domini* until *octabas epiphanie* and from *septuagesima*, until fifteen nights be elapsed.) E 71–4.

60 E 164–8.

some go so far as to seem to prioritize the payment of tithes over the sermon's ostensible message of proper Sunday observance, often threatening terrible punishments for those who fail to pay. The Old English *Letters* are unique in their attention to tithe payment, which reveals much about their popularity in this historical context. My aim in attending to tithe payment in the Old English *Letters* is not to identify direct sources for the *Letter*'s exhortations to tithe, but rather to examine the contexts in which they might have been understood, and to suggest what the sources and motivations for the Anglo-Saxon preachers' additions to the *Sunday Letter* might have been.

Comparable medieval *Sunday Letters* do not focus as much on tithes as the Old English *Letters* do, which suggests that Anglo-Saxon bishops, preachers, or scribes were deliberately modifying the text of the *Sunday Letter* to influence tithe payment.[61] As Jonathan Wilcox has shown, midway through one Old English *Sunday Letter* (Haines E) we find inserted, nearly in its entirety, a short text by Wulfstan on tithes and ecclesiastical dues (Napier XXIII), which is itself compiled from several law codes.[62] Other changes are more subtle. For example, where Haines B's Latin source demands only vigils, fasting, and prayer ("Et rogo uos, expurgate uos in uigiliis et ieiuniis, in orationibus ad ecclesias meas ambulate"),[63] Haines B advises its audience to turn to God with prayer, vigils, fasting, confession, penance, and "tithing of all our goods of worldly gain": "Ac ic halsige on Godes naman and eornestlice hate, þæt ge gecyrran to Gode mid gebedum and mid wæccan and mid fæstenum and mid synna andettnesse eowrum scriftan and mid hreowsunge dædbota *and mid teoðunge ealra ura æhta weoruldgestreona*."[64]

---

61 It can be difficult to determine the relationship between Old English *Letters* and their supposed Latin sources because most of these Latin texts survive in manuscripts that postdate the Old English ones.

62 Wilcox, "Dissemination of Wulfstan's Homilies," 207–8.

63 Vienna Österreichische Nationalbibliothek, 1335 (s. xiv/xv), printed in Haines, *Sunday Observance* as Appendix IIa, ll. 22–3. See also Haines, *Sunday Observance*, 181n12.

64 But I implore you in God's name and earnestly command, that you turn to God with prayers and vigils and fasting and confession of sins to your confessor and with the sorrow of penitence and with *tithing of all our goods of worldly gain* (B 29–32; emphasis added). Later medieval vernacular *Letters* also treat tithes differently than the Old English *Letters*. For example, in John Audelay's fifteenth-century poem, Audelay's primary concern is not to remind his audience that tithe payment is required by biblical and secular law, but rather to remind them that tithes support the priests. See Audelay, *Our Lord's Epistle on Sunday*, in Fein, ed., *John the Blind Audelay*, ll. 105–13. The relative

The Old English *Sunday Letters* are unusual not just for the frequency with which they mention tithes, but also in their methods for ensuring prompt payment. For example, in Haines C – a sermon of the Peter of Antioch recension found in London, Lambeth Palace 489, a manuscript produced for Bishop Leofric of Exeter c. 1050–1072[65] – the first portion of a message about tithe enforcement corresponds closely to Anglo-Saxon law codes, but Christ's speech quickly takes a threatening turn:

And, gif ge nellað teoðian ælc þæra þinga, þe eow God lænð, on swa hwyl-cum þingum, swa ge hit begytað mid rihte, and to Godes cyrcan hit getrywe-lice bringan, ic benæme eow þæra .ix. dæla, and ge sculon þæs teoþan dæles mid teonan brucan. Þæt is, þæt ic asende ofer eower land ælcne úntiman, þæt bið egeslice great hagol, se fordeð eowre wæstmas, and unasecgendlice þun-ras and byrnende ligræscas, þa forglendriað eowre wæstmas ægðer ge on wuda ge on felda. And drugoða eow cymð, þonne ge renas behofedan, and ren, þonne eowre wæstmas wederes beþorftan. And gyt, þæt is egeslicost eow eall to geþafianne: þæt is, þæt ungecyndelic fyr cymð færunga on eowre bur-ga and on tunas and forbærnð þone betstan dæl, þe ge big sceoldon libban.[66]

And, if you will not pay tithe on each of those things which God lends you, on whatsoever things, that you have earned rightfully, and faithfully bring it to God's church, I will take away from you nine parts, and you shall en-joy the tenth part with injury. That is, that I will send upon your land ev-ery misfortune, that is, terribly great hail, which will ruin your crops, and

---

lack of attention to tithes in the Irish versions of the *Sunday Letter* is likely due to the fact that tithes were not introduced to Ireland until several centuries after the compo-sition of the Irish *Epistil* (dated to the ninth century), so emphasizing tithe payment would have required authors or ambitious scribes to insert new material when the texts were recopied in the later manuscripts in which they survive. There is one reference to something like tithe payment: "It is enacted: a third of each profit to God; and the sec-ond third to princes and churches; and the third third to tax-gatherers and guarantors" (O'Keeffe "Cáin Domnaig," §33 [O'Keeffe's translation]). This is the final section of the text, a logical place for later additions.

65 Determining whether a manuscript reflects current concerns or has been mindlessly copied from an exemplar can be difficult. Donald Scragg argues that the scribe respon-sible for one of the *Sunday Letter* manuscripts was "basically a mechanical scribe." "Cotton Tiberius," 30. By contrast, one of the Old English *Sunday Letters* was inserted into the Bath Gospels where there was room between two gospels, which suggests a more enterprising scribe.

66 Haines C 118–27.

indescribable thunder and burning lightning, which will devour your crops both in the woods and in the fields. And drought will come upon you when you need rain, and rain when your crops need good weather. And still, that is the most terrible of all for you to suffer: that is, that unnatural fire will come suddenly to your cities and towns and it will burn up the best share, by which you should live.

This is typical of the alterations made to the Old English *Letters* – not only is the message about proper Sunday observance frequently interrupted so that the preacher may conduct a pledge drive, but instead of simply levying fines for failing to pay tithes, as legal codes do, the preacher imagines in vivid detail exactly how God might accomplish taking away nine-tenths of the sinner's tithable resources. It is quite common in other Anglo-Saxon sources for God to allow the non-payer to keep his tithe but then punish him by taking the rest for himself – this idea appears in homilies by Wulfstan[67] and Ælfric,[68] in Blickling Homily IV (which draws from Caesarius of Arles's sixth-century sermon on tithes), as well as in Anglo-Saxon law codes, beginning with I Athelstan 3 (926 × 930).[69] I have been unable to locate direct sources for the specific maledictions, although they have many similarities to the curses in Deuteronomy 28 and Psalm 77. They may also be inspired by Caesarius's sermon, which explains that in order to take away the nine parts, God will take away the rains and send in their place hail and frost to destroy the vineyards.[70] Strikingly, this passage is omitted in Blickling IV. Massive hail, along with thunder and fire, is also one of the plagues of Egypt.[71] The curses found in the *Sunday Letter*, insofar as they often draw upon Deuteronomy, may well be connected to the

---

67 *De decimis dandis*, ed. and trans. by Thomas N. Hall in "Wulfstan's Latin Sermons."

68 "First-fruits and Tithes," in John C. Pope, ed., *Homilies of Ælfric*, 806–8.

69 Haines, *Sunday Observance*, 187n16.

70 "Avare, quid faceres, si novem partibus sibi sumptis tibi decimam reliquisset? Quod certe iam factum est, cum messis tua pluviarum benedictione subtracta ieiuna defecit, et vindemiam tuam aut grando percussit, aut pruina decoxit." (Avaricious man, what would you do if He had taken nine-tenths for Himself and left you the tithes? Surely, this already happened when the meager harvest failed because your blessing of rain was withdrawn, or when hail struck your vintage or frost killed it.) Willard, "Blickling-Junius Tithing Homily," 75. Translation from Mueller, *Saint Caesarius of Arles*, 164.

71 Haines writes that "the impression created by the Sunday Letter is that of a collection of statements which are meant to sound like scripture while they do not, in fact, quote it directly." She believes the authors may have been working from memory (*Sunday Observance*, 58).

tradition of monastic cursing studied by Lester K. Little, among others.[72] The curses associated with failure to tithe in the *Letters* include blind, deaf, and crippled children; winged adders sent to devour the crops; and "wedende wulfas and wedende hundas, þe etað eowerne lichaman to deaðes tocyme" (raving wolves and raging hounds, which will eat your bodies up to the point of death).[73] Most of these punishments would affect the whole community rather than the individual sinner, which is in keeping with the general message of the *Sunday Letter*. In fact, in another Old English version of the *Letter*, Christ promises a similar sequence of punishments (storms, hailstones, winged adders, fire, and heathen invaders) not for failing to tithe, but for failing to observe Sunday rightly:

> Soþ is iow sæcge, gef ge ne healdaþ þone halgan sunnandeg mid rihte, þæt ic sænde gyt ofer iow micele stormas and hagolstanas and fleogende neddran, þa ge abera ne megan, and sweflicne leg; and ic lete hæþen folc ofer iow, þa iow fornimaþ and iowra bearn.[74]

> It is truth I say to you, if you will not correctly observe holy Sunday, that I will send upon you yet great storms and hailstones and flying adders, which you will not be able to bear, and sulfurous fire; and I will allow the heathens [to come] upon you, who will destroy you and your children.

Such threats contrast with Anglo-Saxon law on tithes, which punishes only the person who fails to pay, but they are typical of the Old English *Letters*, which work to ensure their continued circulation by levying punishments on the group rather than the individual, thus making it in everyone's best interest to preach the message to others so that your neighbour's transgression will not lead to your own suffering.[75] Moreover, this passage

---

72 Little, *Benedictine Maledictions*. For the Irish tradition, see Wiley, "The Maledictory Psalms," and Bray, "Malediction and Benediction." For Anglo-Saxon bishops who curse, see Cubitt, "Archbishop Dunstan." Cubitt concludes that "by the early eleventh century English Benedictine monks had begun to practise liturgical cursing" (161).

73 B 76–7.

74 F 178–81.

75 Obviously, Anglo-Saxon law, promulgated by kings and archbishops, could not hope to ensure such divine punishments as are named in the *Sunday Letters* even if they had so desired. If a person failed to pay his tithe, early Anglo-Saxon law stated merely that he had to pay a fine of unspecified amount or he would be excommunicated (I Edmund 2; 941 x 946). Beginning with II Edgar (issued 960 x 962) and continuing until the end of

illustrates another key fact about tithes in the Old English *Letters*, which is that preachers seem more interested in punishment than in any other aspect of tithe collection, and few pragmatic details regarding tithe payment are included. Only the Wulfstan interpolation specifies the dates by which tithes must be paid, and none of the *Letters* address how they will be collected. Instead, the *Letters* simply promise generic blessings for those who tithe correctly.

It is especially difficult to understand why the Old English *Letters* fail to specify to whom the tithes must be paid, given that tithe collection was part of a substantial shift in late Anglo-Saxon England away from the old *minsters,* which were ecclesiastical houses (and not necessarily monasteries) in which everyone in the community was responsible for pastoral care, rather than having a single priest assigned to each parish.[76] Proponents of the minster thesis believe that these minsters began to break up around 950, when aristocrats began building manorial churches on their own property, which drew attendance and, more importantly, funds away from the old minsters. On the other side of the debate are scholars who claim that the

---

the Anglo-Saxon period, the law on tithes becomes much more specific. If anyone fails to pay, the king's reeve, the bishop's reeve, and the mass-priest of the church to whom the tithe is due are allowed to seize the nine parts and divide them among the church, the lord, and the bishop, much like the passage cited above in which God removes the nine parts by destroying them. Fines are specified for failure to pay ecclesiastical dues – for example, anyone who fails to pay Peter's Pence (a penny due on St Peter's day) must take the penny to Rome along with thirty pence, obtain certification of payment, and then pay 120 shillings to the king upon his return from Rome. "7 se ðe þonne to ðam andagan gelæst næbbe, læde hine to Rome 7 þærto eacan XXX pænega, 7 bringe þonne þanon swytolinga, þæt he þær swa micel betæht hæbbe; 7 þonne he ham cume, gylde þam cynge hundtwelftig scill." II Edgar 4.1 (manuscript G; *Gesetze* I, 198). Later laws remove the requirement to go to Rome but preserve the fee structure. Citations from the law codes are from Liebermann, *Die Gesetze der Angelsachsen.* While Anglo-Saxon laws on tithes punish the individual, later Anglo-Saxon laws in general are more likely to punish the community.

76 For a challenge to the minster hypothesis, see Cambridge and Rollason, "Debate." For a defence, see Blair, "Debate." I tend to disagree with Blair – it seems much more convincing to me that this is all part of a new structure that is imposed as part of the Benedictine Reform, but, in either case, the *Letter* is clearly linked to this historical fact of change. It is true that, as Carole Hough writes, "the Anglo-Saxon law-codes were not primarily intended for practical use," but, given that tithe payment was indeed a matter of dispute, and that the codes are more specific about payment of other church dues, it is striking that they are relatively silent on the practicalities of tithe payment ("Legal and Documentary Writings," 175). Still, the Anglo-Saxon law codes are more specific regarding to whom tithes must be paid than the sermons are.

new hierarchical system of churches in late Anglo-Saxon England was deliberately adapted from the Carolingian model and spurred by the Benedictine reform. They argue that the new churches, and the new tithe laws meant to respond to them, were intentionally created in order to establish new organizational systems, rather than being a desperate attempt to shore up a crumbling system of mother churches. Whichever side in the minster debate has it right, it is clear that the Old English *Sunday Letters'* obsession with tithes must be bound up with the fact that new tithe legislation had been introduced in the second half of the tenth century, and that the construction of new, smaller churches on manorial land posed a challenge to the revenues once enjoyed by the old churches. It is therefore difficult to understand why preachers of the *Sunday Letter* would not be intent on either teaching the people new requirements for tithing to new churches or supporting payment to the mother churches.[77] The only clue regarding to which institution payment should be made is a single moment in one of the six *Letters* in which the preacher tells the audience to pay their tithes to a *minster* – in all other cases the *Letter* says merely that tithes must be paid to God's churches.[78] It is also possible that, because the new legislation was introduced in the mid-tenth century, while the *Sunday Letter* is found in manuscripts dating to the eleventh century, the preachers of the *Letter* felt that they could trust their audiences to know to whom the tithes should be directed, or perhaps they believed that such details were best left to the reeves and vicars who were responsible for collecting the tithes. However, the law codes are always careful to state which portions of the tithe and ecclesiastical dues are to be paid to the minster and which to manorial churches, even as late as Cnut's law codes of the early 1020s, which specify that a thegn who has a church on his bookland that includes a graveyard must give one-third of his tithe to his church, while thegns whose churches lack graveyards must pay the priest out of the other nine parts (which were generally reserved for the payment of alms).[79]

---

77 Haines suggests that the addition of Wulfstanian materials on tithes and other matters may be because "the compiler had to hand some contemporary, authoritative material regarding Sunday observance and tithing and found it more or less germane to the Sunday Letter" (*Sunday Observance*, 92).

78 B 110. Because both *minster* and *cyrice* (church) are used in the same sermon, the author of that sermon may have considered the terms to be interchangeable (B 73, 121).

79 To the old minster was due all churchscot (an old tax proportional to one's wealth), and soulscot (payment for burial of a body), and in some cases it is stated that the tithe itself is due to the minster. 1 Cnut 11–13.

There are several other contexts in which we might understand the Old English *Letter*'s fascination with tithes. The *Sunday Letters* frequently threaten that the world is near its end, or that those who fail to observe Sunday rightly will bring upon themselves pestilence and war. At least one Anglo-Saxon law text states that tithes were in that year collected as a response to a heavy pestilence, which the king believed to have been a punishment for the sins of the English people, and especially because they had not paid their tithes.[80] It is also worth remembering that during the eleventh century (when the Old English *Sunday Letter* manuscripts were produced), England was conquered first by the Danes and then by the Normans, so the *Letter*'s threats of war and death must have seemed all too real. Beryl Taylor has shown that Norman and English tithe systems were different at the time of the Conquest but that, immediately after the Conquest, Normans allowed the English to continue to pay tithes under the English system while requiring Normans to pay under the Norman system.[81] This might provide another explanation as to why tithes would have been so important to preachers of the *Sunday Letter*, as well as explaining why it might have been in their interest not to go into too much detail: because the *Sunday Letter* sermons were not assigned to any particular day in the church calendar, but were designed to be preached at will, providing concrete detail about payment might actually have been a disadvantage. This would have been true in pre-Conquest England as well, because the Danelaw had different requirements for tithe payment than did standard Anglo-Saxon law. In other words, perhaps the lack of specificity was one more way that the *Sunday Letter* tried to ensure its popularity and continued circulation, by making itself adaptable to many situations.

The second command directed to all audiences of the Old English *Letter*, to enforce proper behaviour, is implied by the fact that the punishments levied for improper Sunday observance affect not just the individual transgressor, but whole communities.[82] For example, in Haines C, working on Sunday will cause famine and disease:

---

80 IV Edgar (962 x 963).

81 Taylor, "Continuity and Change."

82 By contrast, the Old Irish *Cáin Domnaig* is quite clear that even someone who merely observes a transgression is liable for it: "the fine for someone who looks on and who does not act as identifier and who does not thereupon levy is equal to the fine for the person who violates the sanctity of Sunday" (Hull, *Cáin Domnaig*, §2; Hull's translation).

Swa hwa swa ænige cypinge on þam dæge begæð oððe oðre þing, þæt man
claðas waxe, oððe ænig cræftig man him on his cræfte tylige, oððe man efesige oðerne man oððe bread bace oððe ænig ungelyfed þing bega on þam
dæge, he scel beon utlaga wið me and ealle þa, þe him to þam unrihte fylstað
and him þæt geþafiað. Forþan þa men, þe swylc þing begað, ne begytað hi na
mine bletsunge ne mine myltse, ac heom becymð færlice min grama ofer for
þæs dæges forsewennysse. And ic asende ofer eow mancwealm and orfc-
wealm, swa þæt þa lybbendan nyton, be hwan hig lifian, and þa deadan man
nat, hu man delfe, for þære untrumnysse, þe heom an becymð eal for minra
beboda forsewennysse.[83]

Whosoever engages in trading or another thing on that day, so that a person
washes clothes, or any craftsman works at his craft, or someone cuts another
person's hair or bakes bread or engages in any illicit thing on that day, he and
all those, who helped him to the sin and permitted him that, shall be cursed
from me. Therefore those people who do such things will never get my blessing nor my mercy, but my rage will come to them suddenly because of their
contempt of the day. And I will send upon you pestilence and murrain, so
that the living will not know by what means they will live and one will not
know how the dead will be buried, because of the sickness which will come
upon them all for contempt of my commands.

Not only is the punishment directed at the whole community, which
will be crippled by hunger and disease, without sparing those who may
not have sinned, but by naming "all those, who helped him to the sin and
permitted him that," this passage stresses that co-conspirators, and even
those who merely allow an infraction to be committed, will be punished
along with the sinner. This is typical of the punishments promised in the
Old English *Sunday Letters*, which also include five-pound hailstones,
destruction by a foreign army, sulfurous fire, poisons, and gnats, all of
which would have affected the community rather than just the individual
transgressor.[84] In this way, the *Sunday Letter* makes its audience responsible not just for their own behaviour, but for policing the actions of their
community as well. We might expect that a culture of gossip would have
arisen to shame into compliance all those who violated Sunday observance. If you saw your neighbour gathering plants from the garden or

---

83 C 97–105.
84 Other representative passages include Haines A 39–47, C 75–83, and D 42–53.

going hunting on Sunday,[85] for example, you might feel compelled to inform them about the message of the *Sunday Letter* in order that your own plants would not be destroyed by hail or locusts. In this way, the *Sunday Letter* encourages the formation of self-regulating textual communities. Furthermore, this passage promises that those who violate the rule of Sunday will be banished from God (literally made "outlaws"). In the moral law of the *Letter*, then, one of the worst punishments imaginable is to be excluded from the community the *Letter* forms.[86] The community is defined both positively and negatively, as something to which one might belong and from which one might be disbarred. By levying punishments on the community rather than the individual, the *Sunday Letter* creates out of its audience a self-policing population. It creates not just a Christian subject, but a community of Christians subject to the law of the *Letter*.

The third thing the *Sunday Letter* asks its audience to do is to disseminate the message. All but one of the Old English *Sunday Letters* include a specific command to the audience to circulate the message further. The circulation injunction is usually directed at priests, bishops, and other learned men, and it is no coincidence that the only sermon without a circulation injunction is Haines C, which is the most emblematic of the sermons addressed to a mixed lay audience. Yet, even Haines C includes general statements on the importance of preaching and implicitly encourages its audience to spread its message if they want to avoid a terrible fate. This raises two questions: why would the preacher address any portion of his catechetical message to preachers and bishops, and how would the lay members of the audience have understood this command? To a certain extent, circulation of the *Letter* by the laity would have been accomplished by the culture of gossip and self-policing behaviour I have just suggested – if you saw your neighbour breaking the law of Sunday, you would feel compelled to tell him or her about the importance of Sunday observance in order to prevent punishment from befalling you and your community. At the same time, the injunction to circulate the message invites members of the audience to become like preachers. This command to disseminate the *Letter* transforms the audience from passive to active

---

85 A 17.

86 According to Stephen J. Harris, "in Anglo-Saxon England, the moral law was primarily to be understood as a collective phenomenon. It was, in the imagery of Scripture, a law given to a people, not separately to individuals, although individuals could independently accept it" (*Race and Ethnicity*, 17).

participants in the mass communication of the message. But because it specifically addresses preachers as well as audience, the circulation injunction also reminds the preacher that he is a member of the audience and of the community that they form. Assuming preachers preached the command to priests regardless of the composition of the audience (rather than reading it in the manuscript but omitting it during oral delivery), the preacher is transformed from proximate audience of the manuscript (or whatever audience he was part of when he learned the *Sunday Letter*), to preacher, and back again to audience member, but this time of his own sermon. Because the *Letter* equates the responsibilities of the preacher to preach with responsibility of the lay people to behave rightly and enforce the message, it suggests that the continued safety of the community depends on everyone's participation in the circulation of the message.

Part of the reason that the command to circulate the message is able to function in this complicated way is due the fact that the *Sunday Letter* is a *letter* and, as such, is reproducible as either an oral or a written text. Letters were often delivered orally by their messengers (as the *Sunday Letter* sometimes claims to have been delivered orally by the angel who brought it to the holy site), so no literacy was required of the recipient, only of the original sender or scribe. This means that the replicability of the sermon's message was not dependent on literate members of the audience. In this section of the chapter, I will explore further the circulation injunction, asking to whom the injunction is addressed, and showing that it displaces the burden of the preacher onto his audience, transforming them from passive to active participants in the dissemination of the message, creating a potential for mass circulation of the content, if not the exact form, of the message. I argue that the fact that the Old English *Sunday Letters* do not claim to be apotropaic and yet are able to gesture towards tangible benefits for believers is due to the fact that the Old English *Letters* are all contained in sermons that would have been preached orally. Paradoxically, the fact that the object is not magical might also account for its popularity – because what is important is *speaking* the message, more people are able to participate in its circulation. You need not be literate or wealthy enough to purchase a physical copy of the *Letter* in order to have access to its message; at the same time, being illiterate or poor does not release you from the negative consequences of not believing in or circulating the message orally.

I begin by surveying the most basic circulation injunction, before turning to some examples that are more complicated. Haines A, a letter of the Effrem Gate type, is very explicit in its circulation address, which asks bishops and mass-priests to preach the letter to the people frequently, and to "send" the letter throughout their districts so that people will believe it and recognize that it was not written by human hands:

Ge bisceopas and mæssepreostas kyðaþ þis gelomlice eallum folce and send-að þis gewrit geond ealle scira þæt eal folc hit geornlice underfoo and his ge-lyfan þæt hit nis þurh nanne man geworht, ac þurh þæs hehstan hælendes handa gewriten.[87]

You bishops and mass-priests make this known frequently to all people and send this letter throughout all the districts so that all people might eagerly receive it and believe of it that it was not made by any human, but written by the hands of the highest savior.

The sermon should be preached orally ("mak[ing] this known frequently to all people") and should also be supplemented by "sending" the document throughout England. Does this imply that a special copy of the document itself might have been circulating within England? How else would sending the letter increase the chance that audiences would be convinced it was not made by human hands? Would Anglo-Saxon audiences have been so moved by the content of the message that seeing a physical copy, even if not the original, would somehow have amplified their belief in it? This is an atypical sermon, much shorter than other *Sunday Letter* sermons, and perhaps directed at a more ecclesiastical audience.[88] It also offers very little introductory framework for the letter, presenting itself almost as though it is an independent letter, not a sermon (except that it begins with a long account of the letter's transmission from Effrem Gate to St Peter's in Rome, surely not part of the "original" letter). I take this lack of explanatory framework as a sign that this sermon, if copied and sent to other priests, might have been interpreted as representing the content of the letter itself, unmediated by human interpretation, except for the editorial preface describing its provenance. It would therefore be all the more important to copy the message directly and accurately from the manuscript rather than simply circulating a paraphrase, whether textual or oral. Comparison with similar messages in other Old English *Sunday*

---

87 Haines A 83–5.

88 It is more ascetic than other sermons; it suggests that its audience fast and wear haircloth, for example (A 28–9).

Letters suggests that priests were meant to send physical copies of the letter, or send an exemplar (but not an original) from which other priests could make copies, but not that any priest claimed to have in his possession the "actual" letter written by Christ in heaven. Regardless of whether Anglo-Saxon preachers had some kind of *Sunday Letter* stage prop, my main point here is that circulation injunctions in Anglo-Saxon *Sunday Letter* sermons, even the ones aimed at more ecclesiastical audiences, encouraged transmitting the message of the letter orally as well as textually, and not just to priests but to *eallum folce* (all people).

The circulation injunction in Haines A raises another question: why would priests be conceived as the audience of this message if they do not seem to be the audience of most of the *Sunday Letter* sermons? If this sermon were ever preached, would this address to the bishops and priests have been included? Or is this formula only part of the letter as a written document, one for priests to read in preparation of preaching – and meant to convince them to preach the message – but not intended to be read aloud? This is not an unimportant question, but it is not perhaps one that we can answer. Given that this sermon was directed at a mixed lay and ecclesiastical audience, it is not inconceivable that the directive to priests and bishops could have been included when the sermon was performed. Whether intended for public proclamation or private reading, because priests and bishops were the proximate audience of these sermons, this directive to priests shifts their role from preachers to receivers of the message. If the sermon were read aloud in this form, it would signal to the congregation that the priest was, like them, part of the immediate audience. Even if it were only read by the priest, and omitted from the sermon, it would still signal to the priest that he was only one in a chain of receivers-turned-preachers of the message.

It might be argued that, because Haines A is an atypical sermon (it asks its audience to perform acts of asceticism, for example), it might have been directed at a more ecclesiastical audience or that, because it presents the text of the letter almost as though it is an independent letter rather than a sermon, the above is not a useful example of how the priest becomes part of the audience, or how a lay audience might have been expected to circulate the message. Fortunately, there are also much more "typical" *Sunday Letter* sermons whose circulation injunctions also address priests. In the two Pehtred homilies (Haines E and F), the message of the *Letter* is preached by a reincarnated Irish deacon named Niall who has been sent to warn those who have not believed the veracity of the *Letter*'s message. Both are preserved in manuscripts associated with bishops and archbishops.[89] Because both are so similar at this point in the sermon, I have presented them in parallel in the table on the next page.[90]

The typical Old English *Sunday Letter* circulation injunction is directed most immediately to priests, and there are hints of that here – in the E sermon, the injunction is preceded by a reference to evangelical teaching (omitted in F), and both sermons suggest that learned men are responsible for its transmission. The F sermon adds that anyone who has access to the letter must allow an ecclesiastical person (*mynstermon*) to preach it. However, these injunctions also implicate unlearned or lay members of the audience in the demand to circulate the message. The passages are at least nominally aimed at "every person ... whatsoever person, who has this gospel in his possession," and they contain the possibility that an unlearned person might have the letter "in his possession" (*geweald*). *Geweald* may mean either "possession" or "control."[91] I find it tempting to translate this phrase, by extension, to mean that the message must be circulated by anyone who can read this letter or who has learned its message, perhaps by having memorized it rather than owning a physical copy.[92] I admit that this is stretching the meaning somewhat but, given that the sermon specifies that the person who has the letter in his *geweald* should "make it known ... either by his own self, or by another learned person," it seems clear that this passage obligates an illiterate person who owns a copy of the *Letter* or has memorized its message to find a learned person, perhaps from his textual community, to help him make it known. The modification of the phrase in F also supports this claim, adding that

---

89 Haines E is in a manuscript (CCCC 419) that also contains Haines B. CCCC 419 + CCCC 421 was a homiliary produced in Canterbury that eventually became part of Bishop Leofric of Exeter's personal library (Treharne, "Producing a Library"). This was one of two *Sunday Letter* manuscripts owned and used by Leofric. Haines F is in BL Cotton Tiberius A.iii, a large miscellany possibly produced in the 1020s and including the *Benedictine Rule*, *Regularis Concordia*, saints' lives and homiletic materials, charms, and Ælfric's *Colloquy*, along with two major illustrations. Tracey-Anne Cooper has called it "a pragmatic archbishop's handbook" ("Homilies of a Pragmatic Archbishop's Handbook"). See also Cooper, *Monk-Bishops*.

90 Emphasis added.

91 BT, *s.v.* "geweald," is both physical power ("power, strength, might") but also control ("power over any thing ... rule ... mastery, sway, jurisdiction, government, protection, keeping").

92 Wilcox likewise considers the use of *geweald* to be a deliberate attempt to signal both oral and written circulation. However, he contends that "the explicit appeal to *gelæredne mon* shows the need for an authoritative intermediary, here someone who can preach (*bodian*) the message" ("Voice of the Irish," n.p).

Haines E, 182–93

Haines F, 203–10

And þa ðe nu get ne gelefað þisses,
þonne bið heom, swa swa þam bocerum
bið, þa ðe nellað heora boccræftas Godes
folce wel nytte gedon. Forðon þæt Godes
folc sceal becuman to lifes wege þurh þa
godspellican lare. And *æghwylcum men*
is beboden þurh God sylfne on Cristes
naman and on þære halgan þrynnesse
naman and on þære soðan annesse
naman and on drihtnes rode naman,
þe he sylf on þrowade, *ðæt swa hwylc
man, swa þis godspell hæbbe on his
gewealde, þæt he hit cyðe Godes folce
swyðe genehhe swa þurh hyne sylfne,
swa þurh oðerne gelæredne man, swa
he þonne eðest mæge.* And gif he þonne
gemeleas læt licgan þis gewrit unnyt
Gode and Godes folce, þonne cweð
se hælend and að swerað, þæt he sy
awerged fram him and fram his halgum.

Ond *eghwilcan men* is beboden þurh
God selfne in Cristes noman and in
þaræ halgan þrinnesse naman and in
þare halgan anesse naman and in þare
halgan rode naman, þe drihten self an
þrowade, *se þe hebbe þis gospel an his
gewealde, þæt he hit bodige and cyþe
swiþe gelomlice Godes folce swa þurh
hine selfne, gef he gelæred sie, swa
þurh oþerne gelæredne mon, þonne
he him to cume.* And gef he þonne þæt
agemeleaseþ, þæt he lætaþ licgan þis
godspyl unnet Godes folce, *þæt hit ne
nan mynstermon na sægþ,* þonne cweþ
drihten and þus aþ swor, þæt he wære
awyrged fram him and fram eallum his
halgum in þa æcan witu.

And those who still do not believe this,
then it will be for them, just as it will be
for the scholars, who do not wish to make
their book-learning useful to the people
of God. Because the people of God must
come to the way of life through evangelical
teaching. And it is commanded *to every
person* by God himself in the name of
Christ and in the name of the Holy Trinity
and in the name of the true Unity and in
the name of the cross, that he himself
suffered on, *that whatsoever person, who
has this gospel in his possession, that he
make it known to the people of God very
frequently either by his own self, or by
another learned person, as he most easily
can.* And if he then should allow this letter
to lie neglected, useless to God and to
God's people, then the Savior says and
swears an oath, that he will be damned by
him and his saints.

And it is commanded *to every person* by
God himself in the name of Christ and
in the name of the Holy Trinity and in the
name of the Holy Unity, and in the name
of the holy cross, which the Lord himself
suffered on, *he who has this gospel in his
possession, that he proclaim it and make
it known very frequently to the people of
God either by himself, if he be learned, or
by another learned person, if he should
come to him.* And if he then neglects
that, so that he allows the gospel to lie
useless to the people of God, so *that no
ecclesiastical person says it*, then the
Lord says and thus swore an oath that
he would be damned by him and all his
saints in eternal torment.

the person should make the message known himself "*if* he be learned, or by another learned person," thus implying that one need not be learned to have the letter in his *geweald*. Moreover, there is precedence for a metaphorical interpretation of the word *geweald*: in Book 1 of the Old English translation of Gregory the Great's *Dialogues*, for example, Julian has been sent with a message for Equitius, but in the presence of the holy man is so frightened that "he bifode 7 forhtode to þam swiðe, þæt he earfoðlice hæfde his tungan geweald, þæt he mihte abeodan þæt ærende, þe he þyder fore com"[93] (he trembled and was so afraid, that he with difficulty had power over his tongue, that he might announce the message, which he came thither for). Regardless of what happened in actual practice, the passage in E and F implies that, in an ideal world, all Christian men could potentially form the community of preachers, or at least messengers who transmitted the *Sunday Letter*, and it acknowledges the possibility that an uneducated person might have a copy of the letter and require the aid of a learned person to help him circulate the message. Nor does the passage specify that the only way to spread the message is through preaching; rather, it should be spread through any means possible. While F emphasizes the role of the learned preacher, what both E and F imply, in their appeal to all people, is that even an unlettered person who has heard the message could speak it to others. In conclusion, while there are indications that this message is directed primarily at preachers or holy men, I argue that these sermons imply that *all* people have both the ability and the responsibility to participate in the circulation of the message, not just more elite or religious audiences. These sermons nominally direct the circulation injunction to *all* people and, because the punishments for bad behaviour encourage believers to disseminate the message at all costs or risk having their neighbours' bad behaviour cause the entire community great suffering, this mandates that the lay audience participate in the oral enforcement and transmission of the message.

Haines D also addresses priests directly, and it does so in a way that both complicates and simplifies the question of the roles of preacher and audience, or messenger and addressee:

Gif þonne hwilc bisceop oððe hwilc gelæred man, æfter þan ðe he þis ærendgewrit him on handa hæfð and hit næle þam folce underþeodan ne him rædan, buton twyon anrædlice he þolað Godes domes, forðan ðe swa hwilc

---

93 Hecht, ed., *Bischofs Waerferth von Worcester*, 4.37.27–30.

sacerd swa ne gebodað þam folce heora synna, huruþinga on domes dæge heora blod bið fram him asoht, and he scildig þonne stent be heora synnum on Godes andweardnysse.[94]

If then any bishop or any learned person, after he has this letter in his hands and does not want to submit it to the people or read it to them, without doubt he will definitely suffer God's judgment; because whatever priest does not preach to the people on their sins, indeed on Doomsday their blood will be sought from him, and he will stand guilty of their sins in the presence of God.

The language here complicates the distinction between preacher and audience. It is very specifically addressed to preachers ("any bishop or any learned person," "priest"), but it is also very careful to state that the priest is preaching from a physical copy of the *Sunday Letter*. Unlike E and F, he has the text "in his hands," not "in his possession." There is a stronger sense that one may not alter Christ's words, and ought not to preach from memory but "read" a written text. There are two ways of accounting for this. First, the attention to the physical letter in D makes it all the more remarkable that other *Sunday Letters* do not specify that future disseminators have access to a written document. Second, we know that oral culture and written culture existed alongside one another in Anglo-Saxon England.[95] Written documents purport, much like Scripture, to offer direct and uncorrupted access to Christ's words, but this need not preclude the possibility that an illiterate peasant might pass along the message, orally, to his neighbour. Even if D gives primacy to the written text, it is still possible to say that the tradition of the *Sunday Letter* in Anglo-Saxon England illustrates the importance of oral culture.

Taken together, the shift from passive to active audience participation in the transmission of the *Sunday Letter* and the complicated role of the preacher – who is of necessity both receiver and speaker of the message, and sometimes explicitly addresses himself or those in his role, making them part of the audience – create a community of disseminators of the message, a network in which everyone can take an active role. Even where the *Letter* sermons do not explicitly say that everyone can spread the message, there is the implication that anyone can become like the angelic

---

94 D 113–18.
95 O'Brien O'Keeffe, *Visible Song*.

messenger or the deacon Niall who returns from the dead to attest to the *Letter*'s authenticity in the Pehtred homilies, both of whom *speak* the message. Indeed letters were often delivered orally in the Middle Ages. Though the message of a letter was often delivered from a written text, that text might not be complete, just as the lay person's memory of the *Sunday Letter*'s message might not be complete. That the medieval messenger was often expected to extemporize did not make the message any less valid. Thus, although the role of priests, preaching, and the letter as written text may take priority, we ought not to ignore the possibility of oral transmission of memorized or incomplete oral texts, inspired by the transformation of the audience into messengers of the letter.

From Fundraiser to Written Amulet

While Old English *Sunday Letter* texts de-emphasize the letter as physical object, in the post-medieval period, the *Sunday Letter* came to be known primarily as textual amulet or apotropaic object.[96] Of the medieval British vernacular *Letters* I have surveyed, only one Middle English example is apotropaic, and none of the Old English *Sunday Letters* seem to be. In the Old English *Letters*, whether one receives the reward of heaven or the poisons and gnats is entirely dependent on one's own behaviour, and the behaviour of one's community, not whether one owns a protective copy of the text. In this final section of the chapter, I survey the ways in which the Old English *Sunday Letter*'s physical properties *do* matter, despite the hesitation to claim healing powers for the document itself. The Old English *Letters* exemplify epistolary acts by attending to the medium, message, and agents of the letters, including scribe and messenger as well as author and addressee. That tithes, rather than apotropaism, become the focus of the Old English *Letters* demonstrates that the *Sunday Letter* was a highly adaptable document whose content could be modified to suit local needs. Some of this flexibility derives from the fact that the Old English *Letter* does not insist on the importance of access to the original document produced by God. But while the *Sunday Letter* sermons

---

96 "Textual amulets … were generally brief apotropaic texts, handwritten or mechanically printed on separate sheets, rolls, and scraps of parchment, paper, or other flexible writing supports of varying dimensions" (Skemer, *Binding Words*, 1). Skemer adds that, by "textual amulet," he means something worn on the body (18). For more on Anglo-Saxon amulets, textual and otherwise, see Meaney, *Anglo-Saxon Amulets*.

emphasize the importance of the *Letter*'s content, they also attend to an aspect of epistolary acts that is related to materiality: the transmission of a letter from person to person, whether orally or textually. Although the Old English *Letters* make no claim to apotropaism, they do not seek to be fully immediate objects (i.e., they do not desire the audience to ignore their media instantiations entirely). In what follows, I trace the ways in which the Old English *Sunday Letters* create documents that are replicable on something approaching a mass scale, not by promising that the document has apotropaic qualities, but by attending to the letter's provenance and transmission.

Although the Old English *Sunday Letters* do not support their authenticity by claiming to have any special powers, other Old English letters from heaven do. Anglo-Saxon audiences of the *Letter* may have been familiar with a group of charms based on letters from heaven that promised healing or protection. The nearest Old English parallel to the *Sunday Letter* is a magico-medical charm meant to cure diarrhea or dysentery,[97] which was supposedly delivered by an angel to Rome in the form of a letter that is to be written on a piece of parchment and placed on the body:

Wið utsihte, þysne pistol se ængel brohte to rome, þa hy wæran mid utsihte micclum geswæncte. Writ þis on swa langum bocfelle þæt hit mæge befon utan þæt heafod, 7 hoh on þæs mannes sweoran þe him þearf sy, him bið sona sel: "Ranmigan adonai eltheos mur O ineffabile Omiginana midanmian misane dimas mode mida memagartem Orta min sigmone beronice irritas uenas quasi dulaþ feruor fruxantis sanguinis siccatur fla fracta frigula mirgui etsihdon segulta frantantur in arno midoninis abar uetho sydone multo saccula pp pppp sother sother miserere mei deus deus mini deus mi. Amen Alleluia Alleluia."[98]

Against diarrhea. The angel brought this letter to Rome, when they were greatly tormented with diarrhea. Write this on a piece of animal skin long

---

97 Magoun argues that the presence in the text of the letter of what seem to be references to fever indicates that "utsihte" must be referring to dysentery, not diarrhea ("Zu den ae. Zaubersprüchen," 32).

98 Pollington, ed., *Leechcraft*, 236. The charm is found in an Anglo-Saxon medical text that has been assigned the name *Lacnunga*. The manuscript in which it is contained has an uncertain provenance. One of *Lacnunga*'s editors has suggested that it "might be intended for the use of a wealthy tenth- or eleventh-century secular (perhaps even royal) lord or, more likely, his physician" (Pettit, ed. and trans., *Anglo-Saxon Remedies*, liii).

enough that it might surround the outside of the head, and hang it on the neck of the person to whom there be need, and he will soon be better: "Ranmigan etc."

The angel delivers this letter to Rome, one of the sites to which the *Sunday Letter* is delivered, but the similarities between the *Sunday Letter* and this charm end there. Not only do none of the *Sunday Letters* that I have found promise to cure gastrointestinal distress, but the text of the angel's supposed letter is a garbled mixture of Latin, Greek, Hebrew, and Aramaic that makes no mention of Sunday or any of the other common features of the *Sunday Letter*. Several attempts have been made to translate the angel's letter, but only short phrases can be identified, in which the speaker appeals to God for help and refers to the nature of the illness.[99] Here letters are associated with suffering bodies, medical practitioners are encouraged to make their own copies of the letter, and there is no need to have possession of the original document. Moreover, instead of simply placing a letter on the body, in this charm the text of the letter is written on a piece of parchment measured to fit the specific size of the patient, then hung about that person's neck. Unlike the Abgar letter (discussed in chapter 3), which often relies on physical contact between document and body, in the charms it is only through the combination of the special content of the message and its carefully produced physical shape that the document has the power to heal.

There is at least one other Anglo-Saxon charm that associates healing with a letter delivered by an angel to a location associated with the *Sunday Letter*:

---

99 The most thorough attempts, though they at times disagree, are those of Magoun, "Zu den ae. Zaubersprüchen"; Cockayne and Singer, eds, *Leechdoms*, 67; Braekman, "Notes on Old English Charms"; and Pettit, *Anglo-Saxon Remedies*, 313–15. Braekman identifies a fifteenth-century Middle Dutch version of the charm that sees the angel delivering the letter to the pope. For "Beronice," see Swan, "Remembering Veronica." Swan argues that there may have been a particular interest in Veronica at Exeter, and that there may have been a concerted effort "to promote [Exeter's] relic collection" through accounts of the Veronica legend (37–9). Several of the Old English *Sunday Letters* are contained in manuscripts associated with Bishop Leofric of Exeter. If Swan is correct, this would provide further evidence for apotropaic texts circulating in the same environments as the Old English *Letters* without inspiring the Anglo-Saxon authors or compilers to apply apotropaic characteristics to the *Letters*.

Se engel brohte þis gewrit of heofonum and lede hit on uppan Sanctus Petrus weofud on Rome.

Se þe þis gebed singð on cyrcean, þonne forstent hit him sealtera sealma. And se þe hit singð æt his endedæge, þonne forstent hit him huselgang.

And hit mæg eac wið æghwilcum uncuþum yfele, ægðer ge fleogendes ge farendes. Gif hit innon bið, sing þis on wæter, syle him drincan. Sona him bið sel. Gif hit þonne utan si, sing hit on fersce buteran and smere mid þæt lic. Sona him kymð bot.

And sing þis ylce gebed on niht ær þu to þinum reste ga, þonne gescylt þe God wið unswefnum þe nihternessum on menn becumað:

Matheus. Marcus. Lucas. Iohannes. bonus fuit et sobrius religiosus. me abdicamus. me parionus. me orgillus. me ossius ossi dei fucanus susdispensator et pisticus.

M'. M'. L. I. Cum patriarchis fidelis. Cum profetis eterilis. Cum apostolis humilis. Jesus Christus et Matheus cum sanctis de fidelibus adiunctus est actibus.

M. M. L. I. Deum patrem. Deum filium. Deum spiritum sanctum trinum et unum et Iohannem basileus fidelium damasci per suffragium sancti spiritus lucidum omnipotens virtutibus sanctus est in sermonibus.

M. M. L. Iohannes. Panpulo dimisit et addinetum. A et O. per camellos abiunctionibus degestum sit pro omni dolore cum dubitu observatione observator.

Exultabunt sancti in gloria. letabuntur. Exultationes dei in faucibus eorum. et gladii.

Laudate deum in sanctis eius. oð ende.[100]

The angel brought this letter from heaven and laid it upon St Peter's altar in Rome. He who sings this prayer in church, then it will count the same as the psalms of the psalter. And he who sings it at his final day, it will count the same as partaking of the Eucharist.

And it also prevails against every unknown evil, both flying and travelling. If it be internal, sing this over water, give him to drink. Soon he will be better. If it be external, sing it over fresh butter and smear the body with it. Soon he will be cured.

---

100 Storms no. 34. From London, BL Cotton Caligula A.xv, f. 140a (*Handlist* item 411; Ker no. 139a). Storms, *Anglo-Saxon Magic*.

And sing this same prayer at night before you go to sleep, then God will shield you from bad dreams that come to men during the night:
Matthew, Mark, Luke, John, etc.

The Latin prayer that follows calls upon the evangelists, the Holy Trinity, and the Alpha and Omega. Karen Jolly explains that the form of this prayer reveals that the practitioner who might have used this charm would had to have been intimately familiar with the language of the church: "Each of the four invocations is followed by Latin or Greek phrases from psalms or liturgy, with the suggestion in Old English (*oð ende*) that the knowledgeable performer (presumably a monk or cleric) would complete the thought/prayer triggered by the phrase, similar to instructions in liturgical manuals and the Benedictine Rule."[101] In other words, the supposedly corrupt prayer is not gibberish meant to be spoken by a credulous fool, but a prompt designed for use by a learned man (or for a learned man to teach to others). And yet, the charm instructions make claims for its efficacy that surely would have raised orthodox eyebrows. This angelic (and apocryphal) letter, we learn, can substitute for psalms and last rites. What is more, the charm implies that an individual could sing the charm *himself*, potentially without the aid of a priest or other intermediary from the Christian community. The charm's powers are so great that it is a cure-all, designed to protect against internal and external illness, death without final rites, and also nightmares. It may be consumed, spread on the body as a salve, or simply prayed aloud (though only in special locations such as the church or at special times such as the moment of death), and it protects the body and the soul.

Despite the fact that other early medieval letters from heaven and other Anglo-Saxon texts claim to be apotropaic, none of the six witnesses of the *Sunday Letter* extant in Old English (which include representatives from the recension to which the lone apotropaic Middle English *Letter* belongs) claim that the physical document has the power to protect or heal its audience. This is not to say that the Old English *Letters* pay no attention whatsoever to the *Letter* as a material object. To the contrary, many of the Old English *Letters* state that the original letter that fell to earth was a

---

101 Jolly, "Tapping the Power," 64. Thomas Oswald Cockayne suggested Greek analogues for some words in the prayer (Cockayne and Singer, *Leechdoms*, 233–5).

deluxe manuscript written in golden letters by God, Christ, or his angel.[102] If the Old English *Sunday Letters* do not claim to be textual amulets, as *letters*, they still have a special relationship to physical, material form.[103] Haines D, which is the most explicit about the process of creating the letter, repeatedly insists that an angel wrote the letter "with his own fingers."[104] While other Old English *Letters* explain that the angel served as God's or Christ's scribe, taking dictation from him, none of these other *Letters* emphasize the use of *fingers*.[105] The idea that God writes with his fingers can be traced to the Bible, where God writes the Ten Commandments with his fingers (Exodus 31:18) and Christ uses the finger of God to drive out devils (Luke 11:20). This image is also present in other Anglo-Saxon

---

102   E 41, 151–2, 201–2; F 43, 127, 221–2; B 11, 131–2. The use of golden letters is apparently a new development in Old English. Dorothy Haines writes that "no extant Latin Sunday Letter states that the missive was written in golden letters" (77). However, there are certainly references to letters written in gold in other medieval literature, as well as manuscripts written in golden letters, which is called chrysography. For example, in the Anglo-Latin *Vita et Miracula Sancti Kenelmi* (eleventh century), after Kenelm is murdered in England, a dove delivers a letter written in gold to St Peter's altar while the pope is at mass to alert him to the murder (Love, ed., *Three Eleventh-Century Anglo-Latin Saints' Lives*, §§10–11). Likewise, in Book 4 of the Old English translation of Gregory the Great's *Dialogues*, Mellitus has a vision that a young man brought him *ærendgewritu* and when he opened them, he "geseah awritene mid gyldenum stafum" (saw [it] written with golden letters). The message records the names of those who will die of the plague (27.299.9–10). Boniface wrote a letter to Abbess Eadburga in 735 asking her to make him a copy of the Epistles of Peter written in gold (Emerton 26 [Tangl 35]). It is also tempting to associate the golden letters of the *Sunday Letter* with the illustration of the New Minster charter (London, BL Cotton Vespasian A.viii, f. 2v). Not only is the manuscript itself written in gold, but the document Edgar holds in his hands in this illumination (presumably the foundation charter) is golden.

103   On the special physical form of legal documents such as charters in later medieval England, see Steiner, *Documentary Culture*. Like Steiner's legal documents, an independent letter could have a distinctive physical form that identified it as a special kind of document, but the Old English *Sunday Letters* are all copied into codices rather than surviving as single-sheet documents. The Old English *Letters* may not be apotropaic, but they are attentive to some of the special forms of letters as physical documents.

104   "Þæt awrat drihtnes engel mid his sylfes fingrum" (D 3–4); "Godes engel hit awrat mid his agenum fingrum" (D 120–1); "hi wurdon … mid engles fingrum awritene" (D 128–9). It is unusual for the letter to be written by an angel rather than by Christ himself (Haines, *Sunday Observance*, 185n4).

105   "Þa angan drehten selfa dihtan þæt gewrit" (Then the Lord himself began to dictate the letter) (F 149–50); "and þæt gewrit ne awrat nan eorðlic man, ac Godes agen ængel, swa swa seo halige þrynnys hit sylf gedihte" (and no earthly man wrote that letter, but God's own angel, just as the Holy Trinity itself dictated it) (C 15–16).

sermons. For example, Ælfric explains that God uses his finger to write the Ten Commandments because his finger "is the Holy Ghost."[106] By referring to the angel's fingers and to golden letters, the *Letter* emphasizes the act of writing and the production of the manuscript, and marks the original document as a manuscript of value and importance. There is no suggestion that either the original manuscript of the *Letter* or any subsequent copies have any special apotropaic properties but, even without apotropaism, this attention to the agents involved in dictating and writing letters, as well as to the production of the physical medium, reflects Anglo-Saxon attentiveness to the full scope of epistolary acts.[107]

Even those versions of the *Letter* that describe the transmission of the letter in greater detail, the so-called Effrem Gate *Letters,* are ambiguous as to whether it is the original document that is being passed from person to person or whether each recipient is making his own copy:

Men þa leofestan, her onginð þæt halie gewrit þe com fram heofenan into Hierusalem. Soðlice hit gefeol beforan þam gaton Effrem, and þær hit wæs funden þurh anes preostes handa, þæs nama wæs Achor. And he hit sende to anre oðre byrig to oþrum preoste, þe genemned is Ioram, þe hit asende fram Bethania byrig to oðrum preoste, þe genemned is Machabeus. And he hit asende to monte Garganum þær sancte Michaeles circe is þæs heahengles. Soðlice þæt ylce gewrit þurh Cristes willan ures hlafordes com to Rome to sancte Petres byrgene. And ealle þa men þe wæron on þam burgum þær þæt gewrit to com, dydon þreora daga fæsten and halie gebedu and ælmessan, þæt ure milde hlaford heom fultum sealde and geopenode gewitt on manna heortan to oncnawenne ures drihtnes hælendes Cristes mildheortnesse.[108]

---

106 "God awrat ða ealdan æ mid his fingre on ðam stænenum weaxbredum. Godes finger is se halga gast. swa swa crist on his godspelle cwæð …" (God wrote the Old Testament with his finger on the stone writing-tablets. God's finger is the Holy Ghost, just as Christ says in his gospel …) "Dominica in Media Quadragesime," in *CH II*, 240–2.

107 Wilcox also notes the importance of the golden letters and handwritten document in Haines E and F, arguing that the sermon authors' attention to the materiality of the document was intended to grant the sermon more authority, as though it shares the authority of the letter written by God. He argues that the sermons and the original document "almost fuse" ("Voice of the Irish," n.p.). According to Wilcox, the authority granted the homilies is then transferred to and reinforced by the body of the preacher delivering the sermon, much like Niall's oral summary of his vision is an embodied performance of authority.

108 A 1–11.

Dearest people, here begins the holy letter which came from heaven to Jerusalem. Truly it fell before the gates of Effrem, and there it was found by the hands of a priest, whose name was Achor. And he sent it to another city to another priest, who is named Joram, who sent it from Bethany to another priest, who is named Machabeus. And he sent it to Mount Garganus, where the church of Saint Michael the archangel is. Truly that same letter through the will of Christ our lord came to Rome to Saint Peter's tomb. And all the people who were in those cities to which the letter came fasted for three days and made holy prayer and almsgiving, so that our merciful Lord might give them help and open understanding in the hearts of people to recognize the mercy of our savior lord Christ.

Given the prayer and fasting that surround the letter's arrival in a new city, it seems logical to assume that the people believed they were seeing the original document. However, this account of the *Letter*'s circulation is strangely unconcerned with the transmission of the physical document, focusing instead on the chain of people and places through which it moves. This is in keeping with Anglo-Saxon epistolary acts, in which access to the original physical document is far less important that representing the agents involved in its transmission. It remains unclear whether there is a single document that travels from place to place or whether each priest makes his own copy of the *Letter*. It also seems that this transmission account reflects an awareness of, or perhaps even an attempt to reconcile this account with, the existence of other recensions that attribute the *Letter*'s discovery to different holy sites, because the passage locates the letter in the places where other recensions claim the *Letter* appeared.[109] As I have discussed above, this *Letter* suggests elsewhere that any future bishops and mass-priests should also "send" this letter to all their districts.

It is useful to compare this passage to the opening lines of the apotropaic Middle English *Sunday Letter*, which also acknowledges that the *Letter* has appeared in multiple locations:

This is the lettere that owr lorde God sentt to dyuerse places þat þe peple shuld amend thame, and specyally for to kepe the Sonday frome all manere of warkes. And none cwth rede it, to at þe last it come to þe sepulcre of Seynt Petre; and þer semlelyd all þe clergye and dewoutely made thare prayere to

---

109 Jerusalem (Recension I/ Effrem Gate), Mount Garganus (where the archangel Michael is said to have appeared many times), and St Peter's altar in Rome (Recension II).

Ihesu Criste þat þai myght hafe vndrestandyng what it mynt. And, thurght the grace of owr lord, come one aungell to a man that hight Octouiane and he rehersed this lettere, and it sead on this manere.[110]

This treatise, found in the late fifteenth-century manuscript Durham University Library, MS Cosin V.IV.2, has been assigned to the same recension as the Effrem Gate sermons and, like the Old English Effrem Gate sermon discussed above, seems aware of other recensions that place the arrival of the *Letter* in different locations. There are several key differences between the Middle English and Old English accounts of this transmission. First, whereas the Old English states that all the people fasted and prayed together, in the Middle English, it is only the clergy who gather. Also, the Middle English version states that no one could understand the *Letter* until it came to St Peter's ("none cwth rede it, to at þe last it come to þe sepulcre of Seynt Petre"), whereas the earlier Anglo-Saxon text suggests that the *Letter* was being circulated from person to person not because no one could understand it, but because they wished to share its message, or because they were following the circulation injunction found later in the *Letter.* Moreover, the prayers offered in the Anglo-Saxon texts are made not so that the *Letter* may be literally understood, as they are in the Middle English text, but so that the people will believe in the mercy of Christ. In comparing the Middle English account to the record of transmission preceding the Old English Effrem Gate *Letters,* we see that whereas the Middle English presents the letter as a difficult, almost inaccessible text to be understood only through the intercession and mediation of select clergy, the transmission account in the Old English Effrem Gate *Letter* serves both as a kind of provenance and as a model for the behaviour expected of the *Letter*'s audience (nominally all people), with respect both to Christian belief and to its further publication.[111] It offers a model for how audiences may participate in the epistolary acts necessary to translate and transmit the message to new communities.

This attention to modes of transmission, along with the *Sunday Letter*'s chain-letter demands, invites small-scale mass communication, if such an

---

110 O'Mara II 1–7. Octavian has not been identified.

111 Felicity Riddy cites a similar publication history in the *Revelation of the Hundred Paternosters* as an example of what some scholars have imagined as "a world of consumers … who seem to form an orderly reproductive chain," but she argues that the realities of late medieval publication were more similar to "a commercial free-for-all" ("'Publication' before Print," 39–40).

oxymoron may be permitted. In *The Preaching of the Friars*, D.L. d'Avray argues that, during the thirteenth century, the combination of the preaching of a standard set of sermons and a new method for copying manuscripts known as the *pecia* system created "something that can almost be called mass communication."[112] The *pecia* system, under which university students were able to rent individual manuscript quires for copying either by themselves or by professional scribes, made it possible, at least in theory, for the production of large numbers of identical copies of a single exemplar. For preachers, this meant that their sermons could be gathered in model sermon collections and distributed to a wider audience than they had previously been able to reach. Nothing comparable to the *pecia* system existed in Anglo-Saxon England but, in many ways, d'Avray's metaphor of mass communication is useful for thinking about what the Old English *Sunday Letters* were trying to accomplish. Indeed, Jonathan Wilcox imagines that Ælfric's sermon collections, which were copied and distributed throughout England, might have been intended for mass circulation. If distributed to priests, there might have been "thousands of copies" of the sermons. A sermon written for a particular day in the church calendar could have been preached on a single day to people throughout England, in a practice he calls "the beginning of a form of mass communication."[113] The *Sunday Letter* imagines another way in which mass communication, or at least communication to (and by) the masses, might have been achieved, via a combination of manuscript production and oral circulation. Even if the manuscript is not intended for truly mass circulation, this imagined circulation reveals much about Anglo-Saxon transmission networks, the manner by which authors encouraged the spread of Christianity throughout England, and the cultural and social networks involved in that program.

Despite the attention to the golden letters and elaborate transmission routes of the *Letter*, none of the Old English witnesses of the *Sunday Letter* move beyond an acknowledgment of the physical properties of the *Letter* to the suggestion that the *Letter* could be a relic or possess apotropaic qualities derived from its status as a material object.[114] Instead of

---

112 d'Avray, *Preaching of the Friars*, 3.
113 Wilcox, "Ælfric in Dorset," 61–2.
114 For Egeria's recognition that the replicability of letters made them a special kind of relic, see Skemer, *Binding Words*, 97.

promising amuletic properties, the Old English *Letters* offer only curses and threats. The Old English *Sunday Letter* was a highly adaptable document, one that exploited the materiality of the letter as a genre but that also subverts our expectations about how the physical form of letters might have mattered. The Old English *Letters* were not textual amulets offering healing and protection, but they were nevertheless attentive to the production of the original document in heaven, written in golden letters by God or an angelic scribe, and to its delivery to earth. This attention to the materiality of production and transmission allows *Sunday Letter* sermon authors to encourage its further transmission by textual communities on a scale that anticipates mass communication. Everyone in the audience is encouraged to circulate the letter's content regarding Sunday behaviour, whether orally or textually. Much like a chain email, what matters is not access to a special original document, but participating in the continued chain of its transmission and replicability. Although it is not apotropaic, the Old English *Sunday Letter*'s attention to the materiality of its transmission, which focuses on a physical document and its movement through space, is part of what encourages a textual community of believers in and transmitters of the message to circulate it further. Likewise, the authors of this *Letter* shift focus from the healing power of the apotropaic document to the physically destructive punishments that will face both those who misbehave on Sundays and those who fail to share the letter's message. It is not ownership of a special document that will protect an individual, but proper Sunday observance, along with becoming a messenger of the letter's content, modelled for the sermon audiences by the provenance of the original document. In other words, Sunday observance alone will not save a person, unless it is accompanied by participation in a chain of transmission of the message and other epistolary acts.

3 Messengers, Materiality, and Transmission in the Old English *Apollonius of Tyre, Letter of Abgar,* and *Life of St Mary of Egypt*

Anglo-Saxon epistolary acts attend to the materiality of the letter in unexpected ways. In chapter 2, I argued that Anglo-Saxon audiences were curiously unlikely to have been encouraged to believe in the apotropaism potentially associated with a letter from heaven. Although the materiality of the message helped explain its transmission, the adaptability of the letter allowed authors of the Old English *Sunday Letter* to transform written text into a message to be circulated as widely as possible, in whatever forms were available, including oral messages. While Old English *Sunday Letters* downplay the materiality of the letter, in the works examined in this chapter, bodies – whether of written document or of human messenger or recipient – are of central concern. Bodies are responsible for conveying documents across great distances, but also transform and are transformed by contact with letters. This chapter thus extends the previous chapter's consideration of how epistolary acts represent the transmission and delivery of letters by examining the importance of messengers, not just in transporting documents but also in conveying messages, and the ways in which messages are read in and through the bodies of messengers.

The importance of the relationship between bodies and epistolarity has been recognized by scholars such as Elizabeth Heckendorn Cook, who makes generative but context-dependent claims about the relationship between the letter and the body in eighteenth-century epistolarity. Cook argues that letters make recipients acutely aware of the body of the absent writer:

In epistolary narratives, the letter serves as a metonym of the body of the writing subject, vulnerable like it to markings, invasion, violence of all sorts.

While reading, we are intended to imagine a scene of writing: behind the printed page is a manuscript bearing the traces of an authentic bodily origin. Formally as well as thematically, the letter constructs the writing subject as corporeal and thus as an already existing object of knowledge that can be mapped by the transparent medium of print.[1]

The relationship between body and letter was also of central importance in Anglo-Saxon England, but this relationship was conceived differently. In Anglo-Saxon England, the representation of epistolary acts focuses not on the bodies of absent senders, but on the bodies of messengers and recipients. Old English letters exploit the relationship Cook presents between letter and body but, surprisingly, the letter more often writes itself on the body of the messenger or recipient rather than conjuring ideas of violence done to the body of the sender.

This chapter takes as its focus the relationship between epistolary transmission and the bodies of both messages and messengers in three texts: the Old English prose romance *Apollonius of Tyre*; Ælfric's *Letter of Abgar*, in which an ailing king exchanges letters with Jesus of Nazareth; and the anonymous Old English *Life of St Mary of Egypt*, in which Mary's death is miraculously recorded in a message written in the ground. Taking up the question of how the body of a text or a messenger might escape the asynchronicity and absence inherent in communication by letter, these texts imagine communication networks in which contact with the container of the letter can make messages legible in and through the bodies of those who carry them, even as the movement of messengers' bodies through space and time reminds us that letters are always mediated and deferred. Although *Apollonius of Tyre* has famously been redacted to omit explicitly sexual and romantic content, I contend that the affective responses provoked in Apollonius and Arcestrate by contact with a message written on a wax tablet suggest deeply intimate, even erotic, possibilities. By contrast, much like the Old English *Sunday Letters'* lack of apotropaism, the authors of the hagiographic texts occlude the possibility that a saint's letter might become a secondary relic by virtue of its contact with the saint's body. Instead, the potential transfer of apotropaic or erotic power from saint to document is displaced onto the body of the messenger, who speaks

---

1 Cook, *Epistolary Bodies*, 32.

directly with the letter's addressee. This oral communication offers a fantasy (however brief) of perfect conversation with the divine, unmediated by distance or physical document. In fact, what seems like immediacy is always mediated by the messenger, who embodies or risks embodying the message he or she delivers.

Medieval messengers are intimately bound up with the physical documents they carry that authorize them to speak. Not only do medieval messengers orally deliver the messages they carry, but their bodies are sometimes transformed by close physical contact with the material and message of the letter, becoming legible messages in which the content of the document may be read. A messenger may thus supplement a message physically as well as textually – for example, when Apollonius blushes at the message of the letter he carries, his body communicates to the king what the content of the letter he delivered did not. Likewise, in the *Gospel of Nicodemus*, when the Jewish elders want to invite Joseph to return to them, they recognize that sending a letter of contrition alone will not be enough – they supplement the written message with the bodies of seven of his friends, whose presence is intended to convince him of the letter's sincerity in a way that the letter alone never could. Because foregrounding the role of the messenger obscures the inscriptional medium, when documents do appear in Anglo-Saxon literature, they can be problematic. Displaying the physical document in *Apollonius of Tyre* heightens its erotic potential, and Zosimus must delicately avoid turning Mary's body and letter (themselves storage containers) into objects for public consumption by retransmitting her message in an entirely new medium.[2] In the texts I explore in this chapter, the bodies of messengers and sick men are transformed by contact with letters (miraculous or otherwise) whose physical, material form may be as important as the letters' content, if not more so, but whose physical form sees its fullest manifestation in the bodies of messengers, not documents.

---

2 When I describe Mary's body as a "storage container," I mean that her body is the object on which her story has in part been written. Even her physical appearance has changed, owing to her time in the desert. More importantly, I am drawing on the Anglo-Saxon tradition of describing the body as a container for the soul: "the body is itself a part, a container for the spirit, or soul (*sawulhus, feorhhus*, for example)" (Lees, "Engendering Religious Desire," 24).

(Not So) Speedy Delivery: Messengers in Anglo-Saxon England

When letters are moved swiftly and successfully through regular communication channels, they can, like the telegraph, television, or other modern media technologies, appear to completely erase the presence of the human agents involved in their production and transmission. But messengers were of course essential to the transmission of documents in the Middle Ages. Not only were messengers expected to perform messages orally to their recipients after transporting them from one location to another, but messengers could also authenticate or destroy, edit, or block transmission of the messages they were licensed to carry. According to Giles Constable, even in the later Middle Ages, letter delivery could be a slow and difficult process: "Reliable messengers were hard to find, and unless a writer had at his disposal a number of professional couriers, who were available only at the largest courts and chanceries, he might have to wait a long time for a suitable messenger or even for a chance traveller going in the right direction. Many letters were written precisely because the opportunity presented itself in the form of a courier."[3] "Real" Anglo-Latin letters often mention by name the person who was asked to deliver the message, sometimes because the letter served in part as a letter of introduction for its bearer, and sometimes to add another layer of authentication, letting the recipient know that the letter writer had approved of the messenger and potentially considered that person trustworthy. By contrast, many early English vernacular texts describing the exchange of letters minimize the role of the messenger or even omit it entirely.

Medieval messengers exemplify multiple aspects of epistolary acts, especially those involving protocols for the transportation, delivery, and performance of a message. Messengers were expected to perform the message

---

3 Constable, *Letters and Letter-Collections*, 52–3. Frank Stenton's survey of the roads and potential travel routes of England throughout the medieval period focuses on the period after the Norman Conquest, when he believes the most growth occurred ("Road System of Medieval England"). But see Wendy R. Childs, who argues that travel in England after 1200 was relatively easy, that later medieval messengers in England "could regularly travel thirty to forty miles a day," and that "once post services were organised by governments towards the end of the fifteenth century, speeds of seventy to eighty miles a day could be more frequently reached" ("Moving Around," 262). Likewise, Donald Bullough thinks some early medieval continental religious centres may have had a developed messenger system; he argues that in Alcuin's time, St Martin's at Tours had "a frequent messenger-service to a select few destinations" (*Alcuin*, 41).

for its addressee, sometimes supplementing the written script with additional elaboration or interpretation. Although many messengers are represented in Old English texts, their roles are often minimal, and the presence of a messenger does not necessarily imply the presence of a letter. It is often difficult to know whether a messenger has come bearing a written text (containing either a complete or partial message, to be supplemented by the messenger during its delivery) or whether the messenger has been deputized to deliver a purely oral message.[4] When the *Anglo-Saxon Chronicle* describes a sensitive negotiation undertaken in 1014 to restore Æthelred to the throne, it makes no mention of whether the message conveyed was oral or written. After Swein's death, the leaders of England decide to try to lure Æthelred back, as long as he promises to be a better ruler than he was before. To do so, they send a message to him, and in return, he sends a group of messengers with a long, delicate message:

Þa sende se cyning his sunu Eadweard hider mid his ærend(d)racum 7 het gretan ealne his leodscype 7 cwæð þæt he him hold hlaford beon wolde 7 ælc þæra ðinga betan þe hi ealle ascunudon, 7 ælc þara ðinga forgyfen beon sceolde þe him gedon oþþe gecweden wære, wið þam ðe hi ealle anrædlice butan swicdome to him gecyrdon; 7 man þa fulne freondscipe gefæstnode mid worde 7 mid wedde on ægþre healfe, 7 æfre ælcne deniscne cyng utlah of Engla lande gecwædon.[5]

Then the king sent his son Edward hither with his messengers and ordered that they greet all his nation and said that he would be a loyal lord to them and improve each of the things which they all detested, and each of those things ought to be forgiven which were done or said to him, provided that they all turned to him unanimously, without deceit; and the full agreement was ratified with word and pledge on both sides, and they said each Danish king was forever outlawed from England.

Given that this describes a highly ritualized legal agreement, it seems inconceivable that Edward and the messengers were not carrying a written document from Æthelred both to confirm his message and to authorize

---

4 On the use of oral versus written messages in Anglo-Saxon diplomacy, see Chaplais, *English Diplomatic Practice*, 1–45.
5 O'Brien O'Keeffe, ed., *Anglo-Saxon Chronicle*, 98–9. There are similar entries in the D, E, and F manuscripts.

them as his representatives, but the *Chronicle* is unconcerned with clarifying whether the messengers carried a written document.[6] Some of the phrasing of the message does echo language found in Anglo-Saxon legal documents, so perhaps learned audiences could be trusted to fill in the blanks, but this should give us pause about putting too much pressure on whether a text explicitly describes a message as physically present or not. It may also be that some kinds of exchanges would have so obviously required a written document that authors felt no need to spell this out explicitly.

However, there are several Old English texts in which messengers are clearly represented as bearing written communication from sender to receiver, and from them we can learn both how Anglo-Saxons imagined the role of messengers in the communication of messages, and also what Anglo-Saxons feared about failed or corrupt messengers. For example, in a scene from *The Gospel of Nicodemus*, after Joseph miraculously escapes from a sealed prison to Arimathea, and Christ disappears from his tomb, the priests want to recall Joseph to them to find out what has happened. In a charming moment, the elders work out that a letter is the best way to communicate over great distance, asking

> "La, on hwylcere endebyrdnysse magon we Ioseph to us gelaðian and hym wyð specan?" Hig þa swa þeah beþohton þæt hig hym seofon weras gecuron, þe Iosepes frynd wæron, and hym to sendon, and ane cartan myd hym seo wæs þus awryten: "Syb sig myd þe Ioseph and myd eallum þe myd þe syndon."[7]

> "Lo, by what means might we call Joseph to us and speak with him?" However they then considered that they might choose seven men, who were Joseph's friends, and send them to him, and a letter along with them which was written thus: "Peace be with you, Joseph, and with all who are with you."

---

6 But see Pierre Chaplais, who believes this was "an oral message," because it was entrusted to so reliable a messenger as Æthelred's son Edward, and because Edward is named in the *Chronicle*. He argues that "in so far as oral messages were concerned, the trustworthiness and personality of the envoy was of primary importance, and his responsibility was fully engaged. That is why, in the records of the earlier and later Middle Ages, envoys of this type are normally mentioned by name, whereas mere couriers, bearers of written communications, seldom are" ("Anglo-Saxon Chancery," 172).

7 Cross et al., eds, *Two Old English Apocrypha*, XV.2.5–9.

The rest of the message contains an apology and confession that they know they have sinned against God, and this (or the presence of the seven friends) convinces Joseph to return to them to explain what has happened to him. Although we are not treated to an account of the messengers' journey to Arimathea, the text does describe how they handed the message to Joseph, highlighting the moment of physical contact when it is placed in his hand.[8] Moreover, the selection of seven men, surely far more than were actually needed to physically transport the message, is symbolic of the forgiveness the message seeks. Although in this case the *Gospel of Nicodemus* does transcribe the text of the message, it seems that it was the presence of the bodies of the seven friends, perhaps even more than the content of the message itself, that communicated the priests' intent to Joseph.

Not all messengers, however, are so trustworthy. The *Encomium Emmae Reginae* accuses Harold Harefoot of forging a letter to lure Emma's sons into danger; not only is Harold complicit in impersonating Emma, but this letter is said to have been sent "per pellaces cursores" (by deceitful messengers).[9] Anxieties around communication networks are also manifested in the life of Gregory in Ælfric's *Catholic Homilies*. Gregory writes a letter (*pistol*) to the emperor (his godfather) asking not to be made pope, but the emperor's high reeve Germanus intercepts the messenger carrying the letter and tears it up before it gets to the emperor. Usurping the place of the messenger, he tells the emperor only that the people have chosen Gregory as pope.[10] All turns out for the best in the end, since Gregory becomes a successful pope, but this rare example of an intercepted letter reveals the realities of the instability and insecurity of early medieval communication networks. It is especially strange that this failure to communicate happens to Gregory, since he is otherwise known for his erudition, his special aptitude for puns, and his control of language. But saints are supposed to be

---

8 "Þa ærendracan þa foron and to Iosepe comon and hyne gesybsumlice gretton and heora gewryt hym on hand sealdon." (The messengers then travelled and came to Joseph, and greeted him peacefully and gave their letter into his hand) (XV.3.1–2).

9 Campbell, ed., *Encomium Emmae Reginae*, III.iv.2. On the veracity of this story, see Keynes's introduction, ibid., xxxiii–xxxiv and lxiii.

10 *CH II*, 9, 96–108. There are many fewer plots involving intercepted letters in Old English literature than in Middle English, perhaps because early medieval people were more likely to choose as messengers people they knew, members of their household or monastery, rather than professional couriers.

humble, and Gregory cannot be seen to be too eager to become pope. Still, we should keep this moment in mind when we come at the end of this chapter to *Mary of Egypt*, and Mary's anxieties regarding the control over and transmission of her message.

Silent Messages and Speaking Bodies in the Old English *Apollonius of Tyre*

Apollonius of Tyre, an Old English translation of a Latin prose work, is found in an eleventh-century manuscript, Cambridge, Corpus Christi College, MS 201.[11] Often called the first English romance, it tells the story of Apollonius, whose happy life is turned upside down when he correctly solves a riddle in order to win the hand of the daughter of Antiochus, who is having a non-consensual sexual relationship with his own daughter and does not want the riddle to be solved. After a series of disasters, Apollonius, having lost his wealth and title, is shipwrecked off the coast of Pentapolis, where he quickly impresses the king and marries his daughter Arcestrate.

Apollonius of Tyre depicts two sets of letters exchanged not between distant lovers, but between the king's daughter Arcestrate and her local suitors and between Arcestrate and her father. In the first, the king orders the three men wooing Arcestrate to write their names on written documents (*gewrita*) along with the price they would pay for her marriage gift, and he promises he will send (*asænde*) them to his daughter and let her choose.[12] The king gives the documents to Apollonius and asks him to

---

11 *Handlist*, item 65.5; Ker no. 49B. For the medieval and early modern transmission of the Latin version, as well as an edition of the Latin *Historia Apollonii* with English translation, see Archibald, *Apollonius of Tyre*. According to Archibald, at least 114 manuscripts of the Latin from the ninth to seventeenth centuries are extant (3). The Old English is the earliest extant vernacular version. Jennifer Christine Brown, who also studies the epistolary exchange in the Old English *Apollonius of Tyre*, argues that the romance reflects a gradual shift from orality to textuality in Anglo-Saxon England. Whereas oral statements in the romance are associated with deceit in the court of the bad king Antiochus, Arcestrate's written letter declaring her desire for Apollonius is more binding and also more true or "real" than her spoken admissions ("Writing Power").

12 Goolden, ed., *Old English "Apollonius of Tyre,"* 30/22. Because Goolden's edition is not continuously numbered, references to the text will be given in the format page number/ line number. On variations of this scene in other traditions, and Apollonius's relative lack of excitement about marrying Arcestrate in some of them, see Archibald, *Apollonius of Tyre*, 66–7.

bring them to Arcestrate, who responds to the men's requests by writing her own letter (*gewrit*) to her father in which she declares that the man she has chosen is the shipwrecked man.[13] She gives her message to Apollonius to carry it to her father. Her father does not know who she means by "the shipwrecked man," and asks Apollonius to read the letter privately to see if he can figure it out. After Apollonius blushes, the king finally gets the message and together they go to Arcestrate, who confesses her love for Apollonius.

Several scholars have noted that, although the translation is relatively faithful, the Old English translator has greatly reduced the Latin text's references to sexual intimacy, love, and other emotions throughout the romance.[14] That said, erotic potential cannot be completely suppressed; the Old English translator could not omit such crucial scenes as the moment when Apollonius recognizes Arcestrate's love for him. Moreover, this is only one of many scenes still extant, if reduced, in the Old English in which bodies are both important and complicated. From Antiochus's rape of his daughter, which opens the romance, to the boy covered in oil who runs through the streets to announce the opening of the gymnasium, to the games Apollonius plays with the king in the bathhouse, to Apollonius's

---

13 It is difficult to say whether the men's written statements are letters or not; *gewrit* can mean any kind of writing (though it is used for letters), and we are not presented with the text of their messages. Here *gewrita* translates the Latin *codicellos*, which is similarly generic but often indicates either a letter or a legal document. Roman authors sometimes described wax tablets, especially those composed of multiple sheets, as *codices*. Given that Arcestrate's reply is written in a wax tablet, it may also be possible that *codicellos* here was meant to suggest small tablets. For the use of *codices* for tablet, see Rouse and Rouse, "Vocabulary of Wax Tablets," 222. Because the king seals the documents with his ring and promises to have Apollonius bear them to his daughter, they meet the basic criteria for a letter – namely, that it is a written document addressed from one person to another that is sent, often with the aid of a messenger or other intermediary, and often with authenticating seals or tokens.

14 The Old English translator removed many of the Latin source's reference to love, ranging from substituting Apollonius's name for the phrase "her beloved" to omitting entirely a scene where Arcestrate grows so love-sick that doctors are sent for. For the Old English translator's changes to his source, see Riedinger, "Englishing of Arcestrate"; Donner, "Prudery in Old English Fiction"; and Morini, "First English Love Romance." For a consideration of homosociality and the erotic potential of the male body in the Old English *Apollonius*, see Townsend, "Naked Truth." Clare Lees argues that Anglo-Saxon sexuality is deeply ambivalent, and that *Apollonius* reveals sexuality as both positive (because it is a way to access knowledge) and something to be restrained ("Engendering Religious Desire," 38–9).

tears when he tells Arcestrate his story, or his blushing when her love is revealed, this is a text full of potential sexual desire of many kinds, wanted and otherwise.

Arcestrate writes a letter because it allows her to say what she could not otherwise say, but also because her message appears to be legally binding, and as such, needs to be in written form. The text of her letter opens with a salutation formula: "You good king and my dearest father," and the letter is both written and sealed (*geinseglode*):[15]

Þu goda cyngc and min se leofesta fæder, nu þin mildheortnesse me leafe sealde þæt ic silf moste ceosan hwilcne wer ic wolde, ic secge ðe to soðan þone forlidenan man ic wille, and gif ðu wundrige þæt swa scamfæst fæmne swa unforwandigendlice ðas word awrat, þonne wite þu þæt ic hæbbe þurh weax aboden, ðe nane scame ne can, þæt ic silf ðe for scame secgan ne mihte.[16]

You good king and my dearest father, now your compassion has given me leave that I myself might choose what man I wanted, I tell you truly that I desire the shipwrecked man, and if you should be amazed that such a shamefast virgin wrote these words so boldly, then know that I have proclaimed in wax, which knows no shame, what I myself could not for shame say to you.

As a love letter, Arcestrate's message may initially seem surprising, not least because it is addressed to her father, not her beloved. However, the concealment of the lover's name is common in medieval love letters, a trope that might have arisen from the correspondents' need for secrecy.[17] So long as the beloved was not named, if the letter was lost or read by someone else, no harm would come of it, because only the messenger knew to whom the letter should be delivered. By concealing the name of her beloved, Arcestrate ensures Apollonius's privacy and gives the king the chance to accept her request or to reject it without social consequences. Recall also that in the Middle Ages, messengers often acted as interpreters or public performers of the letter. Sometimes the written letter was merely an excuse to get the messenger in the presence of the addressee so that, when the opportunity presented itself, the messenger could deliver

---

15 Goolden, ed., *Old English "Apollonius of Tyre,"* 32/9.
16 Ibid., 32/11–17.
17 Camargo, *Middle English Verse*, 25–6.

the real message orally.[18] Furthermore, although Apollonius is not the immediate addressee of Arcestrate's letter, she knows that he is the messenger who will carry the letter to her father, and she might reasonably assume that he will hear or read the message when it is delivered. Addressing the letter to her father rather than to Apollonius is a way of creating the perception of a safe and proper distance between Arcestrate and Apollonius, which is itself a characteristic gesture in love letters.[19]

Arcestrate specifies that she has written in wax, probably a diptych or polyptych wax tablet (because she is able to seal it), which would have added an extra layer of security and secrecy – a sealed diptych protects the wax, which faces inward, and presents only its outer shell, usually wood, to the casual observer. The choice of wax is important for several reasons. First, Arcestrate desires privacy for her declaration of desire. Second, wax tablets were often used for drafts or note taking. Writing worth keeping would have been transferred to parchment, and the wax scraped clean to be used again. Writing in wax rather than calling for a scribe, ink, and parchment suggests that Arcestrate felt pressured to reply as quickly as possible, and that her message was written in some haste. In theory, medieval letters were to be carefully crafted rather than spontaneous notes. The hastiness of the wax tablet may therefore signal to the audience of the romance that her letter, unlike more deliberately prepared documents, might accurately and transparently represent her emotions in the moment. More significantly, wax tablets were used by students to take notes in class, but also to record their thoughts if they had a question while they were away from their teacher, so that they might better communicate it later.[20] Like a

---

18 For a secret message written in the wood base of a wax tablet, then covered by wax in which was written a more innocuous message, see Liestøl, "Correspondence in Runes." For a similar secret message sent by Demaratus in Herodotus, along with wax tablet technology in antiquity, see Kilgour, *Evolution of the Book*, 51. A shorter account of Demaratus's secret message also appears in the Old English *Orosius*: "Þa wæs mid him an wræccea of Læcedamania, Creca byrg, se wæs haten Demerað, se þæt facn to his cyþþe gebodade 7 hit on anum brede awrat 7 siþþan mid weaxe beworhte" (Then there was with him a messenger of Laecedamonia, the Greek city, who was called Demaratus, who made known that treachery to his people and wrote it on a tablet and then covered it with wax) (Bately, ed., *Old English Orosius*, 2.5.46.8–10). The *Orosius* also includes secret messages by Hamilcar written below the wax of tablets (4.5.90.20–3).

19 "The letter is both a reflection of the gap [between suitor and lady] and an instrument for gap closing" (Altman, *Epistolarity*, 189).

20 Mews, *The Lost Love Letters*, 14; Brown "Role of the Wax Tablet," 8.

good student, Arcestrate uses her wax tablet to communicate with her teacher, even if she does not address him directly. In writing the message herself, she also obeys Apollonius's instruction, showing off what a good pupil she has been. When Arcestrate plaintively asks whether Apollonius wouldn't be sad if she chose one of the suitors, Apollonius demurs, saying he only wants her to demonstrate her new skills by writing the message herself, and making her own choice: "Na, ac ic blissige swiðor ðæt þu miht ðurh ða lare, þe þu æt me underfenge, þe silf on gewrite gecyðan hwilcne heora þu wille"[21] (No, but I would rejoice the more that you might through the instruction, which you received from me, yourself make known in writing which of them you desire). Finally, most wax tablets were not held in the hand but were placed on the thigh in order to stabilize them while they were being written upon.[22] Although the romance does not describe how Arcestrate's body was positioned while she wrote (it merely states that she wrote and sealed a reply), given that Arcestrate is sitting in the presence of her teacher Apollonius when she writes her letter, placing the tablet on her thigh would have suggested the intimate physical contact she wished to have with its subject, belying her protestations of pure love and modesty. Even if she did not place the tablet on her thigh to write, she certainly touched it and prepared it while in Apollonius's presence, then placed it into his hands to deliver it for her. As Janet Gurkin Altman argues, a letter, which makes physical contact with both sender and recipient, may be a figure for the lover, and to accept the letter may therefore be to symbolically accept the lover.[23]

Apollonius's medial position as shipwrecked but part of the king's household, nameless but the king's physical equal, is made literal when he is asked to serve as go-between, delivering messages from the suitors to Arcestrate and from Arcestrate to the king. Although Apollonius is notionally the messenger, when he is asked to examine Arcestrate's letter, he realizes that he is in fact the subject (and intended audience) of the letter, despite the fact that it is written to her father. A common medieval metaphor explained that wax could grow dark from overuse; this was

---

21 Goolden, ed., *Old English "Apollonius of Tyre,"* 32/4–5.

22 Rouse and Rouse, "Vocabulary of Wax Tablets," 221.

23 "The letter as a physical entity emanating from, passing between, and touching each of the lovers may function itself as a figure for the lover (rejection of the letters is the 'signal' for rejection of the lover)" (Altman, *Epistolarity*, 19).

sometimes extended to include the shame of the one who wrote in it.[24] Although Arcestrate's letter declares that she has written in wax because it "knows no shame," this association between wax and affect is reflected in passages such as one in which the narrator of *The Life of Christina of Markyate* refuses to write about what a sinful man did, "lest I pollute the wax by writing it" (*ne vel scribendo ceram ... polluam*).[25] Moreover, even if Arcestrate believes wax knows no shame, the people who write in it and read its contents certainly do, as Apollonius's reaction to the letter makes clear. When Apollonius blushes in response to the message, his skin turns red, becoming a legible message, just as darkened wax could signify the shame of its users.

Indeed, a letter's message can be supplemented and even supplanted by the body. When Apollonius is asked to read and interpret Arcestrate's message, his blushing is legible to the king in a way that the message alone was not. Unable to understand who "the shipwrecked man" might be, the king gives the letter to Apollonius, saying:

> "Nim ðu, Apolloni, þis gewrit and ræd hit. Eaðe mæg gewurðan þæt þu wite þæt ic nat, ðu ðe þar andweard wære." Ða nam Apollonius þæt gewrit and rædde and sona swa he ongeat þæt he gelufod wæs fram ðam mædene, his andwlita eal areodode. Ða se cyngc þæt geseah, þa nam he Apollonies hand and hine hwon fram þam cnihtum gewænde and cwæð: "Wast þu þone forlidenan man?" Apollonius cwæð: "Ðu goda cyning, gif þin willa bið, ic hine wat." Ða geseah se cyngc þæt Apollonius mid rosan rude wæs eal oferbræded, þa ongeat he þone cwyde and þus cwæð to him: "Blissa, blissa, Apolloni, for ðam þe min dohtor gewilnað þæs ðe min willa is."[26]

> "Apollonius, take this letter and read it. It might easily happen that you understand what I do not, you who were present there." Then Apollonius took the letter and read it, and as soon as he perceived that he was loved by the girl, all his face turned red. When the king saw that, he took Apollonius's hand and turned him a little way away from the men and said: "Do you know the shipwrecked man?" Apollonius said: "You good king, if it be your will,

---

24 Rouse and Rouse, "Vocabulary of Wax Tablets," 226.
25 Talbot, ed. and trans., *Life of Christina of Markyate*, 114–15 (Talbot's translation). For this example, as well as more examples of this metaphor by Baudri of Bourgueil and Propertius, see Rouse and Rouse, "Vocabulary of Wax Tablets," 226.
26 Goolden, ed., *Old English "Apollonius of Tyre*," 32/26–34/5.

I know him." When the king saw that Apollonius was all overcome with rose redness, then he understood the saying and said to him "Rejoice, rejoice, Apollonius, because my daughter desires that which is my desire."

This scene reveals two key things, the first of which is the fallibility of written communication. Because none of the three suitors are shipwrecked, the king does not understand Arcestrate's message, and he needs the teacher-messenger Apollonius to interpret it for him. It is only through reading Apollonius's reaction and then speaking with Arcestrate directly that the king feels confident in his understanding of her desire. In turning red, Apollonius fulfils his responsibility as messenger, transforming his own body into a legible message. His blush adds the extra-textual information the king needs to understand who the shipwrecked man is, just as a messenger might speak information not written in the document itself. Apollonius's somatic response supplements and becomes the message, allowing the king to interpret the signs on his body even though he could not solve the riddle of the written text alone. This is particularly striking because we normally expect the physical document of the letter to stand in for or even make present the absent sender, but here it is the body of the messenger/recipient, transformed by contact with the message, that becomes the message, replying to and perhaps replacing the emotional plea of the sender with his own response, registered in his own skin. Although Arcestrate declares that she has written in wax because it "knows no shame," Apollonius's reddened visage, like the darkened colour of well-used or shamed wax, is legible to the king as both message and a metaphorical wax tablet, as both textual content and transmission medium.

Apollonius's body becomes the message by blushing, but he also blushes because the document transfers to or induces Arcestrate's affective response in him. If emotion can be said to be communicable, Apollonius is infected through contact with Arcestrate's letter, the emotional content of the message being transferred from her tablet to his body, ostensibly convincing him to love her in return. Having carried the letter on his person, and now seeing himself reflected in it, Arcestrate's shame is transferred – communicated – to Apollonius, his body itself becoming both messenger and message. This brings me back to my point that the scene in which Apollonius watches Arcestrate write her letter, perhaps placing the tablet on her thigh or intimately near her body, is dangerously suggestive. But it also raises, and answers, another question: why, given that Arcestrate is not physically separated from her beloved, would she need to write a letter at all? Because it is only through the conjunction of written message, physical document, and the body of the messenger that the letter can offer the fantasy of a protective distance between sender and recipient but also the fantasy of unmediated access to the thoughts and desires of the lover. The letter written in wax offers modesty, protection, and plausible deniability while simultaneously suggesting the potentially dangerous intimacy of physical and emotional contact across and with the object itself.

Communicating Faith in the *Letter of Abgar*

In *Apollonius of Tyre*, the body of the messenger, transformed by contact with the document, becomes a legible message. *Apollonius* is an unusual text for many reasons, not least of which is that it features a messenger who travels a very short distance, an intermediary who is actually the subject of the message. Instead of uniting distant lovers, Arcestrate's letter induces her beloved to travel away from her, introducing a temporary deferral of her union with him. At the same time, instead of the physical letter being the only object that connects distant lovers, Arcestrate's letter hastens the lovers' very real sexual union. Despite this document's unusual method of delivery, it is crucial for my project not just because it illustrates how the boundary between message and medium, or between medium and messenger, could be blurred, but also because it is a rare representation of interpersonal secular/lay communication in Old English literature. In the rest of the chapter, I turn from love letters exchanged between aristocrats to messengers and miraculous documents in saints' lives. In both the *Letter of Abgar* and *Mary of Egypt*, the physical document complicates transmission of the message. In *Abgar*, the messenger's body stands in place of the physical object that is typically used to heal King Abgar in other versions of the story. Making the presence of the messenger's body rather than the touch of the physical document have the power to heal emphasizes that the truly faithful believe despite the lack of material proof. The presence of the messenger in the story also draws attention to the delays and mediation that are always part of epistolary acts. The suffering body of the king must await the arrival of the letter and, with it, the body of the messenger who carries it. The king's body, like many ailing bodies, experiences time out of joint, reflecting the delays and deferrals inherent to communication as mediated by the letter. Whereas in other traditions of the Abgar legend, it is the letter or Mandylion (a towel or painting of Christ with restorative properties) that heals King Abgar, in Ælfric's version the document is displaced by the power of the messenger's body. As in *Apollonius of Tyre*, the message is embodied by the messenger, whose body performs the healing miracle. The moral seems to be that the truly faithful do not need proof in the form of apotropaic documents, just as the Old English *Sunday Letters* suggest, and that the illusion of unmediated oral communication between Abgar and Jesus (in fact mediated by the messenger) will be sufficient.

The *Letter of Christ to Abgar* is found in Ælfric of Eynsham's *Lives of Saints*, a late tenth-century collection of saints' lives originally written for two of Ælfric's patrons, Ealdorman Æthelweard and his son Æthelmær, elite lay persons with monastic interests.[27] Ælfric was an Anglo-Saxon priest, monk, and later abbot who lived c. 955–c. 1010 and was the author of many homilies and saints' lives, letters, and several language guides intended for students learning Latin.[28] Contrary to Ælfric's explicit wishes, the *Lives of Saints* seems to have circulated always alongside texts that were not written by Ælfric, which complicates the question of the audience of these *Lives*. While it seems likely that Ælfric originally intended the *Lives* for monks or those with monastic taste, it is clear that their circulation included contexts, if not audiences, which Ælfric did not anticipate.[29] This is important because, while it may make sense that monastic audiences would have been familiar with documentary culture and access to textual records, lay audiences may not have been exposed to the same range of documents as a scribe at an ecclesiastical centre.

---

27 Skeat, ed., *Ælfric's Lives of Saints*, vol. 2, XXIVb. Æthelweard and Æthelmær, who were well connected and wealthy, commissioned several works by Ælfric, including the *Lives of Saints* and translations of Genesis and the Book of Joshua. Æthelmær founded Cerne and Eynsham and, when he fell out of favour with King Æthelred, he retired to a monastery for several years. For more on Æthelweard and Æthelmær, see Cubitt, "Ælfric's Lay Patrons." Ælfric's *Lives of Saints* is usually dated no later than 998 (see Hill, "Ælfric," 56). For arguments about why Ælfric might have included the Abgar letter at this point in his manuscript, immediately after the *passio* of Abdon and Sennes, as well as why he did not cite other sources of the Abgar legend known in Anglo-Saxon England, especially as it appears as an apotropaic letter in accounts of the *passio* of Thomas, see Cain, "Apocryphal Legend."

28 For a recent introduction to Ælfric's biography and literary corpus, see Hill, "Ælfric."

29 In the Latin preface to the *Lives of Saints*, Ælfric declares that these *Lives* are "passiones etiam vel vitas sanctorum illorum quos non vulgus sed coenobite officiis venerantur" (the passions and lives of those saints which the monks and not the laity honour with offices) (text and translation from Wilcox, *Ælfric's Prefaces*, 5a.7–9). Ælfric was notoriously anxious about controlling what kinds of texts the laity had access to, believing that they were less capable of correctly understanding more difficult texts.

More properly an exchange of letters between the ailing king Abgar and Jesus of Nazareth, the story of Abgar originates in the mid-third century, and several early writers, including Eusebius and Egeria, claimed to have found evidence of the letters in the archives in Edessa or to have had their own copies.[30] Belief in the letter continues into the later Middle Ages and beyond. According to legend, King Abgar of Edessa (in modern Turkey) is ill, so he writes to Jesus of Nazareth, saying that he has heard that Jesus heals people, and swearing that he believes that Jesus is God or God's son. He asks to be healed. Jesus replies with a letter of his own in which he paraphrases John 20:29, commending Abgar for believing him without seeing him.[31] He says that he has other duties, but will send someone to heal Abgar after he (Jesus) dies. Later, the disciple Thaddeus[32] fulfils Jesus's promise by healing Abgar. In most other versions of the story, Thaddeus heals Abgar by means of either a letter or the Mandylion. However, in Ælfric's version, Thaddeus's mere presence heals Abgar, and there is no mention of the Mandylion or even a letter making contact with Abgar's body. This despite the fact that there are other healing letters in Old English, and even in Ælfric's corpus – in his life of Martin, for example. Moreover, other versions of the Abgar legend circulating in Anglo-Saxon England feature a potentially apotropaic letter. By contrast, Ælfric omits any reference to the use of the Abgar letter to heal, not only because Ælfric is personally wary of any such claims, but also because, for him, the point of the story is that one must simply believe, whether without having seen Jesus or without having seen his letter.

If Ælfric had wanted to represent the Abgar letter as apotropaic, he certainly would not have lacked for sources, both in the Abgar tradition and in the broader Anglo-Saxon literary tradition as well. As discussed in chapter 2, Old English charms associated with heavenly letters could be apotropaic. Other versions of the Abgar legend, including some known in

---

30 For apotropaic documents in medieval England, see chapter 2. For a brief introduction
    to the tradition and a study of Anglo-Latin versions of Abgar's letter in private prayer
    books, see Cain, "Sacred Words"; for Eusebius and Egeria, see ibid., 170–3.
31 John 20:29: *Dicit ei Iesus quia vidisti me credidisti beati qui non viderunt et crediderunt.*
    (Jesus saith to him: "Because thou hast seen me, Thomas, thou hast believed; blessed are
    they that have not seen and have believed.")
32 According to Ælfric, Thaddeus, also known by the name Jude, was one of the 70
    (elsewhere 72) (ll. 127, 134). In the *Legenda Aurea* account of Abgar, Thaddeus is said
    to be one of the 12 disciples (Cain, "Apocryphal Legend," 391).

Anglo-Saxon England, did suggest that owning a personal copy of the letter was important, and that this copy might be apotropaic.[33] The Latin Abgar story found in London, BL Royal 2.A.xx (a late eighth- or early ninth-century private prayer book from England) concludes with the promise that those who believe in Christ will be protected from their enemies and from natural disaster, and "Si quis hanc epistolam secum habuerit secures ambulet in pace" (whoever has this letter with him will go about safely in peace).[34] Accounts of the *passio* of Thomas known in Anglo-Saxon England describe the Abgar letter as apotropaic as well, and it is likely that Ælfric both was aware of this tradition and deliberately sought to suppress it.[35]

There are several letters embedded within the *Letter of Abgar*. Abgar's letter to Jesus, which opens the exchange, begins with a salutation, clearly identifying it as a letter:

Abgarus gret eadmodlice þone godan hælend
þe becom to mannum mid iudeiscum folce[36]

---

33 "In fact, the text of Jesus' letter to Abgar was copied, circulated, and collected by the pious as a material object of devotion" (Cain, "Apocryphal Legend," 386).

34 *Handlist*, item 450; Ker no. 248, quoted in Cain, "Sacred Words," 176–7 (Cain's translation). Another Anglo-Latin version of the letter in London, BL Cotton Galba A.xiv (*Handlist*, item 333; Ker no. 157) does not have a clear apotropaic promise (Cain, "Apocryphal Legend," 388).

35 Cain, "Apocryphal Legend" 390–5. In an exploration of Ælfric's resistance to materialism, Leslie Lockett agrees with and expands on Malcolm Godden's point that Ælfric rarely wrote about miracles that made the immaterial perceptible, and when he did, he stressed that this was atypical (*Anglo-Saxon Psychologies*, 396–7). However, this argument is complicated by the fact that Ælfric did not consistently omit reference to apotropaic letters elsewhere in his corpus. In his two versions of the *Life of St Martin* (*CH II*, 34 and *LS XXXI*), Ælfric describes how a letter of Martin healed a young girl who was suffering from a fever. Ælfric's shorter version of Martin's *Life* in *CH II* presents the story succinctly: "Sumes gerefan dohtor he ahredde fram fefore. ðurh his ærendgewrit þe heo adlig underfeng" (A certain reeve's daughter he delivered from fever through his letter which she received while sick) (*CH II*, 34, 214–16). The longer version adds that the letter was placed on her chest, emphasizing physical contact between the letter and the girl's body: "and he hit lede on hire breoste / ða þa hire hatost wæs and heo wearð hal sona" (and he laid it on her chest where it was hottest for her, and she immediately became well) (*LS XXXI*, 578–9).

36 *LS XXIVb*, 88–9.

Abgar humbly greets the good savior who came to humankind among the Jewish people ...

Unlike *Apollonius of Tyre*, where we watched Apollonius run back and forth delivering letters, we learn almost nothing about *how* the letter was transmitted to Jesus. Ælfric notes only that Abgar had heard about Jesus's miracles and quickly sent an *ærendgewrit* (letter) to him.[37] The letter opens with a salutation formula, which is rare for letters embedded in Old English texts.[38] Note how the address formula already begins to reveal the content of the message – in naming Jesus *hælend* (savior), Abgar asserts his faith in his healing powers, since *hælend* is etymologically related to *hæl* (health, wholeness). This careful address formula also suggests both that Ælfric is familiar with proper epistolary formulae (as we would expect of a prolific letter writer) and also that he expects his audience to be able to register it as such. The form of Abgar's salutation mimics that of Ælfric's *Preface to Genesis* or Wulfstan's writ of c. 1020 addressed to Cnut and Ælfgifu, which both use the construction "[Sender's name and title] gret [recipient's name and title] eadmodlice."[39]

After quoting Abgar's initial letter to Jesus, Ælfric provides no information about how the letter was delivered to and received by Jesus, or about how Jesus drafted and sent his own reply to Abgar, except that Jesus wrote it himself. Instead, the text moves immediately from the end of Abgar's letter to the introduction of Jesus's reply, which Ælfric presents first in Latin and then translates into Old English:

Þa awrat se hælend him sylf þis gewrit
and asende ðam cynincge ðus cwæðende him to
Beatus es qui credidisti in me cum ipse me non uideris.
Scriptum est enim de me quia hii qui me uident non credent
In me et qui non uident me ipsi credent et iuent.
De eo autem quod scripsisti mihi ut ueniam ad te
oportet me omnia propter quae missus sum hic explere.
Et postea quam compleuero recipi me ad eum a quo missus sum.

---

37 Ibid., 87.

38 Salutation formulae were often removed when letters were copied into registers or cartularies (Constable, *Letters and Letter-Collections*, 18); see also chapter 1 above.

39 On these salutation Acts formulae, and the placement of sender before recipient even when the recipient is higher ranking, see chapter 1.

Cum ergo fuero assumptus mittam tibi aliquem
ex discipulis meis ut curet ægritudinem tuam
et uitam tibi atque his qui tecum sunt prestet.
þæt is on engliscum gereorde[:] Eadig eart ðu abgar
þu þe gelyfdest on me þonne þu me ne gesawe.
Hit is awriten be me on witegung-bocum
þæt ða þe me geseoð hi ne gelyfað on me
and þa þe me ne geseoð hi gelyfað and libbað.
Be þam þe ðu awrite to me þæt ic come to þe
ic sceal ærest afyllan þa þincg þe ic fore asend eom
and ic sceal beon eft genumen to þam ylcan ðe me asende.
And ic asende to ðe syððan ic genumen beo
ænne minra leorning-cnihta þe gelacniað þine untrumnysse
and þe lif gegearcað and þam þe gelyfað mid ðe.[40]

Then the savior himself wrote this letter and sent it to the king speaking to him thus:

beatus es etc. ... that is in the English language: Blessed are you Abgar, you who believed in me when you had not seen me. It is written about me in the prophecies that those who see me will not believe in me, and those who do not see me will believe and live. Concerning that which you wrote to me, that I should come to you, I must first fulfil those things for which I have been sent, and I must afterward be taken up to the same one who sent me. And after I have been taken up I will send to you one of my disciples who will cure your illness and prepare life for you and those who believe with you.

Jesus's reply functions differently than Abgar's letter in several key ways. First, unlike Abgar's letter, Jesus's letter has no salutation formula. The salutation formula has been replaced by Ælfric's brief introduction ("the savior himself wrote this letter ...") so that instead of allowing the letter to authenticate itself via the salutation formula, Ælfric's editorial mediation asserts his own faith in the document by proclaiming that it is indeed Jesus's letter. In removing the salutation, Ælfric may also have been thinking of how letters, once archived, require finding aids such as editorial notes. Second, Jesus's letter is preserved in full in Latin as well as Old English. By repeating the letter first in Latin and then Old English, Ælfric

---

40 *LS*, XXIVb, 102–23.

associates Jesus's letter with the authority of Scripture, which is regularly quoted in the *Lives of Saints* in both Latin and Old English translation.

While Ælfric's Old English translation is mostly quite faithful, it does make two small adjustments. In the first, what was in Latin a letter addressed to a nameless "you" (*beatus es qui credidisti*, second-person singular) becomes in Old English a letter directly addressed to Abgar himself (*Eadig eart ðu Abgar*). Hearing the Latin version, any individuals who imagine themselves to be part of the Christian faithful could also imagine themselves into the addressee of the *beatus es*, whereas in Old English, the faithful can only imagine themselves into the Biblical paraphrase (those who do not see me may believe and live), and not as addressees of the letter itself. The second modification to the Latin names the kinds of texts in which these claims about Jesus have been written. Whereas the Latin has simply "Scriptum est enim de me" (for it is written about me), the Old English has "Hit is awriten be me *on witegung-bocum*" (it is written about me *in the prophecies*).[41] This is a tantalizing gesture towards Jesus's awareness of his own presence in the books of the Bible. In addition to increasing his authority by properly citing his sources, Jesus reveals that he knows he is already part of the archival record of Scripture, even as this letter potentially adds to or updates that same record. Ælfric may also be attempting to resolve the temporal paradox raised here: how can Jesus's letter quote John 20:29, when John hasn't been written yet? Although Christ in his divinity knows what, from a human perspective, has not yet happened, this gesture to unnamed Old Testament prophecies as source, rather than to the as yet unwritten John, resolves or at least suppresses the temporal issues raised by Jesus's awareness of the Gospels. It is also significant that Jesus describes himself as both message and messenger, saying "I must fulfil those things for which I have been *sent*, and I must afterward be taken up to the same one who *sent* me."[42] As messenger, Jesus has been sent to earth by God to carry out God's errands and deliver his message of salvation. As a message sent by God, Jesus reminds us, he is also the Word made flesh.

Jesus's letter, in its doubly preserved form, both stores and transmits Jesus's message. As a Latin text, the document joins the ranks of Scripture (a supposedly fixed textual monument) and also records and stores the

---

41 Emphasis added.
42 Emphasis added.

miraculous promise Jesus made to Abgar. But in being translated into Old English and then also into the framework of the *Lives of Saints*, the letter escapes the boundaries of the archive and continues to circulate. Because there is no reference to a messenger or account of the letter's transmission, the letter is stripped of the network in which it was originally embedded and is reinscribed in a network in which the *Lives'* audience might also participate. The communication network does not end when the letter reaches its first addressee. In fact, Ælfric reminds the immediate audience for the *Lives of Saints* that they too are participants in this continuing network of transmission of Christian faith, by prefacing his *Lives of Saints* with a letter – an epistolary preface addressed to the ealdorman who commissioned the work, beginning just as Abgar's letter does: "Ælfric gret eadmodlice Æþelwerd ealdorman" (Ælfric humbly greets Æthelweard the ealdorman).[43]

We might expect there to be one more letter in Abgar's series, sent by Jesus after his ascension to heaven, or a revelation that the Mandylion has accompanied Jesus's letter. However, Ælfric shifts the emphasis from the apotropaic message to the messenger, Thaddeus, who appears on Jesus's behalf. Thaddeus is "sent" just like a letter might have been, as Thaddeus repeatedly reminds Abgar. Ælfric writes that Thaddeus "com ða þurh godes sande" (came then by God's commission).[44] Likewise, echoing Jesus's references to his having been *sent* on God's mission, Thaddeus tells Abgar:

Forðan ðe þu rihtlice gelyfdest on þone ðe me *asende*
forðam ic eom *asend* to þe þæt ðu gesund beo.[45]

Because you rightly believed in the one who *sent* me, therefore I have been *sent* to you that you may be whole.

Whereas the earlier part of *Abgar* is concerned only with the content of the letters and not their transmission, here focus shifts entirely to the messenger, whose body substitutes for the letter and the path it may have

---

43 *LS*, Preface, p. 4, line 35.
44 *LS*, XXIVb, 129. Thaddeus is sent on God's *sande*, which here more idiomatically means "by God's commission," but elsewhere in the corpus also means "sending, message, mission" (BT, *s.v.* "sand").
45 *LS*, XXIVb, 142–3 (emphasis added).

travelled. In the Abgar legend, the messenger usually bears a healing object that takes the place of Jesus's absent body and is of central importance. By omitting any reference to such an object, Ælfric's account displaces potential focus on the letter back onto the body of the messenger, Thaddeus. The messenger has been sent – transmitted across space and time in order to convey a message on behalf of an absent other – just like a letter or other object might be sent, as Thaddeus reminds Abgar ("I have been *sent* to you that you may be whole"). Moreover, since Jesus's message has taken the form of a living person, there is no danger Abgar will misinterpret the message. The messenger, authorized to deliver the message orally and to supplement it as needed, offers an illusion of perfect communication with the divine, a conversation with Jesus mediated through the body of a messenger but unmediated by distance, temporal delay, or writing. The content of Jesus's message is delivered solely orally (as many medieval letters were), in a dialogue with Abgar in which Abgar repeatedly swears his faith. Once Abgar has sufficiently proven his faith to Thaddeus, Thaddeus heals him, not with the touch of a letter or a Mandylion, but with his own hand:

> Tatheus cwæð þa gyt to ðam wanhalan cyninge
> forþi ic sette mine hand on ðæs hælendes naman
> ofer ðe untrumne and he [eac] swa dyde
> and se cyning wearð gehæled sona swa he hine hrepode
> fram eallum his untrumnyssum þe he ær on þrowode.
> Abgarus þa wundrode þæt he wearð gehæled
> butan læce-wyrtum þurh ðæs hælendes word
> swa swa he him ær behet þurh his ærendgewrit.[46]

Thaddeus said then further to the unhealthy king: "Therefore in the name of the savior I place my hand over you who are unwell." And likewise he did so, and as soon as he touched him the king was healed from all his sicknesses which he previously suffered from. Abgar then was amazed that he was healed without medicinal herbs by the word of the savior just as he had promised him in his letter.

The normal barriers of communicating by letter – distance and asynchronicity – fall away, and the word, like the absent author of the letter, is

---

46 Ibid., 154–61.

made present in the body of Thaddeus, whose simple touch heals Abgar. Thaddeus models intermediacy and immediacy – the mediatory intercession of a saint joined with the fantasy of pure communication with the divine, free from signal noise, interference, or distance. The story of Thaddeus suppresses the reality of the many deferrals inherent in this exchange of messages, since Abgar must wait first for Jesus's initial letter, then for Jesus to die, and finally for Thaddeus to travel to him to fulfil Jesus's pledge.

Similar New Testament messages about the importance of faith emphasize Christ's omnipresence, even in his apparent physical absence from the site of the miracle, and his concomitant ability to heal without delay, whether by his own hand or via the power granted to his disciples. Instead of *Abgar*'s message of patience in the face of deferral, these miracles offer the possibility of immediate healing, without intermediary, delay, or even touch. For example, John 4:46–53 offers a very similar message to that of John 20:29, namely that one must believe without seeing, and that, for Jesus, healing is possible even without his physical presence. When a powerful man asks Jesus to come to his house to heal his son, Jesus admonishes him for being unwilling to believe unless he sees physical signs of his divine power.[47] When the man once again asks Jesus to come heal his son, Jesus says he has already been healed. In one version of a sermon by Ælfric on this passage, Ælfric explains that "Gif he rihtlice ilyfde, he sceolde ðonne witen / þæt God sylf is æghwær, on ælcere stowe, / þurh his mycele mihte, and mæg æfre hælpan / allum ðe to him clypiæð on ælcere stowe"[48] (If he had believed rightly, he ought to have known that God himself is everywhere, in each place, through his great power, and might ever offer help to all who call to him in each place). In at least two versions of sermons on John 4:46–53, one *Ælfric's Catholic Homilies* I, 8, and the other a twelfth-century version of Ælfric's sermon "The Healing of the King's Son" found in Oxford, Bodleian Library MS Bodley 343,[49] Ælfric contrasts the ruler's doubt with the faith of the centurion who, in Matthew 8:5–13, recognizes that Jesus can heal through his word alone and need not

---

47 The Vulgate describes this man as "quidam regulus" (a certain ruler) (4:46), but the Ælfrician homilies on the subject substitute the more specific *underkyng* (underking), and include an explication of the term not found in the Bible (Irvine, ed., *Old English Homilies*, 9–13).

48 Homily I, "The Healing of the King's Son," in ibid., 74–7.

49 Ker no. 310.

be present to accomplish miracles. When the centurion tells Jesus his servant is ill, Jesus offers to go to him to heal him, but the centurion says "Lord, I am not worthy that thou shouldst enter under my roof, but only say the word, and my servant shall be healed."[50] Unlike the ruler, the centurion recognizes that Jesus requires neither presence nor the delay of travel to heal the servant. Whereas the twelfth-century sermon criticizes the ruler in John for not recognizing Christ's presence, Ælfric's earlier version praises the centurion in Matthew for understanding the same: "He hæfde micele snoternysse þa ða he understod þæt crist is æighwær andwerd þurh godcundnysse se þe lichamlice betwux mannum gesewenlic eode"[51] (He had great wisdom, because he understood that Christ is everywhere present through divinity, he who bodily travelled visible among men). Without the complication of epistolary communication, Christ is able to perform the immediacy the Abgar miracle seeks to invest in Thaddeus. As the centurion knew, Christ can heal instantly, even across distance, but Abgar, despite all his faith, was like the ruler who believed his son could only be healed by Christ's physical presence. It is for this reason that Abgar's healing must be first deferred and then accomplished without the letter, the symbol of Christ's presence in his absence.

Ælfric's audience did not expect to examine Abgar's document to find proof that the letter was hundreds of years old, nor did they expect to be able to see Jesus's handwriting. Likewise, Ælfric's audience could not have seen Abgar's suffering and then healed body, because the events of the miracle took place hundreds of years earlier and far away from England. The miracle, like the original letter, is inaccessible. Ælfric's audience must instead rely on faith in something they have never seen, and faith in the communication networks through which the letters have circulated before reaching Ælfric and then them. Excising the messenger from the initial exchange temporarily joins together the letters' transmission and storage, but the return of the messenger in the person of Thaddeus separates them again. As I suggested in the introduction, whereas the age of print united transmission and storage, both new media and medieval media physically separate the two. Just as the computer on which I am typing this document inscribes my file on a hard drive I cannot see (without opening up

---

50 "Domine non sum dignus ut intres sub tectum meum sed tantum dic verbo et sanabitur puer meus" (Matthew 8:8).
51 *CH I*, 8, 109–11.

the laptop case, at the very least), and I do not know in what country or countries the servers and other storage media I use to back up this file when I save it to the Cloud are located, when medieval messengers performed letters orally, they did not necessarily need to make present the inscriptional storage media on which the letters were recorded and stored. Thaddeus is pure transmission – he presents no letter, and therefore no storage, or at least offers no visible storage at the site of the miracle. It may seem that by removing the messenger, and thus his potential for mediation, Ælfric takes the initial exchange of letters between Abgar and Jesus out of circulation, stripping them of (some of) their epistolary formulae, removing them from the networks in which they initially participated, and preserving them in an entirely new format and context (i.e., the *Lives of Saints*). However, I would argue that, freed from the context of the original medium, these letters are in fact just as, if not more, able to transmit Christian culture. Unbound from the original physical format, the original audience, and the letter's original temporal context, these letters are transformed into infinitely repeatable messages of Christian faith not by promising to re-enact Abgar's healing miracle (after all, it was the unpreservable touch of Thaddeus, not any letter, that effected the cure), but by addressing to new generations of the Christian faithful the miracle's broader message – that is, be like Abgar: have faith, and you too will be healed of your sins, so that you might go to heaven.

Not Ready for My Close-Up: Memorializing *Mary of Egypt*

Early medieval letters between male and female religious reflect a thorny problem: how could the authors' potentially passionate expressions of true friendship and love reinforce the intimacy of their *spiritual* bond without implying an inappropriately *physical* intimacy?[52] As we saw in

---

52 For Boniface's correspondence with Leoba, Eangyth, and other religious women, see Hollis, *Anglo-Saxon Women*, 130–50. While Aldhelm's letter to the nun Sigegyth is written in what Lapidge and Herren describe as a "simpler Latin style … [that] would appear to characterize Aldhelm's 'official' correspondence" (148), Aldhelm's prose *De Virginitate*, addressed to Hildelith and the nuns of Barking, emphasizes how he *looked* at their previous letters "naturali quadam … latentium rerum curiositate" (with a certain natural curiosity about hidden things) and compares the nuns to athletes wrestling "delibutus lubrici liquoris nardo" (smeared with the ointment of (some) slippery liquid) (Ehwald, ed., *Aldhelmi Opera*, 229, 230; Lapidge and Herren, trans., *Aldhelm*, 59, 60). Male religious did not escape this difficulty when writing to other male religious; Alcuin

chapter 1, Anglo-Saxon letters could be personal or emotional, but this content came with certain risks. As the example of *Apollonius of Tyre* demonstrates, letters are especially dangerous because they enforce the physical distance between sender and recipient while encouraging affective language and allowing the body of the letter to stand in for the body of the absent sender. On the one hand, the letter form is predicated on the physical and temporal distance between correspondents, yet, at the same time, it insists that it offers unmediated, intimate access to the thoughts of the sender. More dangerously still, the exchange of letters depends on the intimacy of correspondents holding the same object (and many letters ask the recipient to keep the letter on his or her person for future reading).

My final case study in this chapter explores how the miraculous writing that appears beside Mary of Egypt's body after her death resists the possibility of erotic or affective transfer between the body of her text and the bodies of those who might receive it. Like *Apollonius of Tyre*, the anonymous Old English *Life of St Mary of Egypt* features a letter whose material support is unusual, if not miraculous. Like *Abgar*, it also reflects anxieties about who maintains control of a message once it leaves its initial network, with Zosimus problematically assuming the role of messenger who carries Mary's story to his monastery and the larger community of Christian faithful. Like both *Apollonius of Tyre* and *Abgar*, the *Life* reflects the intimacy of the relationship between the body of a letter and the body of a messenger. Whereas in *Apollonius of Tyre*, Apollonius is a messenger who comes to discover that he is also the subject of the letter he carries, in *Mary of Egypt*, Zosimus first receives a written message from Mary, then realizes he can be its messenger.

Above all, Mary's *Life* is a story about the dangers and possibilities inherent in communicability. In chapter 4, I explore miraculous writing that invites preservation – letters that become public records of miracle as well

writes to Arn, "If only I could fly like Habbakuk, how quickly I would rush to embrace you and how eagerly I would kiss not only your eyes, ears and mouth but also each finger and toe not once but many times" (translation from Allott, *Alcuin of York*, Letter 135, p. 140). For friendships between women and between men and women in the early Middle Ages, see Schulenburg, *Forgetful of Their Sex*, 307–63. There were several precedents for cross-gender friendships, including the friendship of Christ with Martha and Mary, or the friendships between Paul and Thecla, or between Jerome and several female friends, for example (322). For letters, gifts, and friendship between men and women in Anglo-Saxon England, see 328–42.

as documents whose destruction or erasure creates a storable record of the absence or forgiveness of sins. But here I explore a miraculous text that *resists* being brought into the archive – the message written on the ground after the death of Mary of Egypt. This resistance to preservation can tell us much about Anglo-Saxon documentary culture and who has the right to circulate messages. I argue that Mary's atypical use of writing, which is immediate, temporary, and almost oral, reflects special dangers of communicability for the bodies (and texts) of female saints. I end by suggesting that, while Mary of Egypt insists that her message be private, impermanent *communication*, Zosimus must learn how to transform it into public, long-enduring cultural *transmission* without access to such physical proof as the saint's body, and without turning the reformed prostitute's body into an object for public consumption. Moreover, Zosimus must learn the lesson with which the narrator opens the *Life*: whose secrets must be kept (i.e., which eremitic monasteries must be closed off from the world), and whose (God's) must be told. In this way, the *Life of St Mary of Egypt* is predicated on the tension between models of enclosure or storage (monasteries, hermits, letters that do not circulate) and models of openness, circulation, and access reflected in the unlocking of the monastery gate in the Lenten season, the circulation of the monks' bodies into the desert, and Zosimus's transformation of Mary's narration of her life.

The anonymous Old English *Life of St Mary of Egypt* tells the story of Zosimus, a proud monk who, having left his monastery during Lent for the purpose of solitary contemplation (and to seek a male teacher), encounters a mysterious woman in the desert.[53] This woman, Mary of Egypt, tells Zosimus that she once lived a life of prostitution but has since repented and has lived alone in the desert for forty-seven years. Mary has much to teach Zosimus, including not only the story of her life, but also which practices need to be corrected at his monastery. Mary frequently warns Zosimus not to tell her story to anyone, including his fellow monks, until after she has died. On his third visit to Mary, Zosimus finds her miraculously preserved corpse and a letter written in the ground directing

---

53 Magennis, ed., *Old English Life*. While earlier scholarship on the Old English *Mary of Egypt* focused on authorship and source study, sometimes condemning it as inferior to the Ælfrician *Lives*, in recent decades the text has received much positive attention. For early medieval accounts of Mary of Egypt, see the essays in Poppe and Ross, eds, *Legend of Mary of Egypt*, especially those by Jane Stevenson, Andy Orchard, and Hugh Magennis; as well as the essays by Catherine Brown Tkacz, Andy Orchard, Clare A. Lees, and Robin Norris in Scragg, ed., *Old English Life of Mary*.

him to bury her and revealing her name and date of death (which had occurred one year prior).

Although not written by Ælfric, the *Life* is preserved in an early eleventh-century manuscript of Ælfric's *Lives of Saints* (BL Cotton Julius E.vii),[54] where it follows the anonymous *Legend of the Seven Sleepers*. Two incomplete Old English versions of the *Life* are also extant, in BL Cotton Otho B.x (most of which was destroyed by fire)[55] and Gloucester, Cathedral Library 35.[56] The Old English versions of the life have their source in a ninth-century Latin *vita* by Paul, deacon of Naples, itself a translation of a Greek text possibly by Sophronius dated to the late sixth to early seventh century.[57] As I argued in the introduction, epistolary acts include acts of translation, both linguistic and cultural. The Old English *Life of St Mary* is quite faithful to its Latin source, and its lexical choices for describing Mary's document are no exception: Old English *gewrit* for Latin *scriptura*; Old English *stafas* for Latin *litteras* (letters of the alphabet). That said, the choice to produce a faithful translation is still a *choice*, in this case a surprising one. While most Old English authors and translators would have omitted as many references to Mary's prior sexuality as possible or refused to translate the text at all, this translator preserves even the more risqué elements of the story. This suggests that the audience may have been more trusted not to be misled by them, as the *Life*'s inclusion in a manuscript containing Ælfric's *Lives of Saints*, a collection Ælfric intended for an elite lay audience, might support. The translator appears very comfortable translating Latin vocabulary for writing as well as translating the appearance of mysterious writing to an Anglo-Saxon context, which implies that both translator and audience were familiar with documentary culture. In fact, many miraculous or mysterious documents and letters appear in Old English religious texts, including the *Sunday Letter*, the document that falls to the altar in the life of Giles to confirm the king's sin, and the three documents prepared or destroyed by Basil in the Old English *Life of St Basil* (discussed in chapter 4). Moreover, as scholars have pointed out, the story of Mary of Egypt was frequently modified to meet

---

54 *Handlist*, item 339; Ker no. 162.

55 *Handlist*, item 355; Ker no. 177. It has been newly edited by Linda Cantara, "*Saint Mary of Egypt*."

56 *Handlist*, item 262; Ker no. 117.

57 Magennis, ed., *Old English Life*, 3. On the Greek and Latin *vitae*, and their sources and contexts, and Anglo-Latin reflexes, see Stevenson, "Holy Sinner."

the demands of new audiences, putting more focus on Zosimus as opposed to Mary, more or less explicitly saying Mary was a prostitute, and so on.[58] Thus the choice to translate the Latin source into Old English with minimal modification must have been a deliberate act, one founded on the belief that the Anglo-Saxon audience had documentary and religious competency.

Mary spends much of the *Life* telling Zosimus the story of her conversion, though she cautions him that he must keep the story of her life concealed until after her death. But even after her death, the written message conveying Mary's wishes refuses to be archived, and she refuses to allow her body to be fetishized as a relic.[59] Her message, written in the ground, is intended to be immediate rather than to be preserved across time. It is neither transportable nor replicable, and she asks for her uncorrupt body to be buried so that it may return to dust – decompose – rather than being preserved, displayed, and even ogled as a witness to God's miracle:

Þa ongan he þencan hwæðer hit hire licode. Þa he þis ðohte, þa wæs þær an gewrit on þære eorðan getacnod, þus gecweden: "Bebyrig, abbud Zosimus, and miltsa Maria lichaman. Ofgif þære eorðan þæt hire is, and þæt dust to þam duste geic. Eac gebidde þeahhwæðere for me of þyssere worulde hleorende on þam monðe Aprilis þære nigeþan nihte, þæt is Idus Aprelis, on þam drihtenlican gereorddæge, and æfter þam huslgange."

Þa se ealda þa stafas rædde, þa sohte he ærest hwa hi write, forþan þe heo sylf ær sæde þæt heo næfre naht hwilces ne leornode.[60]

Then he began to consider whether [the burial] would be pleasing to her [Mary]. When he was thinking this, then a written document was marked on the ground, saying thus: "Abbot Zosimus, bury and have mercy on the body

---

58 Karras, "Holy Harlots," 6–10.

59 It is unclear who was the scribe of Mary's message. Mary is illiterate (695–8) and the message seems to appear after her death. However, medieval letter writers frequently employed scribes to transcribe letters for them, so it is not unlikely that Mary might have had a letter issued on her behalf. The letter switches from third person (common in salutation formulae) to first person ("pray for me"), just as the bodies of letters do (see chapter 1). See also Paul E. Szarmach, who calls this message "a writing from Mary" and adds that "she effectively has signed the message!" ("More Genre Trouble," 157–8). For another miraculous message on an unusual medium, see the discussion of the writing on the wall as metaphorical letter in chapter 1.

60 Magennis, ed., *Old English Life*, 890–901.

of Mary. Give up to the earth that which is the earth's, and add that dust to that dust. But also pray for me, having departed from this world on the ninth night of the month of April, that is the Ides of April, on the Lord's feastday, and after the Eucharist."

When the old man had read the letters, he first tried to find who had written them, because she herself had said that she never learned anything of the sort.

Mary's written message opens with an address formula, naming Zosimus as the intended recipient of the message. By naming Zosimus directly, Mary reveals that she intends this to be a private, one-to-one communication between herself and Zosimus, and not a general message directed to all Christian faithful. Because it appears miraculously in the very spot where Zosimus is standing, her message requires no messenger, attempting to remain outside public channels of communication and the involvement of (living) human agents and institutions. It also seems as though the letter, which answers Zosimus's question clearly and directly, has just appeared in response to Zosimus's concerns about what Mary wants. By erasing the notion of travel across distance, the text creates a fiction of immediacy or instant messaging, a perfect communication, but without the chance of reply. Because the miracle defamiliarizes standard letter-writing protocol, the materiality of the medium becomes more important, not because it is apotropaic (as with other miraculous documents in medieval England), but because it is so miraculously unusual. The unusual choice of material support (the earth) on which the miraculous letter is written attempts to control both Zosimus's and the audience's access and response to the letter's content and their participation in the continued transmission process.

Zosimus had entered his monastery in order to learn humility, but his response to the message suggests his troubling susceptibility to pride remains. First, his communication is inwardly directed: he prays throughout the *Life*, sometimes to himself, and he receives miracles and visions in reply, but he makes these messages all about him.[61] His question was about Mary's reaction to burial but, when he receives the letter, he quickly shifts from being comforted that his actions have been approved to focusing on his new knowledge of her name and death, which could help him establish a feast day for her, and, should he be successful in creating a cult around

---

61 As Robin Norris notes, when he discovers Mary's corpse, "Zosimus seems capable of feeling sorry only for himself" ("*Vitas matrum*," 107).

her, through which he could commodify her body (not something the former prostitute desired).[62]

Mary's written message, which might at first seem to be like a *titulus* or label to accompany a body displayed at a religious centre's collection of relics, in fact refuses public memorialization. Because Mary's letter is written in the ground, rather than a more traditional material support, the original document cannot be preserved, and it can never circulate in its original form. It is only by repeating the letter within the *Life* that her message can survive and bear witness to her miracle. A crucial distinction can be made between Mary's letter to Zosimus and Zosimus's oral message to the monastery relating the miracle of her life and burial. Whereas Mary's written letter is *communication*, Zosimus's oral message, and the *Life* that is created from it, is *transmission*. I borrow these concepts from Régis Debray, who argues that while communication strives to be immediate and to travel across space, a transmission seeks to continue its message across time.[63] A transmission is better understood as the attempt, always in process, to preserve and memorialize – to transmit collective ideas, cultures, or institutions so that they last beyond the lifetime of a single individual (Debray's examples include flags, which transmit the nation).[64] Mary's

---

62 There are many similarities between the story of Mary of Egypt and the story of Pelagia. Like Mary, Pelagia is a sinner who reveals her name for the first time in a letter written to bishop Nonnus, and like Mary, Pelagia's corpse remains problematically an object of desire, even compared to gold and silver. On Pelagia's letter written on a wax tablet, see Burrus, *Sex Lives of Saints*, 141.

63 Debray, *Transmitting Culture*, 3. Because most media theorists do not use "transmission" in this specialized sense, I am using Debray's sense of "transmission" only in this section on Mary of Egypt. Elsewhere in this book, I use "transmission" in its more familiar, more general meaning. Although I have attempted to reduce the use of "transmission" elsewhere to avoid confusion, the word in its more general sense is so fundamental to media theory that its use cannot be avoided entirely.

64 "We transmit meanings so that the things we live, believe, and think do not perish with *us* (as opposed to *me*)" (ibid., 3; emphasis original). The *Life* explains that Zosimus told the monks everything about his encounters with Mary. It does not include the exact speech of Zosimus's message to the monks, but it does not need to; the *Life* itself serves as transmission of his message. On this point, see also Paul Szarmach, who argues that "the story speaks for itself [rather than being retold by Zosimus to the monks at the end] in the presence of the Old English monks who constitute the present audience for the *vita*" ("More Genre Trouble," 150). By spreading Mary's message, Zosimus fulfils the commands of the prologue to this *Life*, in which the story of Tobit is recalled as an example of the importance of revealing God's works. On this point, Lees, "Vision and Place," 64–7.

letter is a *private communication* (not transmission) directly addressed to Zosimus with instructions for burial. It proves her identity but directs her physical erasure. Just as she asks for her body to be buried – that is, returned to the earth – her posthumous letter is written in the earth. Mary uses the same material her body will become as the material support for her letter because this gestures to the close connection between her body and her message. Her document is *not* transportable or replicable in its original material form, and it is not meant to be displayed as documentary proof of the miracle, except to Zosimus himself. Moreover, one gets the sense that if she could have avoided a written record entirely, she would have. She writes only because she is dead, and therefore cannot have an oral, interactive, real-time conversation with him as she previously did. As such, the letter is the most immediate, effective way to communicate (rather than transmit) her message, offering a fantasy of immediate and unmediated communication with the dead as replacement for the oral conversation they had while she was alive.[65]

How does Mary's uneasy manipulation of the written text (transforming it from written transmission to almost oral communication) reflect what we know about women's participation in Anglo-Saxon documentary culture? It seems that most letter writers and recipients in Anglo-Saxon England were men, usually associated with the church, although the laity had epistolary legal documents produced on their behalf, and kings issued letters as well.[66] There are fewer extant letters by and to women. Mary Garrison argues that this is not because women did not write letters, but because most surviving medieval Latin letters were preserved in letter collections organized around the letters of and to famous men. For whatever reason (and Garrison suggests several hypotheses), women's letters were less likely to be preserved in their own letter collections, whether collections of letters sent to them or written by them.[67] Among Garrison's

---

65 Zosimus is not the only male author or narrator to struggle with how to transmit the *Life* of a holy woman. As Virginia Burrus remarks, one almost begins to wonder, "Does every female Life give way to the *confession* of a masculine autobiography?" (*Sex Lives of Saints*, 60; emphasis in original).

66 According to the *Enlarged Rule of Chrodegang*, porters were responsible for receiving and replying to any *ærende* that came to them, though this may mean oral messages. Langefeld, ed. and trans., *Old English Version*, chap. 10.195.3–4.

67 Garrison, "Send More Socks," 76–7. But see Fell, who argues that the Boniface correspondence depends on "haphazard survival," not a sense that Boniface's letters were more important than those of his correspondents. Fell argues instead that letters to and

examples of known female letter writers are those associated with Jerome, Boniface, and Alcuin, the most famous of which include Eadburga and Leoba.[68] According to Christine Fell, the best evidence for Anglo-Saxon female letter writers comes from the Boniface correspondence, which includes sixteen letters written to women and nine or ten by women (out of 150 total letters).[69] Stacy Klein notes that the correspondence of Popes Gregory the Great and Boniface V includes several letters written to Anglo-Saxon queens, perhaps because queens were seen as natural counsellors to their husbands.[70] To these I might add women who are represented as sending or receiving letters within Old English literary texts. The *Husband's Message* is addressed to a woman, and in the Old English *Apollonius of Tyre* the king's daughter, Arcestrate, receives written messages from her suitors, then writes her own message in reply. These two works, one poetic, one prose, are rare representations of interpersonal, secular lay communication in Old English literature, but they suggest that it was not unheard of for some Anglo-Saxon laity (albeit elite) to exchange interpersonal communication, not just public letters required for business or state matters. Women writers appear in hagiography as well: in the *Life of St Basil*, a rich woman writes a confession of her sins and brings it to Basil to have them erased, and the emperor Aurelianus's wife sends an *ærende* to him warning him to stop torturing Christian martyrs or he will die (*CH II*, 18, 177.98). Jezebel sends (and perhaps also writes) a letter directing that Naboth be killed (*LS* XVIII, 187–93), and in the Old English *Orosius*, a group of women send *ærendracan* (messengers) to their husbands telling them that, if they don't come home from their military campaign, the women will choose new husbands (1.10.29.10–12). Prohibitions against receiving letters also hint at a more robust system of epistolary communication among Anglo-Saxon religious. The Benedictine Rule stipulated that

---

from women in the Boniface correspondence may have been preserved because they were copied on the Continent rather than England and because some of them were perceived to be literary rather than private letters (Fell, "Some Implications," 29, 31, 41). On the expression of women's emotions in letters written by and to nuns, especially in the Boniface correspondence, see Stevenson, "Brothers and Sisters."

68 Joan Ferrante has gathered the letters of medieval women from the fourth to the thirteenth century at the website "Epistolae: Medieval Women's Latin Letters" (which also includes English translations): https://epistolae.ccnmtl.columbia.edu/, accessed 30 January 2016.

69 Fell, "Some Implications," 31.

70 Klein, *Ruling Women*, 11.

monks were not supposed to receive letters or gifts without permission of their abbot.[71] Likewise, The Old English *Enlarged Rule of Chrodegang* cautions that priests should avoid contact with women, explaining that men and woman should neither speak together, nor even "ne sendon him gretinge ne sanda betwynan" (send greetings or messages between them).[72] In other words, it is certainly possible that some women participated in the regular exchange of letters and other documents, even if Mary of Egypt resists this, shaping writing to her own ends. If Mary's letter is unlike typical letters, this is not because women could not be imagined to participate in an epistolary exchange. Instead, her letter is atypical because her communication is bound up with her desire to prevent both her body and the body of her message from being converted into desired, collectable objects.

In contrast to Mary's refusal to be made an object, Zosimus explicitly sees her body as treasure to be uncovered.[73] When Zosimus returns to the

---

71 "Ne si natoþoshwon munece alyfed, þæt he ænig gewrit oþþe sende, oðþe lac fram hyra magum, oþþe fram ænigum oþrum men, oðþe him betweonum underfon, oþþe sellen, butan þæs abbodes hæse." (It is by no means permitted that a monk receive or send any written document, present, or gift/message from their relatives or from any other person, or among themselves [that is, among monks], without the abbot's bidding.) Schröer, ed., *Die Angelsächsischen Prosabearbeitungen der Benediktinerregel,* 54.87.10–13.

72 Langefeld, *Old English Version,* 54.285.15–16.

73 Bodies held multiple meanings in late antique and early medieval religious thought. While Origen viewed the body and everything associated with it, including sexuality, as temporary and unimportant compared to the long purification of the soul, fourth- and fifth-century ascetic desert lives "became a repository of vivid anecdotes concerning sexual seduction and heroic sexual avoidance … Women were presented as a source of perpetual temptation to which the male body could be expected to respond instantly" (Brown, *Body and Society,* 168, 242). On the thorny question of the gender and sexuality of holy harlots like Mary of Egypt, see Burrus, *Sex Lives of Saints,* 147–55. Burrus argues that "the 'holy harlot' of ancient hagiography is just that: already holy, and still, unrepentantly, a 'harlot'" (131) and also notes that that Pelagia's corpse, which is also compared to treasures, remains "disturbingly seductive" (146). Paul E. Szarmach recognizes the erotic possibilities in the earlier part of Mary's story, but concludes that, once buried, "Mary's body can be no temptation, real or imagined, as it becomes in effect an immediate relic, giving witness to her holy ascetic life" ("More Genre Trouble," 158). I agree that her body becomes a relic, but I see this happening against her will. Szarmach reads her *body* as continuing to transmit her story, but the hagiography ends soon after her burial, and no miracles happen at the site of her corpse. All this suggests that Mary felt there was a danger in her body being displayed. Women's bodies were often understood as texts to be read, but reading their bodies could invite inappropriate

desert to look for Mary and cannot find her, he prays: "Geswutela me, Drihten, þæt gehydde goldhord þe þu me sylfum ær gemedemodest æteowan"[74] (Reveal to me, Lord, that hidden gold-treasure which you previously vouchsafed to show me). Given Mary's former profession, it is deeply problematic that Zosimus imagines her as material wealth to be put on display. Moreover, upon returning to the monastery to tell the monks what has happened, he *rehte* (related) the whole story and *naht ne bediglode* (concealed nothing).[75] Though Mary gave Zosimus permission to tell her story after her death, the fact that he follows the burial of her body, during which he *oferwreah* (covered) her body in the earth,[76] by proclaiming her story without any concealment is the first step in his appropriating Mary's private communication for public transmission.

That Zosimus imagines the body of the former prostitute as treasure to be displayed cannot simply be explained by the veneration of saintly relics, themselves often decorated with gold and gems. As Clare Lees has argued, Anglo-Saxon female saints must transcend the sexual to become saintly, but nevertheless must remain female and sexual. The inescapable reality of the female saint's gendered body creates the always present danger of temptation or improper looking at that body. Female saints must learn to "ren[ounce the] material sexual body," but it is only through looking at their bodies that audiences of their lives gain knowledge: "The act of looking, always problematic in Anglo-Saxon culture, is indeed a potent moment in these lives, with the acquisition of correct knowledge its

---

attention. Shari Horner argues that the bodies of Ælfric's female saints appeal on the surface, but conceal mysteries beneath, which must be read and interpreted (*Discourse of Enclosure*, 133–6). Renée R. Trilling suggests that the bodies of Ælfric's female saints remain necessarily material, but do so in order to be objects of masculine desire (sexual or otherwise) ("Heavenly Bodies," 267). For Andrew P. Scheil, Mary's *Life* is primarily about the *masculine* ascetic body, which is contrasted with Mary's feminine and sexual body that, even after her death, "retains its subversive potential" ("Bodies and Boundaries," 143). On the pitfalls of reading Mary entirely in terms of either heterosexuality or gender, and the possibility of reading Mary as trans* or genderqueer, see Watt and Lees, "Age and Desire."

74 Magennis, ed., *Old English Life*, 878–9.

75 "Sona swa he to þam mynstre becom, þa rehte he heom eallum of frymðe þa wisan, and naht ne bediglode ealra þæra þinga þe he geseah oððe gehyrde, þæt hi ealle Godes mærða wurðodon, and mærsodon þære eadigan forðfore dæg." (As soon as he came to the monastery, he related the story to them all from the beginning, and he did not conceal any of those things which he saw or heard, so that they all honoured God's glories and celebrated the blessed one's day of death.) (Ibid., 950–4.)

76 Ibid., 943.

correlative: even when naturalized by the ideology of spiritual love, the dangers of the unspiritual gaze, the pleasures of eroticized scopophilia, sadism, and masochism, lurk everywhere."[77] The dangers of the female body are not limited to unsafe looking. According to Andrew P. Scheil, Mary's body is "communicable"; the female body, unlike the pure male ascetic body, "like a disease ... can leap across boundaries and 'infect' others."[78] The threat is that Mary's body might communicate its sexuality to Zosimus. To put it another way, the threat is that her body is a message to be delivered to Zosimus. If her message were only the oral account of her life, followed by a standard written message, both might safely be contained by the framework of Zosimus's transmission of her story. Mary's fear, which eventually becomes Zosimus's concern, is that Zosimus may be "infected" by contact with her, and that he will not be able to find a less embodied way to transmit her message.

We might also contrast Zosimus's problematic material desire with the monastery's more perfect withdrawal from the world. The gate of the monastery is always locked, even though the monks have no goods to store or treasures to protect.[79] During Lent, when most of the brothers travel into the desert for private contemplation, a few stay behind, but not because they have any material wealth to guard: "Ænne oððe twegen on þam mynstre hi forleton, næs na to þam þæt hi þa begytanan gestreon heoldon – næs þær swilces nan þincg – ac þæt hi þæt gebedhus butan þam godcundan symbelnyssum ne forleton"[80] (They left one or two in the monastery, not at all to protect treasure they had won – there was no such thing there – but so that they did not leave the prayer-house without the divine solemnities). The monastery is a place for *oral*, non-storable prayer. There is nothing to archive, and nothing to guard, except the religious institution the monastery represents. During Lent, the gate is opened and the monks all go out on separate paths, deliberately turning away from anyone they might see. The Lenten season is thus a time for private contemplation in which the monks flow freely out of the monastery. Although

---

77 Lees, *Tradition and Belief*, 150. Elsewhere, Lees argues that looking at Mary's body is the means by which Zosimus comes to knowledge of God, and this represents his progression through the levels of devotional reading ("Vision and Place").

78 Scheil, "Bodies and Boundaries," 143. Scheil notes that Mary is initially afraid to share even a private, oral communication with Zosimus because she is so worried she might "infect" him with her words.

79 Magennis, ed., *Old English Life*, 125–30.

80 Ibid., 151–4.

the monks' bodies circulate into the world, they remain apart from it, never truly joining social or communicative networks. By contrast, Zosimus turns the season into an opportunity for cultural transmission, bringing back with him to the monastery the news of Mary's life and her suggestions for improving the conduct of the monastery. Having perhaps finally learned from his fellow monks that there is no reason to keep an archive of worldly treasures, because good monks reject the body in favour of the spirit,[81] he is able to free Mary's story to circulate without being attached to the potentially dangerous treasure of her body.

In *Mary of Egypt*, the written text, like Mary's body, resists being converted from temporary communication to public transmission. She wants her body concealed and buried, not revealed as proof of a miracle or commodified as a relic. Mary controls the script of her letter and testimony, but Zosimus controls the transmission of her story. Their conversation and her (oral) confession are extant in the written *Life* only because Zosimus was there as witness and messenger capable of delivering her story to others. It is because the letter arrived through miraculous rather than standard human communications channels, and because it was written on an unusual material support, that the process of communication is defamiliarized to such an extent that Zosimus is inspired to neatly solve the question of how to honour Mary's request for non-preservation by transmitting his own account instead. Her letter, ultimately, does not become a relic, and her body remains buried, because Zosimus has found a way to preserve and transmit the miracle without requiring material proof.

The story of *Mary of Egypt* reflects anxieties about who maintains control of a message once it is sent into the world. Mary, the reformed prostitute, jealously guards her body against becoming an object of either erotic or spiritual desire, and her desperate attempts to regulate access to her body are echoed in her attempt to deny her letter portability and transmission. Yet her interlocutor, Zosimus, initially dangerously attracted to the mysterious woman, eventually finds a way to adapt her message without

---

81 "And þær næfre unnytte spræce næron ne geþanc goldes and seolfres oþþe oþra gestreona, ne furðon se nama mid him næs oncnawen, ac þæt an wæs swiðost fram heom eallum geefst, þæt heora ælc wære on lichaman dead and on gaste libbende." (And there [in the monastery] there was never unnecessary speech nor thought of gold and silver or other treasures, nor even were the names known among them, but that alone was most hastened to by them all, that each of them would be dead in body and living in spirit." (Ibid., 108–12.)

entirely violating her trust, turning it from mere interpersonal communication to cultural transmission, an attempt to preserve and promote her within a larger and more temporally vast network. Zosimus delicately avoids turning Mary's body and letter (themselves symbols of containment and enclosure) into objects for public consumption only by retransmitting her message in an entirely new medium. Stored offsite, both body and text remain buried, inaccessible, while transmission of the message continues in Zosimus's new form.

I opened this chapter by noting that, whereas Elizabeth Heckendorn Cook argues that eighteenth-century letters stand in for the body of the absent sender, in these Old English texts, focus lands not on the sender, but on the body of the messenger or recipient, who is present, not absent. In *Apollonius of Tyre*, Apollonius's body is transformed by contact with the letter he carries, and his blushes become a legible message to the king. Arcestrate's desire is transferred from her tablet to her teacher-messenger's body, making his body more legible than the message itself. King Abgar must believe he can be healed not by a Mandylion, but by the body of the messenger Thaddeus, whose body's presence substitutes for Jesus's letter and Jesus's body, absent and yet omnipresent. Only in the case of *Mary of Egypt* does the letter become coterminous with the sender's body; written in the dirt, Mary's message must not be transmitted, and Zosimus must find a less embodied way to become the messenger who transmits the story of her life. Embodied conversation between messenger and recipient, or between message and messenger, may threaten (*Mary of Egypt*), heal (*Abgar*), or improve communication (*Apollonius of Tyre*). While the materiality of the letter was of minimal importance in the heavenly letters studied in chapter 2, materiality becomes crucial in the texts studied in the present chapter. It is the materiality of bodies – whether of message or messenger – that speaks to recipients.

Because Old English representations of letters frequently reduce or omit both formulaic language (chapter 1) and attention to the physical form of the original document (chapter 2), they are more able to focus on the interactions between material documents and the human bodies that touch, send, carry, and receive them. Documents become merely storage containers or authorizations for messengers to speak, and it is in and through the body of the messenger that the message is truly transmitted. Moreover, these documents are not permanent storage containers, because the fantasy of presence and immediacy necessarily makes the communication of the message ineffable, unable to be fully recorded or preserved. By making the body a document, the absent sender may be made present to the recipient, and affect or healing properties may be transferred from the body of the sender to the body of the messenger or even the body of the recipient. While Old English letters may de-emphasize the materiality of the physical document on which a letter is written, the letter's message remains fully material, whether through its textual incarnation or through the somatic, embodied responses of messengers and recipients.

I have argued that Mary's message is written in the ground as a way of warning Zosimus not to transform her body or her letter into a relic. In the next chapter, I turn to ways in which letters and other epistolary documents were used to preserve and circulate miracles that left no tangible trace. In fact, even writing a message in the ground may not have prevented enterprising worshippers from venerating the site, if they could locate it. Although Mary's message written in the ground is neither transportable nor replicable, the location of her body, and the dirt in which her message was written, could have been turned into a portable secondary relic. In Bede's *Historia Ecclesiastica*, for example, we learn that the place where Oswald was killed became so popular that a large hole was created by lay worshippers taking dirt from the location.[82] Although Zosimus found a way to transmit Mary's miracles without having tangible proof, the popularity of relics and reliquaries in the Middle Ages suggests an abiding desire for tangible proof and memorials that flies in the face of Mary of Egypt's resistance to being made relic, and Ælfric's disavowal of the Mandylion or other physical relic to heal Abgar. It is to the rise of lay interest in saints' cults in late Anglo-Saxon England, and the desire to memorialize miracles through epistolary documents, that we next turn.

---

82 Miller, ed., *Old English Version of Bede*, 3.7.178.8–11. On the appeal of this soil to the laity as well as religious, see Rollason, *Saints and Relics*, 101–3. On relics that came to be associated with Mary of Egypt in the later Middle Ages, see Lavery, "Story of Mary," 114–15.

4 Bodies of Record: Witnessing, Memory, and Erasure in Ælfric's *Life of St Basil* and the Anonymous Old English *Legend of the Seven Sleepers*

How do we remember and memorialize transitory events? In the twenty-first century, many of us are inundated with portable, relatively affordable recording technologies, as attested by the ubiquity of cellphone camera photos and videos of everything from the mundane to the spectacular. Mass production of souvenirs and commemorative plates, coins, and tea towels allows us both to remember events and, in some cases, to anticipate them. In Anglo-Saxon England, by contrast, unless an event left a tangible trace (such as a scar on the landscape or on the body), there were few options for recording it. This was particularly true of miracles: if they did not leave physical proof, or if that proof was non-portable or difficult to verify (a healed body, for example, whose proof of healing may be an absence rather than a presence), how could believers produce and circulate evidence of the event? I argue in this chapter, and I have been suggesting throughout the book, that epistolarity offered one way of recording events (albeit after the fact), which allowed believers to produce and circulate evidence even of events that left no tangible trace. Letters could most obviously transmit the event's message, but they could also store or record the event itself, though in a mediated way. Through the subjective lens of a human witness or author, an event could be recorded first in the written format of the letter, and then within the archive or repository into which the letter might be placed.

The final step in epistolary acts often involves storing the message. Chapter 1 traced the form and composition of letters, chapters 2 and 3 their delivery and transmission. This chapter focuses on what happens after the messenger's delivery is done, and the letter must be archived or destroyed. I articulate the ways in which epistolary materials could capture miraculous events by examining documents that take epistolary form but also function as records. Whereas a letter's primary purpose is, first, to communicate a message and, second, to authenticate that message (by the use of a personal signature, seals, etc.), letters that become archival records witness and authenticate by virtue of their existence or destruction, and by the physical form they may take (possibly including seals or other markers of identity). In chapter 2, I argued that Old English *Sunday Letters* prioritize the content of the message rather than the physical document. In chapter 3, I examined texts in which the body of the messenger trumps the materiality of the document or its content. In this chapter, which focuses on Anglo-Saxon vernacular hagiography, what matters most about embedded epistolary documents is not the precise content of their messages, but the material forms in which they exist and are preserved, or the miraculous ways in which they are erased or invalidated. Ultimately, I demonstrate that treating letters not simply as private two-way communication but as records opens up new ways of understanding medieval miracles, medieval memory, and medieval media.

The reason I am using "record" to describe certain epistolary documents embedded in Anglo-Saxon hagiographies is because this term captures the sense of how such documents claim to *represent* an objective, unmediated truth and of how they *produce* that truth.[1] The word "record" implies a conduit through which something is being recorded, an active agent, who interprets via the act of recording, selecting what content should be preserved, and what content should be ignored or filtered out. By these acts of omission and inclusion, the scribes who collected, preserved, and copied epistolary records created the narrative of the past of a

---

1 My understanding of "records" has been shaped by Lisa Gitelman and her demonstration of how the word takes on new meanings in the age of the phonograph (*Always Already New*). Likewise, Friedrich Kittler argues that the phonograph introduced a new kind of storage that recorded (and later transmitted) events as they happened, but that writing was unique as a storage medium in that it necessarily filtered everything it recorded through that writing. It could not capture anything that was not deliberately recorded or added to the written account, and it also could not record anything that could not be conveyed by written language (*Gramophone, Film, Typewriter*, 7–8). Obviously, while phonographs may have initially seemed to offer unmediated recording, they are necessarily influenced by the choices of their users and makers. Where the machine is placed, for example, will determine what it can and cannot detect and audibly record. Still, it is crucial to acknowledge the ways in which recording devices (whether human or machine) can create the illusion of unmediated preservation, even to the point of denying the role of the recording agent in selecting or excluding what becomes record.

particular individual or institution.[2] As archival records, letters and other epistolary documents are monuments and memorials to miracles and, as such, they claim to present an unmediated access to the miracle itself, even as we know that they have been collected within the hagiography by a scribe or author who deliberately chose to record the document. When stored in an institutional archive or embedded within a hagiography, letters may be valued for the content of their message, which can be retrieved and studied by users temporally or geographically removed from the event itself. By emphasizing the immediacy and agency of the letter, and minimizing the intervention of the human recording agent, authors of documentary records create an illusion of documentary agency in which specific content is less important than the presence of the record. The physical object, and its durability or erasure, bears witness to the miracle by the fact of its existence, finding a way to make even miracles enacted on the soul material, sometimes by inscribing the miracle on a piece of parchment that takes the place of the human skin on which healing miracles are more often inscribed. In the texts I study in this chapter, both message and medium are imagined to communicate intelligibly, and both are valuable components of the documents' transmission. But ultimately, the authenticating speaker (who says I was there, I did or saw this) gives way to the authenticating document or record.[3] The subjective human experience of the miracle is rendered unnecessary or ancillary in the presence of the seemingly more authentic, more objective presence of the material record of the letter. In this way, epistolary documents, even those produced by fallible human witnesses, produce records, and in some cases are archived or become archive. To put it another way, these letters and documents do not just make miracles material, or even record miracles – they also bring miracles into the archive.

---

2 Even cartularies are not merely copies of all the documents in the possession of a single institution, but rather are mediated and created by their makers. See Geary, *Phantoms of Remembrance*, 83–4.

3 This claim is inspired by and yet dissimilar to Emily Steiner's claim about the importance of formulae in legal texts of later medieval England. Steiner argues that the formulae in the late medieval *Charters of Christ* "effectively collapse action and [authorial] will" (*Documentary Culture*, 65–6). While I am interested in authorial will in epistolary records, in this chapter I make no claims about the use of specific epistolary formulae (in part because Old English letters frequently omit such formulae), nor about the ways in which legal documents become binding. Steiner's arguments about the union of will and action in fact contradict the claim I have made about some of the other documents featured in this project, namely that letters separate transmission and storage.

This chapter focuses on the representation of the storage and retrieval of epistolary documents in two saints' lives: first, Ælfric's *Life of St Basil*, and then the anonymous *Legend of the Seven Sleepers*, which circulated along with Ælfric's *Lives* in two eleventh-century manuscripts. In both, letters store, transmit, and are retrieved in service of remembering the past. Erasure or destruction of letters cannot lead to forgetting the past. Only rewriting, producing new narratives and new documents, can do that. Unlike *Mary of Egypt*, in which Mary's life story is retained and transmitted in the hagiography, in *Basil*, we learn how epistolary acts might record a saint's miraculous intervention without creating a record of a sinner's transgressions. In *Seven Sleepers*, by contrast, we see how letters form part of the literal and cultural archive. The story features a letter that travels to its addressees across time, not space, along with the bodies of the sleepers. Once this letter is stored in the archive that is the cave in which the sleepers are found, it transmits its message and can be replicated for users who cannot access the archive of the cave directly. Moreover, the *Legend* reveals how the archivist mediates letters, determining what is preserved, and what lost.

Consulting Letters in the Archives

Letters and other documents considered worth preserving were held in high esteem in Anglo-Saxon England and were often kept with relics and other treasure. According to Simon Keynes, "documents may have been kept with the relics because they gained additional strength from the association, for ease of access should reference need to be made to them, or because their intrinsic value meant that they were regarded as properly a part of the royal treasures."[4] We find evidence for the consultation of archived Anglo-Saxon letters both in the format and structure of extant manuscripts and in references to the retrieval and use of documents as witnesses in Anglo-Saxon literature. Turning first to internal evidence for the consultation of epistolary records, in Blickling Homily 15 (Peter and Paul), Nero is trying to adjudicate between Simon, a false magician who claims that he is the son of God, and Peter, who denies Simon and supports Jesus of Nazareth. As proof of his claims, Peter asks Nero to

---

4 Keynes, *Diplomas of King Æthelred*, 149. See also David Rollason, who cites as evidence Sawyer charters nos 939, 981, 1478, and 1521 (*Saints and Relics*, 162–3).

consult the letter (*ærendgewrit, gewrit*) that Pilate sent to the previous emperor, Claudius, regarding the death of Jesus. This scene demonstrates that letters could be conceived as records, as well as illustrating the process by which letters might be verified as legal witnesses. Peter tells Nero to have the letter brought to him ("You honourable king, if you wish to know what was done with respect to Christ in Judea, command Pilate's letter that he sent to Emperor Claudius about Christ's suffering to be brought to you").[5] This suggests both that the letter has been stored as a witness of the events and also that this record has been stored in such a way that it is relatively easily retrievable. Peter believes this letter may be sufficient evidence to prove his claim regarding the true son of God. However, it transpires that, contrary to Peter's belief, the letter is insufficient proof. After Nero reads the letter, he turns to Peter to confirm the written message, asking "Saga me, Petrus, wæs hit eal swa swa þæt gewrit sæg þurh hine geworden?" (Tell me, Peter, did it all happen to him [Christ] just as that letter says?).[6] Peter immediately swears that the letter is true, but even this does not end the debate. It is significant that Nero, while willing to treat the letter as evidence, prefers to confirm its account with the living witness standing before him, much like the king asking Apollonius to interpret Arcestrate's letter discussed in chapter 3. A written record is good, but gathering living witnesses still seems to be a crucial part of Nero's decision-making process.

By the late tenth and eleventh centuries, Anglo-Saxons avoided the difficulty of gathering living witnesses to an event by developing increasingly sophisticated ways of recording and retrieving documentary witnesses.[7] Even in ninth-century Anglo-Saxon legal disputes, documents were often more essential than oral testimony. As Patrick Wormald argues in regard

---

5 "Þu þonne, dugoþa cyning, gif þu witan wille hwæt be Criste gedon wæs on Iudea lande, hat þe niman Pilatus ærendgewrit þe he sende to Claudio þæm casere ymb Cristes þrowunga." Morris, ed. and trans., *Blickling Homilies*, 15.177. Translations from the Blickling Homilies are my own, but done in consultation with Morris's translation.

6 Ibid., *Blickling* 15.179.

7 On the production and use of legal documents in Anglo-Saxon England, see Wormald, *Making of English Law*; Keynes, *Diplomas of King Æthelred*; Keynes, "Royal Government"; Chaplais, "Origin and Authenticity"; Chaplais, "Anglo-Saxon Chancery"; Snook, *Anglo-Saxon Chancery*; and Hough, "Legal and Documentary Writings"; see also chapter 1. For Anglo-Saxon wills, see Tollerton, *Wills and Will-Making*. On chirographs, see Lowe, "Lay Literacy." Even Michael Clanchy's much-welcomed revisions to the first chapter of his *From Memory to Written Record* do not adequately develop a theory of literacy and documentary culture in England before the Norman Conquest.

to an 824 dispute over Westbury, "the most one can ... say for the oath in this sort of dispute is that it could be important for conflicts irresolvable by other means, and that it may have been the formal means of ending litigation ... There was a premium on the written word."[8] Francesca Tinti traces the ways in which late Anglo-Saxon Worcester carefully preserved, reread, and recatalogued the documents they had in their possession, writing finding aids on the outside of their stored files, so that users might more easily locate and consult the documents.[9] Scribes wrote the name of the place to which the document pertained on the dorse of single-sheet documents soon after they were made, and sometimes a later hand added the name of the king during whose reign the document was produced. In both cases, these names were visible after the document had been folded, which made it easier to search original documents chronologically or geographically.[10] By the end of the Anglo-Saxon period, documents were also beginning to be copied into cartularies.[11] As Tinti reveals, these early English cartularies were designed to be accessible. Texts in the *Liber Wigorniensis* were organized according to both shire and estate, which

---

8 Wormald, "Charters, Law and the Settlement of Disputes," 154. Wormald notes that written records remained crucial in the late tenth century, including to the laity: "Thus, precisely those most accustomed to pre-literate transactions were exploiting the implications of literacy" (161). Anglo-Saxon legal culture did not have a fully developed concept of written law, although Wormald argues that "the point is emphatically not that texts did not matter, but that they did not resonate as they might have" (*Making of English Law*, 482). By contrast, in one of the earliest arguments for Anglo-Saxon lay literacy, Susan Kelly asserted that, to the laity, "the transfer of land was effected and guaranteed by the rituals which marked the transaction, and ... the diploma was important as a part and symbol of these ceremonies, not on its own account as a written record of the transaction." According to Kelly, some Anglo-Saxon charters were prepared before the oral ceremony, with blank spaces left for witness names (which were written by the scribe and not the witnesses themselves). Kelly argues that the ceremony was done for the benefit of the laity, who might otherwise have been mistrusting of ecclesiastical document production ("Anglo-Saxon Lay Society," 29). The overemphasis on oral witnesses in Anglo-Saxon England in previous scholarship may have been influenced by Norman materials. Clanchy points out that, in contrast to Anglo-Norman practices, relatively few symbolic objects are known to have been used in Anglo-Saxon conveyance ceremonies (*From Memory to Written Record*, 39). He also argues that, "in the twelfth century to 'record' something meant to bear oral witness, not to produce a document" (78–9).

9 Tinti, *Sustaining Belief*, esp. 75–150.

10 Ibid., 83–5.

11 There are three extant eleventh-century cartularies from England: Hemming's Cartulary, the *Liber Wigorniensis* (early eleventh century; in the same manuscript as Hemming's Cartulary), and the Oswald or Nero-Middleton Cartulary (ibid., 75–6).

would have made specific leases or charters easier for future users of the cartulary to locate.[12] Nor were cartularies necessarily static collections. The leases in the *Liber Wigorniensis* were updated with the names of later heirs, and notes indicating to which estate a group of documents pertained were also added to some leases.[13] Tinti argues that the careful arrangement and updating of the *Liber Wigorniensis* "testifies to a very strong interest in preserving the memory of how Worcester had acquired its vast estate on the one hand, and on the other, a practical need to keep track of the leases beneficiaries' heirs."[14] Likewise, according to Hemming, St Wulfstan (1062–95) was directly involved in updating and preserving the files of the Nero-Middleton Cartulary, sorting existing documents kept in the *scrinium* and copying important documents into a Bible (the Nero-Middleton Cartulary) so that they would survive even if the originals were lost or destroyed.[15]

Interest in documentary records was not restricted to the church, but was beginning to spread to the laity as well. While Anglo-Saxon charters were usually written in Latin, writs and wills were more often written in the vernacular, and some were produced in duplicate or triplicate by using the process of making a chirograph. Kathryn Lowe has shown that the late Anglo-Saxon popularity of vernacular chirographs suggests that not only elite churchmen, but even laymen, desired to cultivate record collections; she argues that the portion of the chirograph given to and kept by a layman, written in Old English rather than Latin, "was intended to form part of a working archive for the layman."[16] Likewise, Charles Insley argues that although there are no extant Anglo-Saxon lay archives, the laity knew how to use (if not produce) documents, and stored them in accessible ways across multiple generations.[17] The chirograph made it possible for

---

12 Ibid., 91–2.

13 Ibid., 111–18.

14 Ibid., 124.

15 Ibid., 125–7.

16 Lowe, "Lay Literacy," 176. Lowe does not necessarily think the laymen were literate enough to read these documents, but rather that they could recognize them by their shape and know what they were for. A chirograph could, in theory, "be matched and checked" against its "counterpart" by a layman (or in his presence) (178).

17 As Insley points out, "very few surviving Anglo-Saxon documents are genuinely 'lay documents,' in the sense that there was no clerical involvement in their production or use" – but this does not mean that the laity were not involved in the cases the documents recorded, or that they did not collect documents relating to their own interests ("Archives and Lay Documentary Practice," 340).

the laity to keep their own copies of documents, or to have copies sent to their allies. As Insley puts it, "the example of the chirograph suggests that these documents were not just put somewhere and forgotten ... To be of use, the charter had to be a recoverable object."[18] In fact, when documents were lost, their owners sought to have them replaced, as in the case of an ealdorman who successfully petitioned to have his charters reconstructed from memory after they were destroyed in a fire.[19] This is all to say that not only were Anglo-Saxons more literate than was once believed, at least insofar as they participated in literate culture (whether they could read or not), but also that they valued the preservation and accessibility of documents. These documents, become records, communicated not just to the present, but also to the future. By the end of the Anglo-Saxon period, if not earlier, individual records were being stored in ways that maximized their ability to be consulted. Stored in ways that made them retrievable, the function of these records becomes practical rather than symbolic. All this suggests that Anglo-Saxons, even those who could not read, would have valued the storage and retrievability of letters in the archive. In the rest of this chapter, I turn to the ways in which the archivability and easy retrieval of letters is crucial to the recording of miracles in two saints' lives: Ælfric's *Life of St Basil* and the anonymous Old English *Legend of the Seven Sleepers*.

Erasure and Destruction: Memorializing Absence in Ælfric's *Life of St Basil*

One of the central questions of this project, and of this chapter, is how Anglo-Saxons recorded, preserved, and circulated news of intangible miracles – miracles that left no physical trace or "proof." If recording the ineffable (and all the problems of mediation bound up with the process of recording) is a major topic of this chapter, then so too is the issue of forgetting and erasure. In this section of the chapter, I examine texts that memorialize absence, erasure, or destruction of a document. How did Anglo-Saxons, and how does anyone, for that matter, record erasure or absence? What do these texts suggest about the relationship between memory, memorializing, and forgetting? Does the act of remembering necessarily require forgetting? That is, when carefully selecting what to remember,

---

18 Ibid., 350.
19 See Lowe, "Lay Literacy," 170, discussing S 367 and S 371.

do we not necessarily (consciously or not) choose not to remember or memorialize other aspects of the event? As Mary Carruthers suggests, and as some of the documents represented in *Basil* illustrate, destruction and erasure of records allowed people to rewrite or overwrite their own records. That is, erasure does not remove an event from private or public memory; it simply allows new associations to be made with that event or object. Erasure is not total obliteration.[20] Moreover, erasure and destruction of letters and other documents constitutes a way of creating a record. By drawing attention to the ways in which certain acts are suppressed, while others are celebrated, Ælfric reveals a deep understanding of how documentary culture allows people to construct narratives of their own past, but also how one can modify one's own permanent record.

Ælfric's *Life of St Basil* represents several of the ways epistolary documents were embedded in hagiographies.[21] There are three major documents or collections of documents represented within the *Life*. The first is an exchange of letters between Basil and an ealdorman, initiated when a woman who owes taxes to the ealdorman requests that Basil intercede on her behalf.[22] When the ealdorman replies to Basil's request, stating that he wishes he could have mercy on the woman, but he refuses to absorb the cost of the taxes, Basil warns that if he has the power to forgive the debt

---

20 Carruthers, *Craft of Thought*, 46 and *passim*.

21 In addition to appearing in Skeat's EETS edition of Ælfric's *LS*, the *Life of St Basil* has been edited and translated by Gabriella Corona, *Ælfric's Life of Saint Basil*. All quotations from the Old English *Basil* will come from Corona's edition, cited by line number. The Old English *Life of St Basil* is based on the Latin *BHL* 1023, of which there are many extant manuscripts (Corona 4). Corona includes the text of *BHL* 1023 in an appendix to her edition. References to this Latin edition will be cited by chapter and line number, following Corona. For the earlier EETS edition, see Skeat, ed. *Ælfric's Lives of Saints*, vol. 1, III. For an introduction to Ælfric's *Lives of Saints*, see chapter 3.

22 Chapter 6. Basil's initial message is quite short but does meet my definition of a letter, as it is a written message sent from one person to another, and brevity was one of the desired qualities of a letter. Moreover, Ælfric once designates Basil's message an *ærendgewrit* (176). Corona suggests that this lexical choice may have been motivated by Ælfric's use of alliteration and paronomasia in this chapter, arguing that the line (*Þa rædde se ealdorman þæt ærendgewrit* [then the ealdorman read that letter]) alliterates both on *þ* and on the vowel (*Ælfric's Life of Saint Basil*, 107–10). However, while Ælfric's translation of the Latin is rather free, it is perhaps worth noting that at this moment the Latin *Vita* names the document an *epistolam* (6.6), whereas elsewhere in the passage it has focused on the letter's materiality, calling it *cartam* (6.3, 5). Ælfric more often refers to this and other letters in the *Life of St Basil* as *gewrit* (any written document) (171, 177, 182).

and will not, bad things will happen to him. When bad things do occur (he is seized by the emperor), the ealdorman repents, asks Basil to intercede with the emperor on his behalf, and pays the woman back double. These letters are typical communicative exchanges, with the messages quoted or paraphrased directly within the *Life*. No attention is paid to the material form the messages take, little is said about how the letters are conveyed between Basil and the ealdorman, and no attempt is made to archive or destroy them after the initial communication ends. However, in this section, Ælfric modifies his Latin source in several key ways. He emphasizes the role of Basil as intercessor, a concept not present in the Latin. The woman solicits Basil's *þingunge* (intercession) with the ealdorman, Basil's letter to the ealdorman says the woman asked him to *geþingian* (intercede) for her, and the ealdorman's reply acknowledges that he would like to be able to forgive the woman because of Basil's *þingunge*. Likewise, after he is freed, the ealdorman explicitly thanks Basil for his *þingunge*.[23] While the woman is poor, and perhaps illiterate (or at least unable to successfully petition the ealdorman on her own behalf), she understands the power of Basil's intercession and what he might be able to accomplish via participation in epistolary culture. The rich ealdorman initially has no such understanding but eventually comes to learn the intercessory power of both Basil and letters. After his imprisonment, the ealdorman proves that he has

---

23 Corona 170, 174, 179, 198. Basil's initial letter to the ealdorman, for example, is in Old English: "Þis earme wif me gesohte, sæde þæt ic mihte / hire to ðe geþingian. Þonne cyð þu nu, ic bidde, / gif ic swa wel mæg wið þe swa þæt wif truwað" (This poor woman sought me, saying that I might intercede on her behalf with you. Then now make it known, I demand, if I can [do] as well with you as that woman believes) (173–5). The Latin is "Haec muliercula pauper accessit ad me dicens posse me apud te. Si ergo possum, ostende" (This poor woman came to me, saying help me [that is, the woman] with you. If I am able to, then prove it) (6.4–5). Moreover, the woman delivers Basil's message in the Latin, while in Old English it is unclear who the messenger is. This suggests the woman's exclusion from communication channels, and heightens the impact of Basil as sole intercessor or mediator. The Latin describes Basil preparing the document for the woman, who takes it from him and delivers it to the man to whom she owes money: "Qui accipiens cartam, scripsit principi ... Et dedit mulieri cartam. Quae abiens dedit epistolam principi" (Who [Basil] receiving the parchment, wrote the nobleman ... and gave the parchment to the woman, who departing gave the letter to the nobleman) (6.3–6). By contrast, the Old English has "Basilius þa awrat þam earman wife an gewrit / to þæm ealdormenn on þisum andgite ... Þa rædde se ealdorman þæt ærendgewrit" (Basil then wrote a letter to the ealdorman for the poor woman to this effect ... then the ealdorman read that letter" (171–6).

learned his lesson by writing to Basil and asking him to intercede on his behalf: he "asende ... sona to Basilie, / biddende earmlice þæt he þone geyr-sodan casere / þurh his gebedu geliðgode"[24] (sent ... immediately to Basil, praying wretchedly that he might soften the angered emperor through his prayers). There is no erasure or destruction of these documents, but I have treated them here, briefly, to demonstrate that readers of this *Life* are expected to be familiar with basic letters and their most standard communicative functions, though not necessarily to expect letters to be framed by epistolary forms such as salutations. Moreover, Basil is initially represented as someone who has knowledge of non-miraculous, even ineffective written communication, which sets up his much more impressive command of two much more complex documents later in the *Life*, both of which are important not for what they say, but for how they are erased, silenced, and removed from the record.

The second major letter is written by a youth who makes a deal with the devil in order to win a woman.[25] Although he swears to the devil that he renounces Christ, the devil insists that this verbal oath is insufficient, so the youth must then also write a document affirming the renunciation. When the youth's crime is discovered, and he wants to repent, Basil locks him up for fourteen days, until the devils stop visiting him and tormenting him with the evidence of the document.[26] When the youth is finally released, the devil appears with the manuscript, and Basil and company pray until the document falls from the sky to Basil, who tears it up. Ælfric uses a variety of terms to describe the object, not all of which we would imagine could name the same thing, but it is clear that the object is a letter. In the Latin *vita*, the document is an *epistola* (11.19, 25), but also a *carta* (11.26) and a *manuscriptum* (11.37, 103, 135–46). In Old English, the document is sometimes called a *handgewrit* (424, 445, 448), a word that, like *manuscript*, could mean any written document but that also underscores

---

24 Ibid., 191–3.
25 Chapter 11.
26 It is important that he is sealed within this place to reverse the pledge made to the devil, a more symbolic act of sealing. The verb used to describe the youth's being locked up is *beleac* (locked) (419, 428). We are not told whether the contract with the devil is sealed, but because it is described as a letter, it is possible that it was. Moreover, the youth admits to Basil that he "on gewrite afæstnode" (confirmed or fixed in writing) that he was the devil's (414). Sealing the youth into a protective place undoes whatever metaphorical sealing was accomplished by the contract.

that the document is written by hand. The word appears only rarely in the Old English corpus, most often describing letters or legal documents.[27] The document is also described as a *carte* (455), which has a range of meanings, from the general (leaf of vellum or anything written on such material) to the specific (charter or other legal document).[28] At another point, the document is clearly understood to have epistolary form, being designated a *pistol* dictated to the youth by the devil and written by the youth's own hand.[29] Although the youth's document gives possession of his soul to the devil (much like a writ might record land transfer), I can find no evidence in the Old English corpus for the word *pistol* being applied to legal documents written in epistolary form. Instead, its use is clearly limited to actual letters. *Pistol* is most often applied to epistles written by the apostles and church fathers, and is occasionally used for other kinds of letters, such as those written by kings to their people.[30] Therefore, I would argue that we *are* meant to understand this document as a letter, not merely a legal text with a salutation formula. While it was certainly not unusual for Anglo-Saxon legal documents to take epistolary form, Ælfric's slippage between terms here confirms that Anglo-Saxons may have had a more capacious concept of documents or other written media than we do today (as discussed in chapter 1).

---

27 *DOE, s.v.* "handgewrit," cites 12 occurences. According to my search of the Toronto *Dictionary of Old English Corpus*, its use is most frequent in religious prose. It appears three times in *Basil*, refers twice to the *Sunday Letter* (Haines E and F) and once to Theophilus's contract with the devil (*CH I*, 30, 435.191), and is found in two Old English hymnals glossing *cyrographo* (in Hymn 51), and glossing *manufacta, s. simulacra* in Aldhelm's *De Virginitate*. The word is also used to signify a signature rather than a document itself in the Old English version of Bede's *Ecclesiastical History* 5.17, and in a grant of land by William I to Baldwin in 1081. In the Old English *Basil*, *handgewrit* usually appears where the Latin *Vita* uses a form of *manuscriptum*.

28 *DOE, s.v.* "carte." It is possible that the lexical choice in line 455 is motivated by alliteration: "He cwæð: 'Ic oncnawe þas cartan ful geare'" (455), but the same cannot be said for the use of *pistol*.

29 "Þa awrat se earming mid his agenre handa / swa swa se deofol him gedihte þone pistol" (Then the wretched one wrote a letter with his own hand just as the devil dictated to him) (381–2).

30 Ælfric frequently uses the word *pistol*, but he may have been concerned that it was too Latinate to be familiar to some members of his audience. In one of the *Lives of Saints* more likely to have been performed before a lay audience, he takes care to gloss the word, explaining that he is drawing on a text written by Paul in a "pistole, þæt is ærendgewrit" (*pistol*, that is letter) (*LS* XVII, 2–3).

In this story, the letter's primary function is to be a symbol of the contract between the youth and the devil. While the content of its message may be significant, the specific words of the message apparently are not. Unlike the exchange of letters between Basil and the ealdorman, the content of the letter is never quoted within the *Life,* even though the message *is* quoted in the Latin *Vita.* The contract records the youth's confession or oath to the devil, and that fact alone is sufficient to bear witness to his sin. In addition to being a record of the bad agreement the youth made, the epistolary contract also becomes a record of Basil's miracle. Basil's power to protect the youth is made visible by his act of regaining and then destroying the now invalid contract, symbolically destroying the record of the youth's sins: "Basilius hi sona totær / and gehuslode þone cnapan and þam Hælende betæhte" (Basil immediately tore it to pieces and gave the Eucharist to the youth and committed him to the Savior).[31] When Basil regains control of the document, the devil loses his power. The stories of the greedy ealdorman and the youth's contract with the devil demonstrate that, in the *Life of St Basil,* written documents can matter both as written messages whose contents are transmitted directly within the *Life* and as physical documents – records of both sin and forgiveness, of acts rather than words.

Although the *Life* does not transcribe the content of the youth's pledge to the devil, it does record the act of destroying the document – and this is intriguing. What does it mean to record destruction rather than creation and preservation? On the one hand, this accords with what I have already been suggesting – keepers of archives, producers of cartularies, and other record makers knew that part of producing textual monuments is deciding what to omit – that is, what to erase from the record. But *Basil* complicates this, suggesting that the youth's crime can be forgiven, but not entirely forgotten. If the youth's crime were to be entirely erased, then that would leave Basil with no record of his own miraculous intercession. The destruction of the epistolary contract thus serves several purposes. First, it gives the youth a clean slate, as it were. Second, it models for the audience how they too may be given fresh starts if they also repent and perform acts of penitence (as the youth does when he is locked away for so many days). Third, this destruction, rather than complete erasure from the record, is also in keeping with what Mary Carruthers writes about memory and

---

31 Corona 457–8.

forgetting in the medieval world. Medieval memory techniques invite the audience not to obliterate all memory of the letter but to overwrite their memory of the dangerous letter with the account of Basil's miraculous destruction of it. Ælfric takes advantage of this, literally erasing the content of the message from the record while preserving knowledge of the textual object. The performance of the letter's destruction allows us to create a new association with the document – to remember it, yes, but to remember it as proof of Basil's miracle rather than as a record of the youth's sin. In doing so, we change what medieval rhetoricians would call our *intentio* towards the letter, taking a new attitude towards it and converting it from record of sin to record of mercy.[32] Finally, it is worth noting that the first thing Basil does after destroying the document is to give the youth the host, thus symbolically rejoining him to the Christian community and restoring his body and spirit to wholeness, reversing what he has done to the document.

The third document in Basil's *Life*, which is called a *gewrit* (any writing, sometimes a letter), *carte* (charter, any written document, or the material on which a document is written), or *ymele* (roll or writing support),[33] is a confession written by a sinful woman.[34] In a note on the woman's document, Jane Roberts consistently refers to it as a "letter" but does not provide a clear justification for doing so, remarking only that "*letter* sometimes feels a more satisfactory choice for these everyday polysemous Old English words."[35] The *Life*'s most recent editor, Gabriella Corona, also translates

---

32 "What forgiveness changes is that *intentio*, the emotional direction … towards the memory images that still exist in one's mind … The key, as usual, is the moral use one makes of them" (Carruthers, *Craft of Thought*, 97). Although medieval mnemotechniques warn that erasure might prevent true forgetting, in actual practice, early medieval responses to dangerous documents varied. See chapter 2 for debates about whether or not to destroy the *Sunday Letter*.

33 *Ymele* is only used once, at line 641. BT defines *ymele* as "a scroll, leaf of paper." The word is incredibly rare in Old English, and a search of the Old English *Corpus* reveals that it is elsewhere found glossing *sceda* and *scedula*, neither of which necessarily mean *roll*. Nor does the corresponding word used in the *Vita* (*carta*) justify the translation "roll." Although both Corona and Skeat translate *ymele*'s appearance in *Basil* as "scroll," I would suggest that it might make more sense to translate *ymele* as "leaf" or "scrap of parchment," rather than "roll."

34 Chapters 14 and 16 (= Latin Chapter 15).

35 Roberts, "Rich Woman," 5 (emphasis in original).

gewrit here as "letter."[36] The document is certainly delivered – first to Basil, and then to Ephrem (who rejects it) – and since it is a confession, we might assume that it was addressed to someone (whether the confessor or God). The fact that the document is sealed also suggests that we are to imagine it as a letter. Anglo-Saxon letters could be sealed, but charters were likely not sealed before 1050, roughly fifty years after Ælfric completed the *Lives of Saints.* T.A. Heslop concludes that the "primary function" of seals in England before 1100 was "closing correspondence."[37] We are meant to connect this document to Basil's letters on behalf of the poor woman and to the youth's epistolary contract, and therefore to place it in the context of documentary, if not also epistolary, culture.

For reasons that are not made clear, the sinful woman had finally decided to heed God, so she "wrote all her sinful deeds on a document and sealed [it] with lead."[38] She takes this document to Basil, saying

"Eala[39] mine synna ic synfulle awrat / on þissere cartan, and ic com to þe leof, / and ic bidde þe for Godes lufan þæt þu ne[40] unlyse þa inseglunge, / ac adylega þa synna to Drihtne me þingiende."[41]

---

36 "and þæt gewrit ageaf" ("and gave that letter back") (549, Corona's translation); "Heo wearp þa mid þam þæt gewrit on ða bære" ("Then at that moment she threw that letter on the bier") (654, Corona's translation).

37 Heslop, "English Seals," 2. By contrast, Jane Roberts argues that Anglo-Saxon audiences understood charters with seals by the 960s to 970s ("What Did Anglo-Saxon Seals Seal When?" 140). Given that most charters were land grants, it is unlikely that the woman's list of sins would have been conceived as a charter. Likewise, while Anglo-Saxon writs could be sealed, the woman's confession bears little resemblance to extant writs. There is relatively little evidence of seals in England before 1100; for primarily later medieval English seals, see Harvey and McGuinness, *Guide to British Medieval Seals.*

38 "ealle manlican dæda / awrat on anre cartan and beworhte mid leade" (530–1). A similar use of the verb *bewyrcan* (meaning "to cover with wax") is found in the Old English *Orosius,* when the Greek Demaratus discovers that Xerxes has secretly been building ships: "se þæt facn to his cyþþe gebodade 7 hit on anum brede awrat 7 siþþan mid weaxe beworhte" (he [Demaratus] made known that treachery to his people and wrote it on a tablet and then covered it with wax) (Bately, ed., *Old English Orosius,* 2.5.46.9–10.

39 Skeat, *LS* III.535: ealla.

40 MS: me. Corona emends to "ne" by comparison with the analogous Latin text: "[t]u autem, sancte Dei, sigillum ne amoueas" (Corona 217). Jane Roberts makes the same argument in "Rich Woman."

41 Corona 534–7.

I, a sinful one, wrote all my sins on this vellum, and I came to you, beloved one, and I ask you for love of God that you not release the seal, but erase the sins, interceding for me to the Lord.

We are not told what her sins were, nor are we shown the content of her document. Instead, Ælfric focuses on the materiality of the written message, which has been prepared as a quasi-legal document by the woman herself (which is unusual) and authenticated by means of seals. The woman cannot unseal the document herself, for reasons that are more symbolic than logical – she cannot release herself from her sins, because only God can do that – and she does not want Basil to unseal her document and thus know her sin, either. Depending on its form, the lead seal could authenticate the document and identify its author, but the seal's primary function is to offer the woman protection.[42] If the seal has been broken, the woman will know the text has been read. As long as the seal remains whole, she trusts that her sins will remain secret. Though she has written a confession, she does not want it to be made public, or even to be read by Basil. Like the poor woman in my first example, she recognizes the power of Basil as intercessor or mediator, and she believes in his power to obliterate the document (even without knowing its contents), as he did the contract the youth made with the devil.

Basil tells the woman that God is the one who erases sins, but he takes the document, and the next day, when he gives the document back to the woman, all but one of the sins has been removed.[43] She cries, but he sends her to Ephrem, a holy man living in the desert. She shows him the document and asks him to erase the final sin, but he tells her that Basil can do it better. She returns to the city but, when she gets back, Basil is already dead. Upset with Basil, she falls to the ground, but then a miracle occurs:

Heo wearp þa mid þam þæt gewrit on ða bære / and cydde þam mannum be hire misdædum. / Þa wolde an ðæra preosta witan þa synne, / and sceawode þa cartan, and clypode to ðam wife: / "To hwi swincst þu, la wif? Þeos carte is adylegod."[44]

---

42 Roberts argues that the seal is less important than that the document is sealed ("Rich Woman," 5).
43 Old English *adiligian* can mean "to erase" as well as "to blot out."
44 Corona 654–8.

Then with that, she threw the writing on the bier [of Basil] and confessed to the people about her misdeeds. Then one of the priests wanted to know the sin, and [he] looked at the document and called to the woman "Why, oh woman, do you struggle? This document has been erased."

The key word here is *cydde*, "made known, swore, or confessed." Although it may seem that her final sin is forgiven when the saint's dead body makes physical contact with the record of her sin, I would, in fact, argue the opposite. It is only when the sinner makes public the heretofore private record of her sins by proclaiming it to the gathered mourners that she may be absolved, and her record of sin, having lost its former purpose, is transformed into a blank sheet, its emptiness now a record of her purity. When the document is wiped clean, it erases all record and knowledge of her sins, not just from her document, but from Ælfric's story as well – the *Life* never directly tells us, even at the moment of her confession, exactly what sins she has committed, unlike *Mary of Egypt*, which preserves the story of Mary's sinful past. In this way, the letter of the sinful woman in *Basil* is similar to the letter that falls to the altar in the story of St Giles.[45] Charlemagne has committed a sin so great that he cannot bring himself to confess it to anyone. When Giles prays for forgiveness on Charlemagne's behalf, a letter appears saying that Charlemagne has been forgiven. Although other versions explain the sin as incest, the Old English *Life* never specifies it, thus preserving Charlemagne's privacy while simultaneously recording and publicizing his forgiveness and Giles's successful intercession. As a sealed, private document, the letter written by the sinful woman in *Basil* bears witness to her sins, which cannot be entirely forgiven, but once she makes her sins public, there is no need for the private document. Instead of being a private record of private sins, it becomes figuratively a record of absolution, and literally a record of erasure. Moreover, this shift from sealed, private, written confession to public, spoken penitence marks her sin's shift from the permanence of an official, written document to the transience of speech, which cannot, in a pre-sound-recording age, be preserved in unmediated form. The deed of confessing her sins aloud allows the woman's record to escape archivability.[46]

---

45 Giles is also known as Ægidius. The eleventh-century Old English *Life of Giles* is edited and translated by Elaine Treharne, *The Old English Life of St Nicholas with the Old English Life of St Giles*. The account of the miraculous letter comprises lines 444–63.

46 Gitelman might say that the woman successfully escapes having a "permanent record" (*Always Already New*, 44).

The woman's oral confession of her sins, though it does not conform to all the standards for official confession, in many ways mimics the requirements for lay confession in Anglo-Saxon England. This is significant because it reinforces that the forgiveness of sins is achieved via a combination of confession and erasure of the letter, whereas unconfessed sins remain permanently marked on parchment. Anglo-Saxon texts provide some information about how lay persons were or were not expected to confess and perform penance. It was not until 1215 that people were officially required to confess once a year, but Allen Frantzen has demonstrated that confession was encouraged in Anglo-Saxon England well before 1215, though perhaps only for major sins.[47] According to Frantzen, Ælfric "insisted on oral confession," unless the sin was minor.[48] In his *Catholic Homilies*, Ælfric explains that sins must be confessed to a priest, and that making private confession to God without also confessing to a priest will not be sufficient for the forgiveness of sins. Ælfric addresses those who believe that they may confess to God without also confessing to a priest, warning them that

Sume men wenað þæt him genihtsumie to fulfremedum læcedome: gif hi heora synna mid onbryrdre heortan gode anum andettað. 7 ne þurfon nanum sacerde geandettan gif hi yfeles geswicað: ac gif heora wena soð wære þonne nolde drihten asendan þone þe he sylf gehælde to þam sacerde mid ænigre lace.[49]

Some people think that it will suffice for them as a complete remedy if they confess their sins with a contrite heart to God alone, and need not confess to any priest if they cease from evil. But if their expectation were true, then the Lord would not have wanted to send the one whom he himself healed to the priest with any offering.

---

47 Frantzen, *Literature of Penance*, 15–17. See also Meens, *Penance in Medieval Europe*. Meens teases out the tension between the fact that many late Anglo-Saxon sources emphasize the important of penance, while "the manuscript evidence does not really substantiate this view" (163). He concludes that penance must have been of special importance to those affiliated with the Benedictine Reform (including Wulfstan and Ælfric).

48 Frantzen, *Literature of Penance*, 158.

49 *CH I*, 8, 243.68–72. Frantzen connects Ælfric's views on confession and penance to earlier Frankish traditions (*Literature of Penance*, 158).

The sinful woman's tearful confession at Basil's bier, then, conforms to Ælfric's mandate that confession must not be kept private but must be made to a priest. Although the woman has written her confession, it is not complete, and the sins are not erased, until she makes her sins known first to Basil and then to the priests surrounding his bier. In late Anglo-Saxon England, particularly serious sins required public penance, so the woman's earlier repentance, and even her written confession, would not meet the requirements for full forgiveness of sins.[50] She must tell her story to the assembled mourners for her sins to be erased.

In fact, many early medieval and Biblical texts feature the erasure of sins where disclosure of sins both metaphorically and also literally erases the record, giving the penitent a clean slate. These acts of erasure may be figured as positive or negative. God's mercy will blot out or erase sins in Psalm 50, while sinners will be removed from the book of life, as in Psalm 68.[51] Likewise, Ælfric (perhaps echoing Colossians 2:13–14) says that Christ's ascension *erases* the chirograph damning humans to mortal punishment: "By his ascension that chirograph of our condemnation is destroyed and the sentence of our corruption is removed."[52] Just as Basil tore to pieces the contract the youth made with the devil, Christ's ascension destroys the record of Adam and Eve's curse. The metaphor of the heart as wax tablet or parchment was also common in the Middle Ages, the idea being that positive images or ideas could be impressed in its wax, while negative characteristics could be scraped clean. By the twelfth century,

---

50   Meens, *Penance in Medieval Europe*, 164.

51   Ps 50:3, 11: "Miserere mei Deus secundum misericordiam tuam iuxta multitudinem miserationum tuarum dele iniquitates meas … Averte faciem tuam a peccatis meis et omnes iniquitates meas dele" (Have mercy on me, O God, according to thy great mercy, and according to the multitude of thy tender mercies blot out my iniquity … Turn away thy face from my sins, and blot out all my iniquities). Ps 68:29: "Deleantur de libro viventium et cum iustis non scribantur" (Let them be blotted out of the book of the living, and with the just let them not be written).

52   "Mid his upstige is adylegod þæt cyrografum ure genyðerunge. 7 se cwyde ure brosnunge is awend" (*CH I*, 21, 348.81–2). Colossians 2:13–14 reads "Et vos cum mortui essetis in delictis et praeputio carnis vestrae convivificavit cum illo donans vobis omnia delicta. delens quod adversum nos erat chirografum decretis, quod erat contrarium nobis et ipsum tulit de medio adfigens illud cruci" (And you, when you were dead in your sins and the uncircumcision of your flesh, he hath quickened together with him, forgiving you all offences, blotting out the handwriting of the decree that was against us, which was contrary to us, and he hath taken the same out of the way, fastening it to the cross).

Bernard of Clairvaux could lament that the parchment of memory could not easily be scraped clean by human hands, because only God's forgiveness could remove the stain of ink (read: sins) without inducing amnesia:

> In what way will my life be displaced from my memory? A thin, fragile parchment deeply soaks up the ink; by what craft may it be erased? ... In vain should I try to scrape [the ink] away; the parchment rips before the messy letters are erased ... Short of [amnesia], what scraper could bring it about that my memory would remain whole and yet its stains be dissolved? Only that living, powerful word, more cutting than any two-edged sword: "Your sins are forgiven you."[53]

Sins imagined as dismayingly indelible ink also feature prominently in the Old English version of Bede's *Ecclesiastical History*. In Book Five, a Mercian layman who would not confess has a deathbed vision of two angels carrying his book of good deeds (which is quite small) being confronted by a group of devils carrying his book of sins (which is enormous). In despair, the man believes it is too late for him to be saved, and he soon dies. The book of sins is written in dark letters, Bede explains, because the man "obscured and blotted out" all the good deeds of his youth with his sins.[54] If only the man had heeded Psalm 31, Bede laments, he would have obscured his sins rather than his good deeds:

> Þær he ða wið þon ða gedwolan his cneohthade gereccan gemde in giguðhade 7 ða þurh gode dæde from Godes eagum ahwerfan, þonne meahte he ðara rime geðeoded bion, be ðam se sealmscop cwæð: *Beati quorum remisse sunt, et cetera*. Þa beoð eadge þe heora wonnesse forlætne beoð 7 þara þe synna bewrigene beoð.[55]

If he had taken care in his youth to correct the errors of his youth and to turn them away from God's eyes through good deeds, then he might have been joined to the number about which the psalmist says: *Beati quorum remisse sunt, et cetera*. Blessed are they who are forgiven for their iniquity, and whose sins are covered.

---

53 *Ad clericos* VX.28. Translation quoted in Carruthers, *Craft of Thought*, 96.
54 "he ... ealle ðurh his unrihte dæde aðeostrade 7 fordilegade" (Miller, ed. and trans., *Old English Version of Bede*, 5.14.440–2.31–1).
55 5.14.442.1–6 (emphasis in original).

In other words, sins may be like excessive quantities of dark ink, covering over the record of good deeds with the stain of sin. But on the other hand, as Psalm 31 reveals, sins may also be concealed (the verb for "covered" used in the Latin psalm, "tego," can also mean "protected, as by a roof") – that is, protected from view – not through deceit, but by God's mercy.

As these examples suggest, forgetting and forgiveness cannot be achieved by erasure alone. Carruthers reminds us that forgetting is not accomplished by erasure, but by overwriting, replacing, or even covering one's sins with a new narrative of redemption. Even "forgetting" can be a re-writing, creating a new association in the memory network.[56] In sum, life is imagined as a draft that can be rewritten. The epistolary documents of a person's life may be records, but these records are not necessarily permanent. By confession and repentance, one may achieve erasure (aided by God) or overwrite sins with a record of forgiveness. In either act (erasure or blotting out), the penitent's sins escape publication and archivability in the public record, just as the sinful woman's past in *Basil* and Charlemagne's sins in *Giles* are not recorded by the hagiographer (unlike Mary of Egypt's oral story of her life, told to Zosimus, which is recorded in her *Life*). This helps explain why we find so many *written* confessions in saints' lives: unlike oral confessions performed before a priest, written confessions can be *visibly* destroyed as well as recorded and stored. Finally, while sinners' stories may be written by the sinners themselves (as is the case with the woman in *Basil*) or by others (as in the confession that falls to the altar in *Giles*), their confessions are rewritten as stories of the *saints'* miraculous intercessions.

To return to my earlier question, how did Anglo-Saxons imagine preserving and/or displaying the miracle of erasure? The miracle of a healed body is proven by the *absence* of illness, wounds, or deformities, but a healed body sometimes also produces a physical token, as in the crutches hung on the wall by grateful recipients of Swithun's healing miracles in the Old English *Life of St Swithun*.[57] In the later Middle Ages, miracles, even intangible ones, might be commemorated by pilgrim badges and other souvenirs, and *ex-votos* might commemorate the healing of a body part by modelling it in wax.[58] But holy erasure, and holy absence, rather than

---

56 Carruthers, *Craft of Thought*, 53.
57 In addition to Skeat, *LS* XXI, see Lapidge, *Cult of St Swithun*, 575–609. The description of the crutch offerings is in chapter 27.
58 Bynum, *Christian Materiality*, 22, 150.

presence, are much harder to memorialize. Moreover, a letter typically bears witness to its own authority by *presence* – of seals, the familiar rhetorical style of an author, and so on. Likewise, one could argue that the book of the man's sins in the example from Bede bears witness by the presence of the dark letters rather than by hidden or covered sins that have been forgiven. What makes *Basil*'s last epistolary document puzzling is that it bears witness via *absence*, not presence. *Basil* seems to actively resist any suggestion that the woman's parchment retains any trace of the text once written on it. Although scraping parchment clean may in reality sometimes leave behind palimpsests or visible (if faint) scars on the manuscript, and blotting out text would leave a dark stain, the miracle here involves perfect erasure of textual and human corpuses. This is the nature of the ideal confession: "it seeks only to cancel itself. A confession does not aspire to inscription as a permanent text."[59] Sometimes the absence of proof generates the anxious proliferation of other texts attesting the miracles (letters saying "I was there" or "I saw this happen"), supplementing the non-existent physical evidence. But in *Basil*, the *Life* speaks for itself. What should we make of the fact that this document produces no corroborating witnesses? Perhaps this has to do with the nature of faith itself. Faith is believing something you cannot or have not seen, as *Abgar* also teaches. After Basil's death, the woman remains the only living person who has *seen* her confession (because Ephrem had refused to accept the document from her). Like the priests gathered at Basil's bier, Ælfric's audience must take it on faith that the blank document once held writing. Our contact with the divine remains mediated, deferred, while the woman's wishes are granted – her sins are removed from her permanent record and escape circulation and archivability.[60]

Entering the Archive: The *Seven Sleepers* and Documentary Memory

In the previous section, I explored how the erasure and destruction of epistolary documents could record a saint's miraculous intervention while simultaneously resisting the sin being archived or the document made relic. In this section, I turn to the anonymous Old English *Legend of the*

---

59 Wright, "Historical Inscription," 7.

60 As discussed in the previous chapter, Mary of Egypt tries (and fails) to accomplish something similar, hoping her letter written in the ground will control her future narrative, rather than ceding control to Zosimus.

Seven Sleepers, which contains an epistolary document as well as a collection of coins, seals, and bodies, all of which attempt to escape the archive, but cannot. While miraculous confessional documents like the letter that falls to the altar in *Giles* or the sinful woman's sealed confession in *Basil* prove their miracles by their destruction or silence, the martyrology buried with the seven sleepers can attest to the nature of their preservation only if the document itself remains legible. That is, rather than being suppressed, its text must be recorded both by the two witnesses who produce it and by the anonymous author of the *Legend*. It is a document that functions like a letter that must be allowed to be transmitted to future audiences, at the same time inviting the mediation of the human agent who transmits it to be foregrounded rather than suppressed. Rather than erasure, then, this section of the chapter examines collection, preservation, and display, asking how Anglo-Saxons conceived the archive as constituted not just by written documents, but by other media as well. As I argue, the Old English *Legend* reveals how matter archived in a cave (bodies, coins, text, seals) bears witness in a way that an individual speaker never could, how archives fix or stabilize narrative, and finally, how the archive demands its own destruction in order that it may become replicable. The bodies of the sleepers cannot be removed from the cave or they will lose their authenticity, but the account of the materials found in the cave – fixed in the archive – *can* be transmitted, circulated, and repeated.

In the anonymous Old English *Legend of the Seven Sleepers*, an epistolary-like document is transmitted across time in order to serve as a witness to and record of a miracle performed by God. As I noted in the introduction, Anglo-Saxon epistolarity operates across a broad range of genres. In previous chapters I have examined letters in sermons, hagiography, and prose romance. In my final case study, I look not at how letters are embedded in other genres, but how the letter's characteristic form and function influenced related documentary genres, and how deeply epistolarity penetrated Anglo-Saxon documentary culture. The *Legend of the Seven Sleepers* has attracted critical attention primarily because it is one of four works in Ælfric's *Lives of Saints* believed not to have been written by Ælfric.[61] The legend, which enjoyed widespread popularity throughout the

---

61 It appears in the early eleventh-century BL Cotton Julius E.vii, and fragments survive from BL Cotton Otho B.x (first half of the eleventh century). Magennis describes the Old English version as "a free and considerably expanded rendering of a text of the Latin version *BHL* no. 2316" (*Anonymous Old English Legend*, 6, 11).

Middle Ages, describes how God saves seven Christian youths from persecution and death by inducing a miraculously long sleep, then wakes them nearly four hundred years later in order to disprove an anti-Resurrection heresy current in the fifth century.[62] In the tradition represented by the Old English *Legend*, an account of the seven sleepers is secretly written on a lead tablet by two faithful Christians who have been ordered to seal the cave in which the seven are sleeping. The tablet is placed in a case, sealed with two silver seals, and hidden with the sleepers before the cave itself is sealed. When the cave is accidentally discovered hundreds of years later, and the sleepers finally wake from their miraculous slumber, the casket containing the martyrology is publicly opened in the presence of witnesses in order to confirm the sleepers' identity and prove God's miracle.

The martyrology is not a letter per se, but I include it in this study because it displays many of the characteristics of letters and epistolary acts. First, it is a written document (*gewrit*) that is intended to address a person or persons who are separated from the authors by time (rather than the more usual space). Although the document remains stationary, it is carried across time to its addressees, much like Mary of Egypt's letter discussed in chapter 3. The author of the *Life* reminds its readers of the future audience of the document more than once, saying that the casket had been sealed with silver seals "þæt þa insægla wæron eft to swutelunge hwæt man þærinne funde, þonne se tima gewurðe eall swa God wolde þæt þa gewurðan sceolde" (so that the seals would be evidence of what someone might find therein, when the time would come just as God desired that it should happen).[63] Second, the document (or rather, the case in which it is placed) is sealed, which, as I have discussed above, was associated in Anglo-Saxon England with letters more often and earlier than with charters. Although

---

62 The text's chronology is confused here. The *Legend* repeatedly asserts that the sleepers were in the cave for 372 years (ll. 443–5, ll. 644–6), though they enter the cave during the third-century reign of Decius and are awoken in the fifth century (ibid., p. 71).

63 Ibid., 697–9. When Theodorus and Rufinus first bury the tablet, the author says they do so "swa man into ðam scræfe gan sceolde, þæt hit mid him þærinne læge to swutelunge oð ðone byre þe hi God ælmihtig awehte and hi mancynne swutelian wolde, þæt ealle men ðurh ðæt gewritt eft ongytan mihton hwæt þa halgan wæron þe man ðærinne funde, þonne þæt Godes wylla wære" (So that when one might go into the cave, it [the tablet] would lie therein with them as evidence until the time when almighty God should awaken them and reveal them to mankind, so that all people might understand by that writing what the saints were whom one would find therein, when it would be God's will) (306–10). All quotations from *Seven Sleepers* will come from Magennis's edition, cited by line number. For the earlier EETS edition, see Skeat, *LS* XXIII.

the martyrology lacks a salutation, it is signed by the witnesses or authors (Theodorus and Rufinus) who produced it. While the martyrology is not a traditional letter, the sophisticated ways in which it adapts the features and functions of letters demonstrate the widespread influence of epistolarity on Anglo-Saxon literary culture. As in *Basil*, the *Legend of the Seven Sleepers* also includes a more recognizable letter: at the end of the legend, Bishop Marinus writes a letter to the emperor Theodosius, telling him to come quickly to the site because of the miracle. This document, clearly a letter (it is called an *ærendgewrit* in line 728, and it opens with a salutation formula), is written in order to spread word of the miracle more widely; more crucially, it reveals Marinus's belief that a person has to witness the tablet and the sleepers' bodies for himself or herself. He cannot transport the evidence of the lead tablet or the resurrected bodies to the emperor, or they will lose their authenticity. They must remain in the place they were found, the archive of the cave.

Along with the sleepers' bodies and the sealed tablet, the cave also contains coins carried by the saints when they first lived. It is the discovery of these coins that leads to the discovery of the miracle. When the sleepers awake, they send one of their number, Malchus, to buy some bread (plaintively hoping he might find better bread than he did on what they believe was the day before). When Malchus attempts to purchase bread at the marketplace, the merchants are surprised by his coins, which they recognize are quite old. They accuse him of having dug up a treasure hoard, which Malchus vehemently denies. In actuality, the coins *have* been dug up by the shepherds who revealed the cave, just as Malchus has been, though he does not know it. Like the sleepers' bodies, and like the seals on the casket (whose image and form the coins might well echo),[64] the coins are preserved, revealed, and interpreted as signs of their authenticity. Eventually, Malchus is brought before the bishop and reeve, who say that the coins were struck in the days of Emperor Decius, and have his appearance and name on them.[65] Moreover, the reeve says, "Here each person who is able to understand anything of arithmetic can see, and the superscription of these coins here openly reveals to all people that it is even more than 372 years since this money was circulating on earth, and all

---

64 There is evidence that some Anglo-Saxon coins and seals shared similar images. See Heslop, "English Seals," 3.

65 *Anonymous Old English Legend*, 603–5.

people procured for themselves what they wanted with it."[66] Taken out of circulation, deprived of their use value, the coins have become evidence or a record of what the merchants incorrectly believe is Malchus's theft. Like the saints' bodies, the coins have not marked the passage of time by decaying, but by being preserved unchanged. If coins have become records, however, this scene also reminds the audience that records can be misinterpreted. Although the reeve claims the superscription is so clear that it should be obvious to all people (*eallum mannum*) that the coins are nearly four hundred years old, it is *mis*read as proof that Malchus has plundered a gold hoard.[67] Malchus attempts to prove his identity by more standard means but, in a heartbreaking turn, when he is asked to name family and friends who might testify to his identity, he finds there are none living who know him. Whereas Charlemagne in the *Life of St Giles* and the sinful woman in *Basil* were trying to escape their records, external supplementary media (coins, seals, casket, martyrology) are the only means to provide the seven sleepers with the record Malchus so desperately seeks. Held in a purse, sealed within the cave along with the sleepers, gathered into the archival space the cave constitutes, the coins, like seals on a letter, authenticate Malchus's identity and testify to the authenticity of the miracle.

In the next part of this chapter, I explore the media of the cave more closely, moving from the seals, to the lead tablet, and then to the bodies of the sleepers. The author of the Old English *Legend* took special interest in these materials, expanding on his Latin source at several key moments. Possibly confused by the Latin *quator*, the Old English author added a long section on the reminting of coins that reveals knowledge of Anglo-Saxon coin practice under King Edgar.[68] In the scenes describing the creation and discovery of the lead tablet, the Old English *Legend*'s emphasis

---

66 "Her mæg geseon ælc man þe telcræftas ænig gescead can, and þisra peninga ofergewrit her eallum mannum openlice þæt swutelað, þæt hit mare is for an þonne þreo hund geara and twa and hundseofontig wintra syððan ðyllic feoh wæs farende on eorðan and ealle men mid him tiledon, and þæt wæs sona on þam fyrmestan dagan þe Decius se casere to rixianne begann, and swilces feos nu nan dæl nahwær nis amang þam feo þe we on þysum dagum notiað and ure neode mide bicgað" (ibid., 642–9).

67 The reeve is otherwise represented in this passage as a shrewd practitioner of the law, so it is all the more surprising that he should stumble here. For the reeve's knowledge of contemporary Anglo-Saxon legal practice, see Catherine Cubitt, who argues, contra Patrick Wormald, that Anglo-Saxons did make use of lawbooks for legal administration ("As the Lawbook Teaches").

68 Whitelock, "Numismatic Interest." See also Cubitt, "As the Lawbook Teaches."

on the materiality of the text also goes beyond that of its Latin source, repeatedly emphasizing how the tablet is made, sealed, and enclosed in a case before being sealed into the cave along with the sleepers. The initial account of the production of the document adds several details that the Latin text withholds until the discovery scene. When the martyrology is first made, the Latin text mentions only that the document is written on lead tablets and sealed:

> ut cogitarent scribere martirium sanctorum in *paginis plumbeis* et cum reliquiis sanctorum deponere illud in medio lapidum constitutorum in ore speluncae ... Et sic cogitauerunt duo socii fidelissimi imperatoris *scribentes litteras, et sigillantes* deposuerunt secrete.

> They [Theodorus and Rufinus] planned to write the saints' martyrdom on *tablets of lead* and to set this with the remains of the saints in the midst of the stones placed in the mouth of the cave ... And thus the two companions, most faithful followers of the emperor, planned, and *they wrote the document and sealed it* and deposited it secretly.[69]

The Old English text significantly expands on the appearance of the lead tablet, describing it as engraved with writing, and adding that the tablet is placed in a casket that is also sealed with two silver seals:

> hi woldon ðisra haligra martyra martyrrace awritan and þæt gewrit mid þam halgum ðærinne lecgan ... And hi ða twegen getreowfæste wæron: dydon þærrihte eall swa hi ær gemynton: eodon into þam scræfe dearnunga onsundran, and þas halgan martyrrace eall swa heo gewearð *on anum leadenum tabulan ealle mid stafon agrofon,* and *hi ðæt gewrit mid twam sylfrenan inseglum on anre teage geinseglodon* and wið þa halgan ðærinne swiðe digollice ledon, and ðæs scræfes locstan hi wel fæste beclysdon.[70]

> they wished to write the account of the martyrdom of these holy martyrs and to lay the writing therein with the saints ... And those two were faithful. Straightaway they did just as they had intended: they secretly went into the cave alone, and they *inscribed* this holy martyrology *with letters on a lead*

---

69 Magennis, ed., *Anonymous Old English Legend*, ll. 154–9 (emphasis added). Translation of the Latin is from Magennis.
70 Magennis, ed., *Anonymous Old English Legend*, 304–15 (emphasis added).

tablet just as it had happened, and *they sealed the writing into a casket with two silver seals* and very secretly laid it therein with the saints, and they very securely closed up the sealing stone of the cave.

By revealing that the tablet is placed within a casket and sealed with silver seals before the cave itself is sealed with the final stone, the Old English text not only emphasizes the materials with which the document was produced, but it also prepares its audience for the idea that the cave is not just an enclosure, but an archive. This awareness of the layers and layers of seals with which the document is secured also reassures the audience that there is no way the martyrology could have been tampered with before it was opened by the reeve and bishop.

It is perhaps unsurprising that the Old English author would emphasize the multiple levels at which the document is sealed.[71] After all, his audience has no means of determining the proof of his account – Anglo-Saxons living hundreds of years after the sleepers reawakened would have had little opportunity to examine the text or seals for themselves. Nevertheless, the remarkable attention to seals here reflects more than just the mark of an

---

71 On the Roman seal box – a small metal container tied closed with strings that were then secured by a ring or cone seal – which may have been used to secure letters, see Holmes, "Seal Boxes from Roman London"; Derks and Roymans, "Seal-boxes and the Spread of Latin Literacy; and Vikan and Nesbitt, *Security in Byzantium*, 23. Such a container would have been more secure than a seal alone. On Anglo-Saxon evidence for seals and seal matrices, see Heslop, "English Seals." In an essay tracing the meanings, both literal and metaphorical, of *insegel*, Jane Roberts discusses the sealed casket of the Old English *Legend* briefly, suggesting that while *insegel* could mean simply "lock," here it is most likely to mean the impression made from king's ring ("What Did Anglo-Saxon Seals Seal When?" 149–50). Roberts does not explain why she thinks this seal must have been produced by a ring, much less a king's ring. According to Elisabeth Okasha, although signet rings were used as seals elsewhere, very few rings from Anglo-Saxon England have been found ("Anglo-Saxon Inscribed Rings"). However, as we have seen in chapter 3, Arcestrate's father seals the three suitors' offers with his ring before sending them to her. Signet rings do become more popular in twelfth-century England; on their re-use of Roman gems, see Henig, "Re-Use and Copying." Perhaps the most famous Anglo-Saxon reference to a seal accompanying a letter to prove the identity of the letter's author is in the Old English translation of Augustine's *Soliloquies*, where Augustine's *sceadwisnes* (reason) rebukes him "geþenc nu gyf ðines hlafordes ærendgewrit and hys insegel to ðe cymð, hwæðer þu mæge cweðan þæt ðu hine be ðam ongytan ne mægæ, ne hys willan þæron gecnawan ne mæge" (consider now if your lord's letter and his seal should come to you, whether you might say that you could not recognize him by that, nor understand his will therein) (Carnicelli, ed., *King Alfred's Version of St. Augustine's Soliloquies*, 62.22–5).

author anxious to prove his case. Seals, unlike some relics, are transformed by their use. The enclosure of the cave and seals can function as proof only for as long as the seals hold. Once broken, a seal may be preserved as a token or relic of the event, but the unsealing of the cave can never be recreated, and the casket cannot be resealed. Once broken, the seal loses its use value and enters the world of the symbolic. While the perfect wholeness of the sleepers' bodies confirms their resurrection, the broken seal confirms Bishop Marinus's testimony to the emperor, and ultimately the hagiographer's account of the discovery of the sleepers, by virtue of its having been broken. Anglo-Saxon seals sometimes had inscriptions or images that might have identified their owners (though portraits tended to represent stereotypes rather than individuals). If the image and/or inscription on the seal matrix or ring identified Theodorus and Rufinus, or if the style of the seal could be recognized as several hundred years out of fashion, then the seal, like the coins, could also speak to the age of the sleepers.

Finally, like both contact relics and letters, seals also offered the fantasy of physically touching the absent being who handled the document, seal, or matrix. Describing twelfth-century French seals, Brigitte Bedos-Rezak argues that at various points in their development, seals offered both something akin to the standardization of mass production and also the reassurance of intimate contact with the unique individual whose sign the seal was: "Seal impressions were products of mechanical reproductive techniques which assured the multiplication of identical images ... That contact between the sealing person's body and the seal, which had originally been so important a factor in establishing the seal's authority, thus came to be displaced by the relationship between image and image."[72] While I am particularly struck by the affective possibilities implied here, what Bedos-Rezak is arguing is that by this admittedly later stage in their development, seals had come to signify not by their relationship to the owner but by the fact that a seal impression could be compared against other seal impressions known to have been produced by the same matrix. The ability to produce copies rendered the original less important, or, rather, all impressions became "originals" as well as copies. I would argue that two aspects of the seals are important to the author of the Old English *Legend*: both physical contact with a unique object that was once touched, perhaps even lovingly cradled, by the absent writer; and the possibility of multiple identical copies produced by a single matrix. If seals (or their

---

72 Bedos-Rezak, *When Ego Was Imago*, 202.

impressions, at least) can be repeated, then what other materials produced in connection with the miracle of the sleepers might be iterable? And once iterable, how might they be circulated or stored as part of the transmission of the story of the sleepers?

What initially drew me to the *Legend* was the martyrology inscribed on the lead tablet, how it imagines communication across time and space, and how it is simultaneously a written record of historical events and an object whose burial and resurrection is clearly meant to parallel that of the sleepers, with similar vocabulary being used to describe the sealing of the document and the sealing of the tomb. Turning to the scene in which the tablet is discovered, we can re-examine both how the tablet might have been understood by Anglo-Saxon audiences and how the Old English author adds details to the discovery scene that emphasize the connection between the lead tablet and the sleepers' bodies.

After Malchus leads the bishop and reeve back to the cave, the tablet is unsealed in a public ceremony. Bishop Marinus, the reeve, and other witnesses enter the cave, and when they get inside,

> þa gemetton hi on þa swiðran hand ane teage, seo wæs geinsæglod mid twam sylfrenan insæglan þe þa twægen getreowfæste menn ðærinne ledon þa Decius se casere het þæt scræf forwyrcan, swa we ær beforan rehton, þæt þa insægla wæron eft to swutelunge hwæt man þærinne funde, þonne se tima gewurðe eall swa God wolde þæt þa gewurðan sceolde ...
>
> Syððan hi ealle þær ætforan þam bisceope gegaderode wæron, þa feng se portgerefa to þære tege, and he on gewitnysse ealles folces hi uninsæglode, and hi sona unhlidode, and þærinne funde *ane leadene tabulan* eall awritene, and þa hi openlice rædde. Þa com he to þære *stæfræwe* þær he þæt word funde awriten, and he hit þa rædde eall swa, þæt hi fram Decie þam casere flugon, and his ehtnysse þoledon: "Maximianus, wæs þæs burhgerefan sunu, Malchus, Martinianus, Dionisius, Iohannes, Seraphion, Constantinus. Ðys synt þa halgan þe æfter Decies þæs caseres bebode on þyson scræfe wæron mid weorcstane beworhte; and wytt Theodorus and Rufinus heora martyrrace awriton and hi herinne mid þyson halgan uppon anum stane ledon."
>
> And þa þa hi þæt gewrit ræddon, hi ealle wundrigende wæron, and God ælmihtigne anon mode wuldredon and mærsodon for þam micclum wundrum þe he þær geswutolode and geuþe eallum mannum; and hi ealle anre stefne Godes þa halgan martyras heredon þær hi on þam scræfe *ealle on geræwe sæton*, and eall heora nebwlite wæron swilce rose and lilie.[73]

---

73 Magennis, ed., *Anonymous Old English Legend*, 694–717 (emphasis added).

then on the right side [of the cave] they [Marinus and the other witnesses] found a case, which had been sealed with two silver seals, which the two faithful men had placed therein when the emperor Decius commanded the cave to be sealed, as we said before, so that the seals would be evidence of what someone might find therein, when the time would come just as God desired that it should happen …

After they all were gathered before the bishop, then the town reeve took the case, and in the witness of all the people he unsealed it, and immediately opened it, and discovered therein *a lead tablet* written all over, and he read it publicly. Then he came to the *row of letters* where he found that account written, and he read it also, that they fled from Emperor Decius, and suffered his persecution: "Maximianus, who was the son of the city reeve, Malchus, Martinianus, Dionysius, Johannes, Seraphion, Constantine. These are the saints who according to the command of the emperor Decius were sealed in this cave with stones, and we Theodorus and Rufinus wrote their martyrology and placed it herein with these saints upon a stone."

And when they read the document, they were all wondering at [it], and with one mind they glorified and praised God almighty for the great wonders which he had revealed and granted to all people; and they all with one voice praised the holy martyrs of God where they sat *all in a row* in the cave, and all their faces were like roses and lilies.

The witnesses must unlock layer after layer of seals and cases before they are finally able to read the text, which turns out to be relatively unimpressive. The document has been carefully witnessed by Theodorus and Rufinus, although even their act of witnessing is diminished by comparison with the finding and unsealing of the tablet. What, exactly, did the Old English author or his audience picture when they read or heard this tablet described? Although I strongly believe that the document is meant to be understood within the context of epistolary culture, I also think that the lead tablet sealed within the cave is meant to suggest lead tablets found in Anglo-Saxon burials that identified the bodies found there.[74] In other words, the tablet is

---

74 In addition to funerary inscriptions on other materials, such as stone, Okasha cites four inscribed lead plates from Anglo-Saxon England, as well as other inscribed lead such as funerary crosses ("Third Supplement"). Jill Hamilton Clements has also connected this scene in *Seven Sleepers* to lead funeral plaques buried with the dead in late Anglo-Saxon England in "Inscribing the Saintly Dead." She argues that inscriptional materials make corpses more legible than the body alone can. I wish to thank her for sharing this pre-publication work with me.

not just an authenticating witness, it is also a finding aid, meant to help catalogue the contents of the cave. The choice of the word *tabula/tabule* is also
significant. Elsewhere in the Old English corpus, it is almost exclusively
used to designate the tablets on which the Ten Commandments were written, and the Latin *tabula* is often glossed by other, more familiar Old
English words for tablet. Why, then, might the author of the *Legend* have
chosen *tabula* rather than *weaxbred* or *bred* (writing tablet)? Above all,
tabula suggests permanence. The martyrology is not a wax tablet used for
making notes or drafting documents, but a potentially permanent record.
The association with the Ten Commandments also lends the lead tablet authority, linking it to both divine authority and the law.

Once again, it is not the content of the message that is important. What
matters above all is the physicality of the proof, both of the written tablet
and of the physical bodies of the sleepers, which now turn red and white,
signalling their miraculous vitality. Just as the alphabetic letters of the martyrology are written in a row on the tablet (in a *stæfræwe* [705]), the sleepers sit "ealle on geræwe" (716–17) while they listen to the account written
on the tablet, having been transformed from living bodies into the text itself.[75] Their bodies, unmarked by death, are also meant to be read. The
bodies of the seven sleepers themselves bear witness to the miracle. Under
pressure from Decius to renounce their Christianity, their bodies were
formerly marked by sorrow: the saints had lost weight and physical beau-
ty,[76] and, when captured and brought before Decius, they were tearful
and covered in dirt from their many prayers.[77] After the tomb is opened,
they are transformed from dirt- and tear-stained bodies of anxious men
into light-filled, healthy bodies of reawakened saints. In a sense, the message of their preservation is recorded on their bodies themselves, which
are "carried through time" to speak to their fifth-century discoverers.[78]
In this transformation, however, the seven are denied the ability to speak

---

75 Neither of these phrases appears in the corresponding Latin passage.

76 Magennis, ed., *Anonymous Old English Legend*, 112–16.

77 Ibid., 137–40.

78 I take the phrase "carried through time" from Eileen A. Joy, who reads the excessive
    torture witnessed and suffered by the seven sleepers as a way for late Anglo-Saxon audi-
    ences to process similar atrocities committed by the Vikings ("Old English *Seven Sleep-
    ers*," 86). In the text's attention to the emotional experiences of Malchus she locates "the
    development of a certain *thick* subjectivity through *eros* … [which refers not to] sexual
    love but to what Freud termed the libido, or 'love force,' without which no interest or
    investment in the world is possible for individuals" (80; emphasis in original). Joy argues

as individuals, bearing witness to their own stories. Their voices are subsumed by the proliferation of documents that claim to speak for them – first the martyrology, then Marinus's letter, then the *Legend* itself. When the seven are given the chance to tell their own story, their account is briefly paraphrased by the narrator, not delivered by one of the seven speaking in the first person, and it is completely devoid of detail.[79] Immediately after this, Marinus writes his letter to the emperor, and the emperor's reaction to the saints brings us nearly to the end of the legend. From the moment Malchus re-enters the cave, then, the seven sleepers lose their individual identities, becoming a single unit that speaks and acts together. They are no longer named individually as Maximianus, Malchus, and so on, but collectively, as *þa halgan martyras* (the holy martyrs). Even when they address the emperor at the end of the legend, they speak as a unit (*Þa cwædon hi …* [Then they said …]), whereas both the Latin source and Ælfric's version in *CH II* have Maximianus alone address the emperor.[80] The saints have become a collection and, what is more, they have been silenced. When God deliberately preserved their bodies, he put the idea of walling up the cave into Decius's head because he wanted them to sleep there *ungehrepode* (untouched/intact) and *stille* (unmoving/silent).[81] Rather than allowing the bodies to buried in a grave, God wanted the bodies preserved in a special place (like an archive), and he wanted them sealed up like writs or letters as proof of their authenticity. In this way, the seven sleepers are made bodies and not speakers, objects and not subjects. Like documentary evidence, the saints bear witness by the changes to and presence of their bodies, but they are denied the agency to narrate and interpret their own experiences, which, following the discovery of the contents of the cave, will always be mediated by the lead tablet, Marinus's letter, Theodosius's prayer of thanksgiving, and the *Legend* itself.

As I have been suggesting, the cave of the seven sleepers is, in fact, an archive: it contains what the *Legend* describes as a *collection* of multiple bodies, coins, and a text inscribed on a lead tablet, which functions as a label or even a catalogue of the archive's contents, meant to guide future

---

that in resisting the account of the saints' reburial, the *Legend* attempts to memorialize without subsuming the experience of the individual to the impersonal generic requirements of a hagiography.

79   Magennis, ed., *Anonymous Old English Legend*, 721–6.

80   Ibid., 765. By contrast, Ælfric has "þa cwæð se yldesta Maximianus to ðam casere …" (Then the eldest Maximianus said to the emperor …) *CH II*, 27, 219–20.

81   Magennis, ed., *Anonymous Old English Legend*, 289.

users. The cave is a cultural archive and an archive of memory, both individual and public. When I use the term "archive," I mean both the cave into which objects are placed and the records themselves; as David Zeitlyn demonstrates, "archives are both the repositories of material (buildings, suites of rooms, or a Web address) and the materials contained therein."[82]

Archives are distinguished from other repositories of treasure by several features: first, archives may be designed to be consulted by future users, and, second, an archive's contents are deliberately gathered and maintained, curated by archivists who guide which materials should be preserved and which destroyed. Archives are repositories of public memory, but they also have much in common with individual memory. Individuals curate their own treasure houses of memory and may cultivate their own memorial archives from texts they read. As Kathleen Davis writes of Alfredian memory techniques, "Alfred emphasizes the responsibility of the individual reader to be an active collector of authoritative texts – that is, to produce an anthology or an archive that can provide the basis for such a constitutive process."[83] In the case of the cave of the seven sleepers, God might be said to be the initial archivist, although the first viewers of the cave, who determine that the saints' bodies should continue to be contained within it, are also responsible for maintenance of the collection.

How is the cave like an archive? First, it constitutes a collection of materials that are fixed, unchanging, and consultable. Like the bodies frozen in time, sleeping within the cave and eventually brought into very public view, an archive stabilizes or fixes its contents in what Jacques Derrida, remembering that "archive" derives from the Greek word for house, calls a kind of *domiciliation* or "house arrest."[84] Second, the cave, like a letter, is

---

82 Zeitlyn, "Anthropology in and of the Archives," 462.

83 Davis, "Time," 219.

84 "It is thus, in this *domiciliation*, in this house arrest, that archives take place. The dwelling, this place where they dwell permanently, marks this institutional passage from the private to the public, which does not always mean from the secret to the nonsecret" (Derrida, *Archive Fever*, 2–3; emphasis in original). Although I rely on Derrida for certain formulations, I do not mean to suggest that I agree with all his claims regarding the role of the archive in state formation, nor about the archive's role in hierarchical, bureaucratic control. For a critique of the relevance of Derridean and Foucauldian archive theory to the early Middle Ages, see the introduction to Brown et al., eds, *Documentary Culture*. The editors argue that Foucault's and Derrida's emphasis on hierarchy and massive, large-scale collections is problematic for medieval archives, as is the fact that "this model of the archive and its development is fundamentally bound up with discussions of the modern state and its development" (13).

a *container* – a storage medium filled with other storage media. Derrida also emphasizes the archive as container, whether of the promise of God's covenant, or of the dead body: "*Arca*, this time in Latin, is the chest, the 'ark of acacia wood,' which contains the stone Tablets; but *arca* is also the cupboard, the coffin, the prison cell, or the cistern, the reservoir."[85] The cave of the sleepers, like the *arca*, can also be understood as a coffin, a container enclosing bodies and text, preserving them in a kind of death or living sleep. Third, for Derrida, the archive is always bound up with the death drive: the archive would not exist without a desire to destroy, because our desire to preserve is bound up with our awareness of mortality. But this destruction is not merely a source of loss. Instead, the archive demands its own destruction in order that it may become replicable. In similar ways, medieval archives respond to loss, erasure, forgetting, and destruction by carefully cultivating materials that might survive that loss. For the seven sleepers, destruction is also necessary – their bodies *must* die in order to be resurrected, made whole eternally. Curiously, their deaths are omitted in this version of the work, which ends abruptly and prematurely. In other versions of the legend, including the analogous Latin *passio* and Ælfric's brief account in *CH II*, the sleepers die soon after their reawakening, then appear in a vision to refuse being buried in ostentatious tombs. They resist being made tourist site – places to be decorated, touched, and consumed – although churches and shrines are still built over their place of burial. In the anonymous Old English *Legend*, there is no death and therefore no reburial, except insofar as the text of the *Legend* itself contains their bodies. Their bodies are resurrected, but also preserved rather than restored, as the Latin ending insists. Thus the omission of the sleepers' deaths in the Old English *Legend* does not mean that the seven sleepers escape obliteration or overwriting. When their bodies, and the other items within the cave, become archived, they also become repeatable, like the seals compared to other impressions made by the same matrix rather than to the matrix itself. No longer proof of miracle, relic, or witnessable witnesses that are reportable but not repeatable,[86] their bodies

---

85 Derrida, *Archive Fever*, 23 (emphasis in original).

86 Here I am thinking of Susan Stewart's definition of the souvenir: "We do not need or desire souvenirs of events that are repeatable. Rather we need and desire souvenirs of events that are reportable, events whose materiality has escaped us" (*On Longing*, 135). The archive in *Seven Sleepers* makes iterable the message, but not the experience of visiting the tomb.

and their story are reproduced and remediated in the form of the Old English *Legend*.

The Old English *Legend of the Seven Sleepers* emphasizes the iterability of the documents it contains by positioning the *Legend* itself as a recreation of the miraculous tablet. In fact, the relatively unexciting text of the tablet (the list of the sleepers' names) also constitutes the opening lines of the *Legend* itself:

> Her efne onginð þera eadigra seofon slæpera ðrowung, ðara haligra naman scinað on heofenum, lihtað eac on eorðan beorhte mid Cristenum mannum. Ðara is se forma his geferena heretoga, Maximianus; ðærto se oþer Malchus, se geþensuma; and se ðridda þærto Martinianus; þonne se feorða Dionisius; se halga Iohannes fifta; þonne ðæs sixtan Seraphion nama is; æt nextan, ðæs seofeþan Constantinus.[87]

> Indeed, here begins the passion of the blessed seven sleepers, whose holy names shine in heaven, and likewise they shine brightly on earth among Christian people. Of these the first is the leader of his companions, Maximianus, in addition the second is the servant Malchus, the third Martinianus, then the fourth Dionisius, the holy Johannes fifth, then the name of the sixth is Seraphion, and lastly, the seventh Constantinus.

There are two key things to note here. First, the opening lines of the *Legend* do not simply repeat the text of the tablet. Instead, the author numbers the saints, thus reinscribing them in an archive, which necessarily, as Derrida might say, sets things *in order*.[88] Second, the *Legend* itself *contains* the martyrology of the lead tablet, both insofar as it represents it and also insofar as it presents itself *as* the message of the tablet, enclosing the whole legend within an envelope structure that begins by declaring the *Legend* itself the thing it represents. In this way, the author of the legend begins to imagine his own *Legend* as a recreation of the lead tablet, producing a text that is not once but doubly resurrected. Moreover, the *Legend* comes to be an archive of the archive, not only putting the saints in order, but assembling the coins, bodies, and text within the cave, in a

---

87 Magennis, ed., *Anonymous Old English Legend*, 1–6.
88 The archive is "*there … in this place* from which *order* is given" (Derrida, *Archive Fever*, 1; emphasis in original).

new, now fully iterable form.[89] Whereas the original bodies could only be read, the bodies contained within the Old English *Legend*, compared to a row of letters, can be read and reinscribed as a promise to the future, a promise of the resurrection to come, here enacted by the author of the *Legend*'s double resurrection of the text and its bodies.

This double resurrection is, in fact, a potentially infinite resurrection, owing to the mediality of both archival space and archival temporality. The temporally mediate space of the cave, at once the third-century reign of Decius, the fifth-century reign of Theodosius, the eleventh-century present of the Old English audience, and the time of the resurrection to come, is fixed or stabilized within the archive. Upon arriving at the tomb, Theodosius says that being in the presence of the saints makes him feel as though he is in the presence of Christ:

> "Eall me þincð þæt ic eow geseo her swa beforan me swilce ic ful gehende wære þam Hælende urum Drihtne, and hine mid minan eagan eahsynes be-heolde þa he Lazarum of byrgenne awehte; and nu me þincð eac swilce ic stande gesewenlice æt his wuldorfullan mægenþrymme foran, and his agene stefne gehyre, swa swa hit toweardlic is to gehyranne, þonne on his micclan tocyme ealle men gemænelice þurhwuniað."[90]

> It entirely seems to me that I see you here before me as if I were very near to our Lord the Savior, and beheld him visibly with my eye when he awoke Lazarus from the tomb; and now it also seems to me as though I stand before his glorious majesty, and hear his own voice, just as it will be heard in the future, when all people will universally persist in his great coming.

The place of the tomb is neither the fifth-century cave, nor heaven, nor Lazarus's tomb, nor the time of the resurrection to come; the saints are neither themselves nor Christ – they are simultaneously both and all, in the in-betweenness of the space of the archive.[91] This is what Carolyn Dinshaw has described as a "gratifyingly multiple *now*" and "the capacious *now* in

---

89 What Derrida calls "that re-producible, iterable, and conservative production of memory … that objectivizable storage called the archive" (*Archive Fever*, 26).
90 Magennis, ed., *Anonymous Old English Legend*, 758–64.
91 Likewise, in the opening lines of the *Legend* (quoted above), we learn that the record of the seven sleepers is kept both in heaven and on earth.

which what we know as past and future time is contained."[92] Likewise, the *Legend* itself is temporally mediate. The *Legend* opens with a reminder of the date of the feast day of the seven sleepers, which carefully locates it within the church calendar: "Ðara seofon haligra freolstid bið on geare fif nihton ær Hlafmæssan" (The festival of the seven saints is in the year five nights before Lammas).[93] The reality of everyday serial, annual time means that the celebration of the miracle reoccurs each year, but (at least in other versions of the legend) so does the saints' death and reburial. Ultimately, the time of the archive is complicated by the time or mediality of resurrection. Although Eileen Joy argues that the sleepers strenuously resist martyrdom and reburial,[94] they must nevertheless die to prove the resurrection, must die to live, must (like letters) be simultaneously present and absent. It is through their containment in the archive that Dinshaw's "gratifyingly multiple *now*" is both made visible and imprisoned.

Anglo-Saxon authors were deeply concerned with the functions and forms of inscriptional media objects that behave like letters. Ultimately, this chapter explores several questions related to these concerns: How did Anglo-Saxons memorialize and circulate miracles in cases where they did not have access to the use of relics, or where saints' stories advocated resistance to being made relics? How could human authors, especially ones as geographically and temporally removed from the miracle as Ælfric and the anonymous author of the *Seven Sleepers*, transform the miraculous into publishable, iterable form? And how do we, as modern scholars, likewise temporally and geographically removed from the Old English saints' lives, make sense of those texts, or of letters whose content is not preserved? One answer, I suggest, can be found in epistolary documents, themselves *always* expected to communicate over distance and/or time, and in the ways in which Anglo-Saxon authors position themselves in relation to them.

---

92 Dinshaw, *How Soon Is Now?*, 56 (emphasis in original).

93 Magennis, ed., *Anonymous Old English Legend*, 6–7.

94 "Therefore, whereas the Latin version is at pains to express that the seven men rose from the earth once and will need to rise from that same earth again (at a later date), implying their status as *buried bodies* (if also 'sleeping'), and to also represent them as 'dying' a second time (or, perhaps, for the first time), the Old English version never emphasizes the *type* of resurrection the Seven Sleepers undergo, nor does it provide a picture of the final, more 'real' death of the martyrs" (Joy, "Old English *Seven Sleepers*," 79, emphasis in original).

In the documents I have examined, there is an important but shifting relationship between message and medium. Within the saints' lives, the message of the miraculous documents is subsumed by the act of bearing witness, whether that is textual, as in the sinful woman's confession in *Basil*, or material, as in the lead tablet and unchanged bodies of the *Seven Sleepers*. But then that act of bearing witness, when contained within the hagiography, is itself subsumed by the hagiographer's desire to control and shape his own narrative. As I have shown, in the *Seven Sleepers*, the author takes this idea one step further, imagining records as archives, then resurrecting and yet still containing the tablet within his own text. In fact, the hagiographer deliberately calls his text a martyrology, and openly agonizes about who should and should not be recorded in it.[95]

The hagiographer necessarily interprets and frames the epistolary document, whereas the lead tablet (like other divinely inspired or produced documents) wishes to present itself as though it offers unmediated access to the divine truth. When the martyrology of the seven sleepers is remediated as an archive of the archive, or when the sinful woman's epistolary confession is transmitted but not preserved or published, these documents are brought under the control of a human author functioning as an archivist who must choose who and what to save, without the benefit of divine power or wisdom. He can only save a memory, not a soul. It is not enough to say, as I did before, that the authenticating speaker of the letter or legal document gives way to the authenticating document. Although that shift momentarily offers the impression of more immediate, less mediated access to the divine, once placed within the archive of the text, control returns to the human author or authenticating speaker of the saint's life. Doubly resurrected, doubly buried, bodies of record are brought back to life only to be killed once again in order to be memorialized in the archive of the archive.

---

95 Magennis, ed., *Anonymous Old English Legend*, 335–7.

Epilogue: Epistolary Afterlives

I see something of God each hour of the twenty-four, and each moment then,
In the faces of men and women I see God, and in my own face in the glass,
I find letters from God dropt in the street, and every one is sign'd by God's name,
And I leave them where they are, for I know that wheresoe'er I go,
Others will punctually come for ever and ever.

– Walt Whitman, Song of Myself

Epistolary Acts ends where other studies of medieval documentary culture begin: the proliferation of administrative documents after the Norman Conquest, including the Domesday Book, and the rise of the *ars dictaminis* in the late eleventh century.[1] Alberic of Monte Cassino's treatise on letter writing was written c. 1087; at Christmas 1085 King William I called for a survey of England that would eventually produce the Domesday Book. The Domesday Book signalled new directions in the use of documentary culture to record and control the movements and lives of the English people. Although the survey of landowners was likely conducted in Anglo-Norman French, English, and Latin, the book itself was written in Latin – an assertion that English documentary culture would no longer be practised in the vernacular, as it had long been in Anglo-Saxon England. While the practice of issuing legal documents in English seems to have

---

1 Clanchy, *From Memory to Written Record*; Steiner, *Documentary Culture*; Justice, *Writing and Rebellion*; Camargo, *Ars Dictaminis*, which focuses primarily on the twelfth to fifteenth centuries; and Camargo, *Middle English Verse Love Epistle*, which focuses on the fourteenth to sixteenth centuries.

continued for a short period after the Conquest, by 1070 William was no longer issuing writs in English.[2] This shift from English to Latin would seem to mark a break with Anglo-Saxon documentary culture, one that greatly reduced the need for the epistolary acts of translation (linguistic or cultural) this book has explored. Indeed, Michael Clanchy and other historians of medieval documentary culture frequently describe the Domesday Book as though it were, in its way, a new kind of documentary act, one that sparked the massive increase in bureaucratic documents in late medieval England. It was a project that generated the production of documents – documents written by surveyors about local land, including records of oral testimony, which were then collected and rearranged in the manuscript that would become the Domesday Book. This project was a massive undertaking and required the ability to organize these materials, collected by multiple people in multiple formats, into a coherent whole (a project that, if not perfectly done, was nevertheless done).

And yet, while Domesday might seem to mark a sea change in documentary culture, it was a project that required epistolary communication and, more importantly, kinds of epistolary communication that reflected Anglo-Saxon epistolary acts. Writs would have been sent to the shires announcing the plan for the survey. These writs were written in epistolary form and would have been recognizable to the English who would have received similar writ-charters before the Norman Conquest as well (though perhaps in the vernacular rather than Latin). The Domesday survey, like epistolary acts, also concerned the movement of bodies – commissioners sent to organizational units called the circuits to collect evidence and return it to the king. The documentary acts that produced the Domesday Book were thus akin to and yet a reversal of the epistolary acts I have described in this book. Just as Anglo-Saxon authors sometimes referred to letters using Latinate terms like *(e)pistol,* the scribes preparing the Domesday Book sometimes had to maintain or Latinize English terms, like *soke,* in order to reflect special legal contexts for which Latin had no equivalent vocabulary.[3] The acts of cultural, linguistic, and documentary translation required to produce the Domesday Book – including locating vocabulary for legal relationships, land rights, individuals' ranks and titles, and so on – required scribes to borrow from the vernacular of the conquered English. Thus,

---

2 Clanchy, *From Memory to Written Record,* 24.

3 On the multilingualism of the *Domesday Book,* see Baxter, "Making of Domesday Book."

whereas the practice of Anglo-Saxon epistolary acts had required converting Latinate protocols for English audiences, the production of the Domesday Book required converting English legal protocols to Latin vocabulary and for non-English-speaking audiences. According to Stephen Baxter, the multilingual nature of the Domesday project was what enhanced its success, because it "meant that the commissioners could draw on a wider range of legal vocabulary and were therefore able to pinpoint phenomena with greater precision than might otherwise have been possible."[4] In the same way, traces of Latinate vocabulary and protocols in Old English representations of epistolarity reflect not a mechanical translation by vernacular authors unpractised in epistolary protocols, but a thoughtful reflection of the ways in which English vocabulary might not always suffice to capture the capacious, slippery genre of the letter.

In one popular version of the history of English documentary culture, the Domesday Book set off new bureaucratic practices that eventually led to the proliferation of documents in late medieval England. But in fact, as I have been suggesting, the Domesday Book grew out of Anglo-Saxon documentary practices, if not in Anglo-Saxon modes. Just as Anglo-Saxon royal and ecclesiastical authorities were deeply concerned with the production, use, and archival storage of legal and epistolary documents, William I was deeply concerned with producing an authoritative, consultable record of land rights in late eleventh-century England. Although *Epistolary Acts* ends with the Norman Conquest and the birth of the formal *ars dictaminis*, the break with Anglo-Saxon epistolary and documentary protocols is not so clear-cut. My argument here is a double one. On the one hand, Domesday and the *ars dictaminis* signal the birth of new documentary and epistolary protocols. The Norman Conquest, which leads to Anglo-Norman French rather than Old English becoming a prestige language in England, along with the birth of the formal *ars dictaminis* in Italy in the late eleventh century, represents a major break with Anglo-Saxon epistolarity. No longer are legal documents with salutation formulae in England written in English, but in Latin, and the Domesday Book attempts to assert Norman control over English lands and bodies. Epistolary rhetoric, which was likely known and taught if not formally codified previously, begins to abound in letter-writing manuals and strict classifications of letter types, but in Latin, rather than English.

---

4 Ibid., 307.

On the other hand, another version of this story might use the same events to entirely different ends. The changes to English epistolary and documentary culture did not happen overnight. The production of Domesday arose out of and in response to an Anglo-Saxon culture that had already been asking how documents, including letters, could be used to record, circulate, and preserve lives, and that had been chronicling its people and places in the vernacular in the *Anglo-Saxon Chronicle*. English did not cease to be a language of record in October 1066; the Peterborough Chronicle continued in English into the twelfth century. The *ars dictaminis*, while important, took time to arrive in England, where it was never as influential as it was in Italy.[5] However, by the time English returns as a literary language in late medieval England, the landscape has changed drastically. Higher literacy rates, the rise of bureaucratic documents (and clerks to produce them), and changing literary tastes, along with developments in epistolary style, mean that when fourteenth- and fifteenth-century writers choose to represent epistolarity, they do so in ways that can be very unlike those practised by Anglo-Saxon authors. Domesday is therefore not the end of early English epistolary acts, though it does mark a transition; when English epistolary acts re-emerge in Middle English in the fourteenth and fifteenth centuries, they do so in altered form. With the rise of bureaucratic documentary culture in England in the later Middle Ages, documentary culture, including epistolary culture, was increasingly practised in the vernacular. Epistolary acts were no longer needed to translate Latinate practices for English audiences; rather, new kinds of epistolary acts were needed to translate new kinds of documents to new audiences. Single-sheet documents were more frequently produced, pragmatic literacy more widespread, and the special forms of letters (whether the physical shape of the document or the five-part structure of the *ars dictaminis*) could be exploited by literary authors to create new poetic forms, as Emily Steiner has ably demonstrated. The *ars dictaminis* was already on the decline in fifteenth-century England, but other kinds of letters, not always shaped by its dictates, continued to be produced in English and to fuel the literary imagination.[6] From the John Ball letters, to the

---

5 Richardson, "Fading Influence."

6 According to Richardson, the *ars dictaminis* was practised only by a select few in England. It was not until the thirteenth century that "Latin letter-writing was probably first taught on a significant scale" in England ("Fading Influence," 226), and the *ars dictaminis* was on the decline by fifteenth century. But other kinds of letter writing,

Paston letters, to Chaucer's *Troilus and Criseyde*, epistolarity shaped the landscape of English literary production.[7] The eventual rise in documentary competency among a larger portion of the population led to new kinds of experiments with the representation of documents in literary culture, and changes in documentary protocols created new epistolary tropes to be explored in English literature: the intercepted message, the brief personal note, the exploration of the subjectivity of the speaker, and the exploitation of the special material and physical properties of the document, increasingly represented in manuscript illustration and eventually leading to more apotropaic documents as well.

The Anglo-Saxon documentary impulse was similar in motivation but not in expression to later medieval documentary culture. Yet the differences between Anglo-Saxon and later epistolarity were to some extent also a question of quantity rather than kind. When Walt Whitman describes creation as "letters from God dropt in the street" (as in the epigraph to this chapter), he is participating in a long tradition of imagining oneself as the recipient of messages from God. In his reading of the letters as objects rather than as written text, Whitman reflects an early medieval understanding that letters can communicate as medium as well as, or even instead of, message. The medieval belief in communication from God continued in more familiar ways as well. The *Sunday Letter* and other heavenly letters, although they continued to mutate as they were adapted to new contexts, were popular in late medieval England and in early printed broadsides, and were in use among Pennsylvania Germans in the nineteenth century.[8]

---

based on other styles and forms, including business correspondence, continued to flourish. Richardson's article appears in a special issue of *Rhetorica: A Journal of the History of Rhetoric* on the collapse of the *ars dictaminis* in the later Middle Ages and Renaissance, introduced by an essay by Martin Camargo called, appropriately, "The Waning of Medieval Ars Dictaminis." Richardson has more recently argued that rhetoricians of epistolarity should pursue three areas of future research: formularies, the "bourgeois 'customal' book," and corpus linguistics ("The *Ars dictaminis*," 60–3). On letters in later medieval England, see also Taylor, "Letters and Letter Collections."

7 On literary adaptations of documentary forms, see Steiner, *Documentary Culture*. On the John Ball letters, see Justice, *Writing and Rebellion*.

8 The earliest known printed *Sunday Letter* broadside is BSB Einblattdrucke VII, 13, which was produced in Munich c. 1501 by Hans Schobser (Yoder, *Pennsylvania German Broadside*, 209). Bayerische Staatsbibliothek, Munich, has made available high quality images of its broadsheets at http://daten.digitale-sammlungen.de/~db/ausgaben/ uni_ausgabe.html?projekt=1046961503&echerche=ja&rdnung=sig. This broadsheet has

Epistolary Acts has traced the representation of epistolary communication in early medieval vernacular literature in a wide range of genres. Rather than seeing epistolarity as the sole province of later medieval England, I argue, we should recognize that epistolarity (broadly conceived) was crucial to Anglo-Saxon vernacular literature. Because no theory of Anglo-Saxon epistolarity exists, the book has sought to recover Anglo-Saxon vernacular epistolarity by studying letters' representation within other texts. Attending to vernacular epistolarity in particular reveals the protocols of what I have called "epistolary acts" – the acts of cultural and linguistic translation necessary to adapt epistolarity to Anglo-Saxon audiences. These acts include protocols of letter writing, delivery, reception, and storage, and necessarily involve the movement of bodies across space; the handling of parchment and ink, or wax and stylus; and the performance of the letter, usually orally, before its recipients. Over the course of the book, expectations about Anglo-Saxon epistolarity have frequently been overturned: I have traced a line from the formal qualities of the epistolary genre to the ways in which Anglo-Saxon epistolary acts subvert our expectations for the genre by de-emphasizing the materiality of the document or the importance of the salutation formula, instead celebrating the production, transmission, and storage of documents, as well as how documents and human messengers and recipients are transformed by coming into contact with one another. This book ends by attending to the storage of letters and other textual objects that behave like letters, demonstrating the broad reach of epistolarity's influence on early medieval vernacular culture.

Although there are many extant Anglo-Latin letters, there is no surviving theory of epistolary rhetoric from Anglo-Saxon England. By examining the extant letters, however, we are able to reconstruct what must have

---

also been reproduced by Gisela Ecker, *Einblattdrucke von den Anfängen*, no. 167. For more on Schobser's life, and a catalogue of his work, see Schottenloher, ed., *Der Müncher Buchdrucker*. Other early *Letter* broadsides, dating from 1497 to 1500, have been linked to printing houses in Munich, Nürnberg, and Memmingen. Some later printers even attempted to replicate the golden letters in which the letter was said to have been written, if not in the text-block itself, then at least for the decorative borders. See, for example, Pennsylvania German Broadsides and Fraktur Collection, F160.G3P463/ Box 4/Item 15/Vault, Rare Books and Manuscripts, Special Collections Library, University Libraries, Pennsylvania State University, at https://collection1.libraries .psu.edu/cdm/singleitem/collection/frak/id/124/rec/1; and Franklin and Marshall, Pennsylvania German Broadside Collection, F & M College, G23, at https:// dspace.fandm.edu/handle/11016/5225.

been some of the central tenets of Anglo-Saxon epistolary theory. English salutation formulae reflect a deep awareness of Latinate protocols and the theories that underpinned them, but also reveal that Anglo-Saxon authors felt free to modify formulae to suit their own purposes. Old English salutation formulae follow their own rules for placement of the names of sender and addressee, in which social rank is not as important as it was in Latin, and editors of letters frequently omitted salutation formulae entirely in order to make the letters appeal more universally to new audiences. Likewise, Old English vocabulary for letters reflects the porousness of the genre. Some Anglo-Saxon audiences must have been expected to have a highly sophisticated understanding of the letter concept in order for it to have been applied, though perhaps sometimes metaphorically, to texts as various as brief notes, long treatises, and the writing on the wall.

While Old English authors and translators were certainly familiar with epistolary form, they, unlike their later medieval counterparts, placed little emphasis on representing salutations or other elements of the five-part structure of what would become the *ars dictaminis*. Neither did they always prioritize the materiality of the letter as physical object. In the case of the *Sunday Letter*, what mattered most seems to have been creating communities of believers in and circulators of the letter's message, not accurate transcription of the content or access to the original document said to have been delivered by an angelic messenger. While the Old English *Letter* does not claim to be apotropaic, as it would come to be in the later Middle Ages, the letter's materiality does matter, as accounts of its creation, delivery, and provenance model for its audiences, whether lay or secular and whether literate or not, how they too might participate in the continued circulation of the *Letter*'s message on something anticipating a mass scale. The Old English *Sunday Letters* are not apotropaic amulets, but they are still invested in how the medium matters to epistolary acts.

Where materiality becomes more significant to epistolary acts is in the transmission and delivery of letters by messengers. Whereas in later epistolary traditions, the letter makes the recipient aware of the body of the absent sender, in Old English, it is the body of the messenger or recipient, or of the letter itself, that is most important. Documents become mere storage containers authorizing messengers to speak, and it is through the body of the messenger that the message becomes legible. Both secular romances and saints' lives imagine the ways in which the body of a messenger, transformed by contact with a letter, may display extratextual somatic information (Apollonius's blushing cheeks) or become apotropaic (as when Thaddeus's touch, rather than the message he carries, heals Abgar).

At times, a messenger must even negotiate how he may safely transmit a letter without being dangerously infected by the body of its sender. While Mary of Egypt's message needs no visible messenger (since it appears at the feet of the one to whom it is addressed), its unusual writing support cautions Zosimus that Mary's letter must not be circulated through normal communication channels, and must not be venerated as a relic, but must remain as humble as the dirt in which it is written. Her non-portable letter reminds him that access to her story, like access to her body, must remain carefully controlled.

Epistolarity was so important in Anglo-Saxon culture that even texts that we might not imagine were letters could adopt the protocols and functions of epistolarity. After being created, transmitted, and delivered, some letters entered the archive. But as the example of *Mary of Egypt* suggests, not all letters could safely be preserved, nor could all miraculous events easily be recorded. In both Ælfric's *Life of St Basil* and the anonymous *Legend of the Seven Sleepers*, letters record, transmit, and are retrieved in service of remembering the past. Just as forgetting is possible in medieval mnemotechniques only when a person actively rewrites his or her memory, destruction of a letter will not erase it from the archive. Letters could preserve the memory of a saint's miraculous act, but only if deliberately stored in the archive – whether institutional, textual, or physical. These texts are particularly epistolary in their conception of temporality, attending to a deferral that far exceeds the typical delay between sending and receiving of letters. They ask how letters can be transmitted across time by being placed in the archive, and how the stories or sins they record can be erased or preserved as records of saintly intervention.

As this book has demonstrated, epistolarity was deeply engaging to Anglo-Saxon authors and audiences, even those who may not have produced or received letters themselves. Throughout, I have striven to make clear not just the fundamental role epistolarity played in shaping Old English literature and memorial culture, but also the many ways in which a media studies framework might help us better understand Anglo-Saxon epistolarity by breaking us out of more traditional conceptions of orality versus textuality or genre studies. This move has larger implications not just for the study of epistolary communication but also for the field as a whole; it is especially important for understanding the abiding relevance of Anglo-Saxon inscriptional media. The rise of print leads to what is often understood as a fundamental change in inscriptional media technology: the union of storage and transmission. In fact, print culture now appears to be a blip, a temporary union of storage and transmission of documents that were neither united before the early modern nor are so now, in an age of computing and Cloud storage. But the later Middle Ages and the Renaissance certainly did usher in a new era of epistolary communication. The gradual transition to a culture in which more and more people could read the letters delivered to them, as well as the development of more affordable print and paper technologies, meant that it was no longer as necessary for epistolary acts to involve the oral translation and performance of written messages. This is not purely a result of print technology; the impulse to unite storage and transmission is already seen in late medieval manuscripts like the illustrated *Charters of Christ*, some of which enclose the text of the message in a box meant to represent the physical shape of a single-sheet document, complete with illustrated seal hanging from the bottom.[9]

Although it might be tempting to claim that the Norman Conquest or the rise of the *ars dictaminis* was ultimately responsible for the end of Anglo-Saxon epistolary and documentary culture, the eleventh century is only one possible place to conclude the story of early English epistolary acts, and traces of these acts remain in late medieval epistolary practices and beyond. It is not that the Norman Conquest happened and England lost its taste for vernacular epistolarity, but rather that epistolarity is an endlessly adaptable, protean genre, and as epistolary protocols change, literary authors respond by reimagining epistolary acts, sometimes continuing or reviving older traditions, sometimes creating new modes. In their tendency towards paraphrase, their omission of epistolary formulae and structure, their relative lack of attention to the special physical form of the single-sheet document, and their almost complete lack of love letters, Anglo-Saxon epistolary acts are in many ways unlike the epistolary acts of late medieval England, late antiquity, or continental medieval Europe. This does not mean that Anglo-Saxons had a limited conception of epistolarity. Rather, as this book has shown, Anglo-Saxon authors writing in the vernacular could engage in the standards of Latinate epistolarity when they desired to do so, but they could also imagine a short inscription transmitted by God to Baltassar's wall as a metaphorical letter, delivered by an angelic hand rather than carried by an angelic messenger. They could imagine letters written on the bodies of the messengers who carried them; letters sent by God or saints that did not become relics and

---

9 London, BL Additional 37049, f. 23r.

whose content was circulated orally, by people of all levels of literacy; and letters that travelled not through space but through time. Anglo-Saxon epistolary acts play a crucial role in Anglo-Saxon conceptions of inscriptional media and communication and, in their acts of translation, reveal particularly Anglo-Saxon forms of epistolarity. Their use of epistolary acts was inventive and playful, and reflects deep understanding of and familiarity with Latinate practices (some of which were being adapted for audiences who would have been much less familiar with the same). Letter writing was not a new technology in Anglo-Saxon England, yet it had to be made new. Epistolary acts adapted Latinate practices for new audiences and, in doing so, revealed both what Latin letter writing was and what English letter writing could be.

Bibliography

Allott, Stephen, trans. *Alcuin of York: His Life and Letters.* York, UK: William Sessions, 1974.

Altman, Janet Gurkin. *Epistolarity: Approaches to a Form.* Columbus: Ohio State University Press, 1982.

Anderson, Earl R. "Style and Theme in the Old English *Daniel.*" *English Studies* 68 (1987): 1–23.

Andrew, Malcolm, and Ronald Waldron, eds. *The Poems of the Pearl Manuscript: Pearl, Cleanness, Patience, Sir Gawain and the Green Knight.* 1978. Reprint, Exeter: University of Exeter Press, 1999.

Anonymous of Bologna. "The Principles of Letter-Writing" (*Rationes Dictandi*). Translated by James J. Murphy. In *Three Medieval Rhetorical Arts.* Edited by James J. Murphy, 1–25. Berkeley: University of California Press, 1971.

Archibald, Elizabeth. *Apollonius of Tyre: Medieval and Renaissance Themes and Variations.* Cambridge, UK: D.S. Brewer, 1991.

Assmann, Bruno, ed. *Angelsächsische Homilien und Heiligenleben.* Kassel, DE: Georg H. Wigand, 1889.

Attwood, Katrina. "Anonymous, *Leiðarvísan.*" In *Poetry on Christian Subjects. Part 1. The Twelfth and Thirteenth Centuries.* Edited by Margaret Clunies Ross, 137–78. Skaldic Poetry of the Scandinavian Middle Ages Vol. 7. Turnhout, BE: Brepols, 2007.

– "Leiðarvísan and the 'Sunday Letter' Tradition in Scandinavia." In *Til heiðurs og hugbótar: Greinar um trúarkveðskap fyrri alda.* Edited by Svanhildur Óskarsdóttir and Anna Guðmundsdóttir, 53–78. Reykholt, Iceland: Snorrastofa, 2003.

Bately, Janet, ed. *The Old English Orosius.* EETS s.s. 6. London: Oxford University Press, 1980.

Baun, Jane. "Taboo or Gift? The Lord's Day in Byzantium." In *The Use and Abuse of Time in Christian History*. Edited by R.N. Swanson, 45–56. Woodbridge, UK: Boydell Press, 2002.

Baxter, Stephen. "The Making of Domesday Book and the Languages of Lordship in Conquered England." In *Conceptualizing Multilingualism in England, c. 800–c.1250*. Edited by Elizabeth M. Tyler, 271–308. Turnhout, BE: Brepols, 2011.

Bedos-Rezak, Brigitte. *When Ego Was Imago: Signs of Identity in the Middle Ages*. Leiden, NL: Brill, 2011.

Bevan, Edwyn. *Sibyls and Seers: A Survey of Some Ancient Theories of Revelation and Inspiration*. London: George Allen and Unwin, 1928.

Biblia Sacra, iuxta Vulgatem Versionem, 4th ed. Edited by Boniface Fischer et al. Stuttgart: Deutsche Bibelgesellschaft, 1994.

Bishop, T.A.M., and P. Chaplais, eds. *Facsimiles of English Royal Writs to A.D. 1100 Presented to Vivian Hunter Galbraith*. Oxford: Clarendon Press, 1957.

Bittner, Maximilian. *Der vom Himmel gefallene Brief Christi in seinen morgenländischen Versionen und Rezensionen*. Vienna: Alfred Hölder, 1906.

Blair, John. *The Church in Anglo-Saxon Society*. Oxford: Oxford University Press, 2005.

– "Debate: Ecclesiastical Organization and Pastoral Care in Anglo-Saxon England." *Early Medieval Europe* 4.2 (1995): 193–212.

Bolter, Jay David, and Richard Grusin. *Remediation: Understanding New Media*. Cambridge, MA: MIT Press, 1999.

Boretius, Alfred, ed. MGH, *Capitularia regum Francorum I*. Hannover, DE: Hahn, 1883.

Borsje, Jacqueline. "The *Bruch* in the Irish Version of the Sunday Letter." *Ériu* 45 (1994): 83–98.

Bosworth, James, and T. Northcote Toller. *An Anglo-Saxon Dictionary Based on the Manuscript Collections of the Late Joseph Bosworth*. 1898. Reprint, Oxford: Oxford University Press, 1972.

Bowman, Alan K. *Life and Letters on the Roman Frontier: Vindolanda and Its People*. 1994. Reprint, London: British Museum Press, 2003.

Boureau, Alain. "The Letter-Writing Norm, a Mediaeval Invention." In *Correspondence: Models of Letter-Writing from the Middle Ages to the Nineteenth Century*. Edited by Roger Chartier, Alain Boureau, and Cécile Dauphin. Translated by Christopher Woodall, 24–58. Princeton: Princeton University Press, 1997.

Braekman, Willy L. "Notes on Old English Charms II." *Neophilologus* 67 (1983): 605–10.

Bragg, Lois. "Runes and Readers: In and Around 'The Husband's Message.'" *Studia Neophilologica* 71 (1999): 34–50.

Bray, Dorothy Ann. "Malediction and Benediction in the Lives of the Early Irish Saints." *Studia Celtica* 36 (2002): 47–58.

Brown, Jennifer Christine. "Writing Power and Writing-Power: The Rise of Literacy as a Means of Power in Anglo-Saxon England." *Medieval Perspectives* 15.1 (2000): 42–56.

Brown, Michelle P. "The Role of the Wax Tablet in Medieval Literacy: A Reconsideration in Light of a Recent Find from York." *British Library Journal* 20.1 (1994): 1–16.

Brown, Peter. *The Body and Society: Men, Women and Sexual Renunciation in Early Christianity*. New York: Columbia University Press, 1988.

Brown, Warren C., Marios Costambeys, Matthew Innes, and Adam J. Kosto. "Introduction." In *Documentary Culture and the Laity in the Early Middle Ages*. Edited by Brown et al., 1–16. Cambridge: Cambridge University Press, 2013.

Bullough, Donald A. *Alcuin: Achievement and Reputation*. Leiden, NL: Brill, 2004.

Burrus, Virginia. *The Sex Lives of Saints: An Erotics of Ancient Hagiography*. Philadelphia: University of Pennsylvania Press, 2004.

Bynum, Caroline Walker. *Christian Materiality: An Essay on Religion in Late Medieval Europe*. New York: Zone Books, 2011.

Cain, Christopher M. "The Apocryphal Legend of Abgar in Ælfric's *Lives of Saints*." *Philological Quarterly* 89.4 (fall 2010): 383–402.

– "Sacred Words, Anglo-Saxon Piety, and the Origins of the *Epistola salvatoris* in London, British Library, Royal 2.A.xx." *Journal of English and Germanic Philology* 108.2 (2009): 168–89.

Camargo, Martin. *Ars Dictaminis, Ars Dictandi*. Turnhout, BE: Brepols, 1991.

– *The Middle English Verse Love Epistle*. Tübingen, DE: Max Niemeyer, 1991.

– "The Waning of Medieval Ars Dictaminis." *Rhetorica* 19.2 (2001): 135–40.

Cambridge, Eric, and David Rollason. "Debate: The Pastoral Organization of the Anglo-Saxon Church: A Review of the 'Minster Hypothesis.'" *Early Medieval Europe* 4.1 (1995): 87–104.

Cameron, Angus, Ashley Crandell Amos, Antonette diPaolo Healey, et al. *Dictionary of Old English: A to H* online. Toronto: Dictionary of Old English Project, 2016. http://tapor.library.utoronto.ca/doe/.

Campbell, Alistair, ed. and trans. *Encomium Emmae Reginae*. 1949. Reprinted with supplementary introduction by Simon Keynes. Camden Classic Reprints 4. Cambridge: Cambridge University Press, 1998.

Cantara, Linda, ed. "*Saint Mary of Egypt* in British Library, MS Cotton Otho B.x." In *Anonymous Interpolations in Ælfric's "Lives of Saints."* Edited by

Robin Norris, 29–69. *OEN* Subsidia 35. Kalamazoo, MI: Medieval Institute Publications, 2011.

Carnicelli, Thomas A., ed. *King Alfred's Version of St. Augustine's Soliloquies.* Cambridge, MA: Harvard University Press, 1969.

Carruthers, Mary. *The Craft of Thought: Meditation, Rhetoric, and the Making of Images, 400–1200.* Cambridge: Cambridge University Press, 1998.

Chaganti, Seeta. "Vestigial Signs: Inscription, Performance, and *The Dream of the Rood.*" *PMLA* 125.1 (2010): 48–72.

Chaplais, Pierre. "The Anglo-Saxon Chancery: From the Diploma to the Writ." *Journal of the Society of Archivists* 3.4 (1966): 160–76.

– *English Diplomatic Practice in the Middle Ages.* London: Hambledon and London, 2003.

– "The Letter from Bishop Wealdhere of London to Archbishop Brihtwold of Canterbury: The Earliest Original 'Letter Close' Extant in the West." In *Medieval Scribes, Manuscripts and Libraries: Essays Presented to N.R. Ker.* Edited by M.B. Parkes and Andrew G. Watson, 3–23. London: Scolar Press, 1978.

– "The Origin and Authenticity of the Royal Anglo-Saxon Diploma." *Journal of the Society of Archivists* 3.2 (1965): 48–61.

Chartier, Roger. *Inscription and Erasure: Literature and Written Culture from the Eleventh to the Eighteenth Century.* 2005. Translated by Arthur Goldhammer. Philadelphia: University of Pennsylvania Press, 2007.

Chase, Colin, ed. *Two Alcuin Letter-Books.* Toronto: Published for the Centre for Medieval Studies by the Pontifical Institute of Mediaeval Studies, 1975.

Chaucer, Geoffrey. *The Riverside Chaucer.* Edited by Larry D. Benson. 3rd ed. Boston: Houghton Mifflin, 1987.

Childs, Wendy R. "Moving Around." In *A Social History of England, 1200–1500.* Edited by Rosemary Horrox and W. Mark Ormrod, 260–75. Cambridge: Cambridge University Press, 2006.

Clanchy, M.T. *From Memory to Written Record: England, 1066–1307.* 3rd ed. Malden, MA: Wiley-Blackwell, 2013.

Clayton, Mary. "Homiliaries and Preaching in Anglo-Saxon England." 1985. Reprinted in *Old English Prose: Basic Readings.* Edited by Paul E. Szarmach, 151–98. New York: Garland, 2000.

– ed. *Letter to Brother Edward: A Student Edition.* *OEN* 40.3 (2007): 31–46.

Clements, Jill Hamilton. "Inscribing the Saintly Dead in the Old English *Legend of the Seven Sleepers.*" Paper presented at at the Annual Symposium on Medieval and Renaissance Studies, St Louis, MO, June 2016.

Clemoes, Peter, ed. *Ælfric's Catholic Homilies: The First Series.* EETS s.s. 17. Oxford: Oxford University Press, 1997.

Cockayne, Thomas Oswald, and Charles Singer, eds. *Leechdoms, Wortcunning and Starcraft of Early England.* Vol. 3. 1866. Reprint, London: Holland Press, 1961.

Colgrave, Bertram, and R.A.B. Mynors, eds. *Bede's Ecclesiastical History of the English People.* Oxford: Oxford University Press, 1969.

Conner, Patrick W. *Anglo-Saxon Exeter: A Tenth-Century Cultural History.* Woodbridge, UK: Boydell Press, 1993.

Constable, Giles. *Letters and Letter-Collections.* Turnhout, BE: Brepols, 1976.

Cook, Elizabeth Heckendorn. *Epistolary Bodies: Gender and Genre in the Eighteenth-Century Republic of Letters.* Stanford, CA: Stanford University Press, 1996.

Cooper, Tracey-Anne. "The Homilies of a Pragmatic Archbishop's Handbook in Context: Cotton Tiberius A. iii." *Anglo-Norman Studies* 28 (2005): 47–64.

– *Monk-Bishops and the English Benedictine Reform Movement: Reading London, BL, Cotton Tiberius A.iii in Its Manuscript Context.* Toronto: Pontifical Institute of Mediaeval Studies, 2015.

Corona, Gabriella. *Ælfric's Life of Saint Basil the Great: Background and Context.* Cambridge, UK: D.S. Brewer, 2006.

Corradini, Erika. "Preaching in Old English: Tradition and New Directions." *Literature Compass* 3.6 (2006): 1266–77.

Cross, J.E., Denis Brearley, Julia Crick, Thomas N. Hall, and Andy Orchard, eds. *Two Old English Apocrypha and Their Manuscript Source: "The Gospel of Nichodemus" and "The Avenging of the Saviour."* Cambridge: Cambridge University Press, 1996.

Cubitt, Catherine. "Ælfric's Lay Patrons." In *A Companion to Ælfric.* Edited by Hugh Magennis and Mary Swan, 165–92. Leiden, NL: Brill, 2009.

– "Archbishop Dunstan: A Prophet in Politics?" In *Myth, Rulership, Church and Charters: Essays in Honour of Nicholas Brooks.* Edited by Julia Barrow and Andrew Wareham, 145–66. Aldershot, UK: Ashgate, 2008.

– "'As the Lawbook Teaches': Reeves, Lawbooks and Urban Life in the Anonymous Old English Legend of the Seven Sleepers." *English Historical Review* 124.510 (2009): 1021–49.

Curtius, Ernst Robert. *European Literature and the Latin Middle Ages.* 1948. Translated by Willard R. Trask. Princeton: Princeton University Press, 1967.

Davis, Kathleen. "Time." In *A Handbook of Anglo-Saxon Studies.* Edited by Jacqueline Stodnick and Renée R. Trilling, 215–34. Malden, MA: Wiley-Blackwell, 2012.

d'Avray, D.L. *The Preaching of the Friars: Sermons Diffused from Paris before 1300.* Oxford: Oxford University Press, 1985.

Debray, Régis. *Transmitting Culture.* 1997. Translated by Eric Rauth. New York: Columbia University Press, 2000.

Delehaye, Hippolyte. "Note sur la légende de la lettre du Christ tombée du ciel." *Académie royale de Belgique: Bulletin de la classe des lettres et des sciences morales et politiques et de la classe des beaux-arts* 1 (1899): 171–213.

Deletant, Dennis. "The Sunday Legend." *Revue des études sud-est européennes* 15 (1977): 431–51.

Derks, Ton and Nico Roymans. "Seal-boxes and the Spread of Latin Literacy in the Rhine Delta." In *Becoming Roman, Writing Latin? Literacy and Epigraphy in the Roman West*. Edited by Alison E. Cooley, 87–134. Portsmouth, RI: Journal of Roman Archaeology, 2002.

Derrida, Jacques. *Archive Fever: A Freudian Impression*. 1995. Translated by Eric Prenowitz. Chicago: University of Chicago Press, 1998.

Dinshaw, Carolyn. *How Soon Is Now? Medieval Texts, Amateur Readers, and the Queerness of Time*. Durham and London: Duke University Press, 2012.

Discenza, Nicole Guenther. "Alfred's Verse Preface to the *Pastoral Care* and the Chain of Authority." *Neophilologus* 85 (2001): 625–33.

Donner, Morton. "Prudery in Old English Fiction." *Comitatus* 3 (1972): 91–6.

Dümmler, Ernst, ed. MGH, *Epistolae* IV.2. Berlin: Weidmannsche Buchhandlung, 1895.

Ecker, Gisela, ed. *Einblattdrucke von den Anfängen bis 1555*. Vol. 2. Göppingen, DE: Kümmerle Verlag, 1981.

Edgar, Swift, and Angela M. Kinney, eds. *The Vulgate Bible: Douay-Rheims Translation*. Cambridge, MA: Harvard University Press, 2010–13.

Ehwald, Rudolf, ed. *Aldhelmi Opera*. MGH, *Auctores Antiquissimi* XV. Berlin: Weidmann, 1919.

Emerton, Ephraim, ed. and trans. *The Letters of Saint Boniface*. New York: Columbia University Press, 1940.

Ericksen, Janet Schrunk. "Runesticks and Reading *The Husband's Message*." *Neuphilologische Mitteilungen* 99 (1998): 31–7.

Farrell, R.T., ed. *Daniel and Azarias*. London: Methuen, 1974.

Faulhaber, Charles B. "The *Summa dictaminis* of Guido Faba." In *Medieval Eloquence: Studies in the Theory and Practice of Medieval Rhetoric*. Edited by James J. Murphy, 85–111. Berkeley: University of California Press, 1978.

Fein, Susanna, ed. *John the Blind Audelay, Poems and Carols*. Kalamazoo, MI: Medieval Institute Publications, 2009.

Fell, Christine E., "Introduction to *Anglo-Saxon Letters and Letter-Writers*." In *"Lastworda Betst": Essays in Memory of Christine E. Fell with Her Unpublished Writings*. Edited by Carole Hough and Kathryn A. Lowe, 278–98. Donington, UK: Shaun Tyas, 2002.

– "Some Implications of the Boniface Correspondence." In *New Readings on Women in Old English Literature*. Edited by Helen Damico and

Alexandra Hennessey Olsen, 29–43. Bloomington: Indiana University Press, 1990.

Ferrante, Joan. "Epistolae: Medieval Women's Latin Letters." Accessed 1/30/2016. https://epistolae.ccnmtl.columbia.edu/.

Foys, Martin K. "Media." In *A Handbook of Anglo-Saxon Studies.* Edited by Jacqueline Stodnick and Renée R. Trilling, 133–48. Malden, MA: Wiley-Blackwell, 2012.

– "A Sensual Philology for Anglo-Saxon England." *Postmedieval: A Journal of Medieval Cultural Studies* 5 (2014): 456–72.

– *Virtually Anglo-Saxon: Old Media, New Media, and Early Medieval Studies in the Late Age of Print.* Gainesville: University Press of Florida, 2007.

Frantzen, Allen J. *The Literature of Penance in Anglo-Saxon England.* New Brunswick, NJ: Rutgers University Press, 1983.

Garrison, Mary. "'Send More Socks': On Mentality and the Preservation Context of Medieval Letters." In *New Approaches to Medieval Communication.* Edited by Marco Mostert, 69–99. Turnhout, BE: Brepols, 1999.

Gatch, Milton McC. *Preaching and Theology in Anglo-Saxon England: Ælfric and Wulfstan.* Toronto: University of Toronto Press, 1977.

Geary, Patrick J. *Phantoms of Remembrance: Memory and Oblivion at the End of the First Millennium.* Princeton, NJ: Princeton University Press, 1994.

Gitelman, Lisa. *Always Already New: Media, History, and the Data of Culture.* Cambridge, MA: MIT Press, 2006.

Gneuss, Helmut, and Michael Lapidge. *Anglo-Saxon Manuscripts: A Bibliographical Handlist of Manuscripts and Manuscript Fragments Written or Owned in England up to 1100.* Toronto: University of Toronto Press, 2014.

Godden, Malcolm, ed. *Ælfric's Catholic Homilies: The Second Series.* EETS s.s. 5. London: Oxford University Press, 1979.

Gonser, Paul, ed. *Das angelsächsische Prosa-Leben des hl. Guthlac, mit Einleitung, Anmerkungen und Miniaturen.* Heidelberg: C. Winter, 1909.

Goolden, Peter, ed. *The Old English "Apollonius of Tyre."* Oxford: Oxford University Press, 1958.

Green, Richard Firth. "Textual Production and Textual Communities." In *The Cambridge Companion to Medieval English Literature, 1100–1500.* Edited by Larry Scanlon, 25–36. Cambridge: Cambridge University Press, 2009.

Griffith, Mark. "Ælfric's Preface to Genesis: Genre, Rhetoric and the Origins of the *ars dictaminis.*" *ASE* 29 (2000): 215–34.

Gwara, Scott, ed. *Aldhelmi Malmesbiriensis Prosa De Virginitate: cum glosa latina atque anglosaxonica.* Corpus Christianorum Series Latina CXXIV A. Turnhout, BE: Brepols, 2001.

Haines, Dorothy, ed. and trans. *Sunday Observance and the Sunday Letter in Anglo-Saxon England.* Cambridge, UK: D.S. Brewer, 2010.

Harbus, Antonina. "Nebuchadnezzar's Dreams in the Old English *Daniel.*" 1994. Reprinted in *The Poems of MS Junius 11: Basic Readings.* Edited by R.M. Liuzza, 261–86. New York: Routledge, 2002.

Hall, Thomas N. "The Early Medieval Sermon." In *The Sermon.* Edited by Beverly Mayne Kienzle, 203–69. Turnhout, BE: Brepols, 2000.

– "Wulfstan's Latin Sermons." In *Wulfstan, Archbishop of York: The Proceedings of the Second Alcuin Conference.* Edited by Matthew Townend, 93–139. Turnhout, BE: Brepols, 2004.

Harmer, F.E. *Anglo-Saxon Writs.* 1952. Reprint, Stamford, UK: Paul Watkins, 1989.

Harris, Stephen J. *Race and Ethnicity in Anglo-Saxon Literature.* New York: Routledge, 2003.

Harvey, P.D.A., and Andrew McGuinness. *A Guide to British Medieval Seals.* Toronto: University of Toronto Press, 1996.

Healey, Antonette diPaolo, John Price Wilkin, and Xin Xiang. *Dictionary of Old English Web Corpus.* Toronto: Dictionary of Old English Project 2009. http://tapor.library.utoronto.ca/doecorpus/.

Hecht, Hans, ed. *Bischofs Waerferth von Worcester Übersetzung der Dialoge Gregors des Grossen über das Leben und die Wunderthaten italienischer Väter und über die Unsterblichkeit der Seelen.* Leipzig: G. H. Wigand, 1900–7.

Henig, Martin. "The Re-Use and Copying of Ancient Intaglios Set in Medieval Personal Seals, Mainly Found in England: An Aspect of the Renaissance of the 12th Century." In *Good Impressions: Image and Authority in Medieval Seals.* Edited by Noël Adams, John Cherry, and James Robinson, 25–34. London: British Museum Press, 2008.

Heslop, T. A. "English Seals from the Mid Ninth Century to 1100." *JBAA* 133.1 (1980): 1–16.

Hill, Joyce. "Ælfric: His Life and Works." In *A Companion to Ælfric.* Edited by Hugh Magennis and Mary Swan, 35–65. Leiden, NL and Boston: Brill, 2009.

Hollis, Stephanie. *Anglo-Saxon Women and the Church: Sharing a Common Fate.* Woodbridge, UK: Boydell Press, 1992.

Holmes, Simon. "Seal Boxes from Roman London." *London Archaeologist* 7.15 (1995): 391–5.

Horner, Shari. *The Discourse of Enclosure: Representing Women in Old English Literature.* Albany: State University of New York Press, 2001.

Hough, Carole. "Legal and Documentary Writings." In *A Companion to Anglo-Saxon Literature.* Edited by Phillip Pulsiano and Elaine Treharne, 170–87. Oxford: Blackwell, 2001.

Howe, Nicholas. "The Cultural Construction of Reading in Anglo-Saxon England." 1993. Reprinted in *Old English Literature: Critical Essays*. Edited by R.M. Liuzza, 1–22. New Haven, CT: Yale University Press, 2002.

Hull, Vernam. "Cáin Domnaig." *Ériu* 20 (1966): 151–77.

Huppé, Bernard F. "Alfred and Aelfric: A Study of Two Prefaces." In *The Old English Homily and Its Backgrounds*. Edited by Paul E. Szarmach and Bernard F. Huppé, 119–37. Albany: State University of New York Press, 1978.

Insley, Charles. "Archives and Lay Documentary Practice in the Anglo-Saxon World." In *Documentary Culture and the Laity in the Early Middle Ages*. Edited by Warren C. Brown, Marios Costambeys, Matthew Innes, and Adam J. Kosto, 336–62. Cambridge: Cambridge University Press, 2013.

Irvine, Martin. *The Making of Textual Culture: "Grammatica" and Literary Theory, 350–1100*. Cambridge: Cambridge University Press, 1994.

Irvine, Susan, ed. *Old English Homilies from MS Bodley 343*. EETS o.s. 302. Oxford: Oxford University Press, 1993.

Jolly, Karen L. "Tapping the Power of the Cross: Who and for Whom?" In *The Place of the Cross in Anglo-Saxon England*. Edited by Catherine E. Karkov, Sarah Larratt Keefer, and Karen Louise Jolly, 58–79. Woodbridge, UK: Boydell Press, 2006.

Jones, Christopher A. *Ælfric's Letter to the Monks of Eynsham*. Cambridge: Cambridge University Press, 1998.

Jones, W. Garmon. "A Welsh 'Sunday Epistle.'" In *A Miscellany Presented to John Macdonald Mackay*. Edited by Oliver Elton, 233–42. Liverpool: Liverpool University Press; London: Constable, 1914.

Jones, W.R. "The Heavenly Letter in Medieval England." *Medievalia et Humanistica* n.s. 6 (1975): 163–78.

Joy, Eileen A. "The Old English *Seven Sleepers*, Eros, and the Unincorporable Infinite of the Human Person." In *Anonymous Interpolations in Ælfric's "Lives of Saints."* Edited by Robin Norris, 71–96. *OEN* Subsidia 35. Kalamazoo, MI: Medieval Institute Publications, 2011.

Justice, Steven. *Writing and Rebellion: England in 1381*. Berkeley: University of California Press, 1994.

Karkov, Catherine E. *Text and Picture in Anglo-Saxon England: Narrative Strategies in the Junius 11 Manuscript*. Cambridge: Cambridge University Press, 2001.

Karras, Ruth Mazo. "Holy Harlots: Prostitute Saints in Medieval Legend." *Journal of the History of Sexuality* 1.1 (1990): 3–32.

Kelly, Susan. "Anglo-Saxon Lay Society and the Written Word." 1990. Reprinted in *Old English Literature: Critical Essays*. Edited by R.M. Liuzza, 23–50. New Haven, CT: Yale University Press, 2002.

Ker, N.R. *Catalogue of Manuscripts Containing Anglo-Saxon*. Oxford: Oxford University Press, 1957.

Keynes, Simon. *The Diplomas of King Æthelred "the Unready," 978–1016: A Study in Their Use as Historical Evidence*. Cambridge: Cambridge University Press, 1980.

– "The Fonthill Letter." In *Words, Texts and Manuscripts: Studies in Anglo-Saxon Culture Presented to Helmut Gneuss on the Occasion of His Sixty-Fifth Birthday*. Edited by Michael Korhammer, 53–97. Cambridge, UK: D.S. Brewer, 1992.

– "Royal Government and the Written Word in Late Anglo-Saxon England." In *The Uses of Literacy in Early Mediaeval Europe*. Edited by Rosamond McKitterick, 226–57. Cambridge: Cambridge University Press, 1990.

Kienzle, Beverly Mayne. "Medieval Sermons and Their Performance: Theory and Record." In *Preacher, Sermon and Audience in the Middle Ages*. Edited by Carolyn Muessig, 89–124. Leiden, NL: Brill, 2002.

Kilgour, Frederick G. *The Evolution of the Book*. Oxford: Oxford University Press, 1998.

Kittler, Friedrich A. *Gramophone, Film, Typewriter*. 1986. Translated by Geoffrey Winthrop-Young and Michael Wutz. Stanford: Stanford University Press, 1999.

Klein, Stacy S. *Ruling Women: Queenship and Gender in Anglo-Saxon Literature*. Notre Dame, IN: University of Notre Dame Press, 2006.

Kleist, Aaron J, ed. *The Old English Homily: Precedent, Practice, and Appropriation*. Turnhout, BE: Brepols, 2007.

Knirk, James E. "Learning to Write with Runes in Medieval Norway." In *Medeltida skrift- och språkkultur. Nordisk medeltidsliteracy i ett diglossiskt och digrafiskt perspektiv II. Nio föreläsningar från ett symposium i Stockholm våren 1992*. Edited by Inger Lindell, 169–212. Stockholm: Sällskapet Runica et Mediævalia, 1994.

Landes, Richard. "Economic Development and Demotic Religiosity." In *History in the Comic Mode: Medieval Communities and the Matter of Person*. Edited by Rachel Fulton and Bruce W. Holsinger, 101–16. New York: Columbia University Press, 2007.

Langefeld, Brigitte, ed. and trans. *The Old English Version of the Enlarged Rule of Chrodegang*. Frankfurt am Main: Peter Lang, 2003.

Lanham, Carol Dana. "Freshman Composition in the Early Middle Ages: Epistolography and Rhetoric before the Ars Dictaminis." *Viator* 23 (1992): 115–34.

– *Salutatio Formulas in Latin Letters to 1200: Syntax, Style, and Theory*. Munich: Arbeo-Gesellschaft, 1974.

Lapidge, Michael. *The Cult of St Swithun*. Winchester Studies 4.ii. Oxford: Oxford University Press, 2003.

Lapidge, Michael, and Michael Herren, trans. *Aldhelm: The Prose Works*. Cambridge, UK: D.S. Brewer, 1979.

Latham, R.E., D.R. Howlett, R.K. Ashdowne, et al., eds. *Dictionary of Medieval Latin from British Sources*. 17 vols. Oxford: Oxford University Press, 1975–2013.

Lavery, Simon. "The Story of Mary the Egyptian in Medieval England." In Poppe and Ross, *The Legend of Mary of Egypt*, 113–48.

Lees, Clare A. "Engendering Religious Desire: Sex, Knowledge, and Christian Identity in Anglo-Saxon England." *Journal of Medieval and Early Modern Studies* 27.1 (1997): 17–45.

– "The 'Sunday Letter' and the 'Sunday Lists.'" *ASE* 14 (1985): 129–51.

– *Tradition and Belief: Religious Writing in Late Anglo-Saxon England*. Minneapolis: University of Minnesota Press, 1999.

– "Vision and Place in the Old English Life of Mary of Egypt." In Scragg, *The Old English Life of Mary of Egypt*, 57–78.

Lendinara, Patrizia. *Anglo-Saxon Glosses and Glossaries*. Aldershot, UK: Ashgate, 1999.

Lenker, Ursula. "The *West Saxon Gospels* and the Gospel-Lectionary in Anglo-Saxon England: Manuscript Evidence and Liturgical Practice." *ASE* 28 (1999): 141–78.

Lerer, Seth. *Literacy and Power in Anglo-Saxon Literature*. Lincoln: University of Nebraska Press, 1991.

Leslie, R.F. *Three Old English Elegies*. Rev. ed. Exeter: University of Exeter Press, 1988.

Lewis, Charlton T., and Charles Short. *A Latin Dictionary*. 1879. Reprint, Oxford: Oxford University Press, 1980.

Liebermann, F., ed. *Die Gesetze der Angelsachsen*. 3 vols. 1903–16. Reprint, Aalen, DE: Scientia, 1960.

Liestøl, Aslak. "Correspondence in Runes." *Mediaeval Scandinavia* 1 (1968): 17–27.

Little, Lester K. *Benedictine Maledictions: Liturgical Cursing in Romanesque France*. Ithaca, NY: Cornell University Press, 1993.

Lockett, Leslie. *Anglo-Saxon Psychologies in the Vernacular and Latin Traditions*. Toronto: University of Toronto Press, 2011.

– "An Integrated Re-examination of the Dating of Oxford, Bodleian Library, Junius 11." *ASE* 31 (2002): 141–73.

Love, Rosalind C., ed. and trans. *Three Eleventh-Century Anglo-Latin Saints' Lives*. Oxford: Oxford University Press, 1996.

Lowe, Kathryn A. "Lay Literacy in Anglo-Saxon England and the Development of the Chirograph." In *Anglo-Saxon Manuscripts and Their Heritage*. Edited by Phillip Pulsiano and Elaine M. Treharne, 161–204. Aldershot, UK: Ashgate, 1998.

Lucas, Peter J. "A Daniel Come to Judgement? Belshazzar's Feast in Old and Middle English." In *Loyal Letters: Studies on Mediaeval Alliterative Poetry and Prose*. Edited by L.A.J.R. Houwen and A.A. MacDonald, 71–91. Groningen, NL: Egbert Forsten, 1994.

Magennis, Hugh, ed. *The Anonymous Old English Legend of the Seven Sleepers*. Durham, UK: Durham Medieval Texts, 1994.

– *The Old English Life of St Mary of Egypt*. Exeter: University of Exeter Press, 2002.

Magoun, Francis P. "Zu den ae. Zaubersprüchen." *Archiv für das Studium der neueren Sprachen* 171 (1937): 17–35.

Meaney, Audrey L. *Anglo-Saxon Amulets and Curing Stones*. Oxford: B.A.R., 1981.

Meens, Rob. *Penance in Medieval Europe, 600–1200*. Cambridge: Cambridge University Press, 2014.

Mews, Constant J. *The Lost Love Letters of Heloise and Abelard: Perceptions of Dialogue in Twelfth-Century France*. New York: St Martin's Press, 1999.

Migne, J.-P., ed. *Patrologia Latina Cursus Completus*. 221 vols. Paris: 1844–65. Full text database: *Patrologia Latina Full Text Database*, Chadwyck-Healey, 1996.

Miller, Thomas, ed. *The Old English Version of Bede's Ecclesiastical History of the English People*. EETS o.s. 95, 96, 110, 111. 1890–8. Reprint, London: Oxford University Press, 1959.

Morini, Carla. "The First English Love Romance without 'Love'! The Old English *Apollonius of Tyre*." *Selim* 12 (2003–4): 109–25.

Morris, Richard, ed. and trans. *The Blickling Homilies of the Tenth Century: From the Marquis of Lothian's Unique MS. A.D. 971*. EETS. o.s. 58, 63, 73. London: N. Trübner, 1880.

Mueller, Sister Mary Magdeleine, trans. *Saint Caesarius of Arles, Sermons*. Vol. 1. New York: Fathers of the Church, 1956.

Muir, Bernard J., ed. *The Exeter Anthology of Old English Poetry: An Edition of Exeter Dean and Chapter MS 3501*. 2nd ed. Exeter: University of Exeter Press, 2000.

Mullett, Margaret. "The Madness of Genre." *Dumbarton Oaks Papers* 46 (1992): 233–43.

Murphy, James J. *Rhetoric in the Middle Ages: A History of Rhetorical Theory from Saint Augustine to the Renaissance*. Berkeley: University of California Press, 1974.

Napier, Arthur S. "Contributions to Old English Literature." In *An English Miscellany Presented to Dr. Furnivall in Honour of His Seventy-Fifth Birthday*, 355–62. 1901. Reprint, New York: AMS Press, 1973.

– *Wulfstan: Sammlung der ihm zugeschriebenen Homilien nebst Untersuchungen über ihre Echtheit*. Berlin: Weidmannsche Buchhandlung, 1883.

Niermeyer, J.F. *Mediae Latinitatis Lexicon Minus*. Leiden, NL: Brill, 2002.

Niles, John D. "The Trick of the Runes in *The Husband's Message*." *ASE* 32 (2003): 189–223.

Norris, Robin. "*Vitas matrum*: Mary of Egypt as Female Confessor." In Scragg, *The Old English Life of Mary of Egypt*, 79–109.

O'Brien O'Keeffe, Katherine, ed. *The Anglo-Saxon Chronicle: A Collaborative Edition*. Vol. 5 (MS. C). Cambridge, UK: D.S. Brewer, 2001.

– *Visible Song: Transitional Literacy in Old English Verse*. Cambridge: Cambridge University Press, 1990.

O'Keeffe, J.G. "Cáin Domnaig. I: The Epistle Concerning Sunday." *Ériu* 2 (1905): 189–214.

O'Mara, V.M. *A Study and Edition of Selected Middle English Sermons*. Leeds Texts and Monographs n.s. 13. Leeds, UK: School of English, University of Leeds, 1994.

Okasha, Elisabeth. "Anglo-Saxon Inscribed Rings." *Leeds Studies in English* 34 (2003): 29–45.

– "A Third Supplement to *Hand-List of Anglo-Saxon Non-Runic Inscriptions*." *ASE* 33 (2004): 225–81.

Orchard, Andy. "Old Sources, New Resources: Finding the Right Formula for Boniface." *ASE* 30 (2001): 15–38.

– *Pride and Prodigies: Studies in the Monsters of the* Beowulf-*Manuscript*. 1995. Toronto: University of Toronto Press, 2003.

Oxford English Dictionary Online. Oxford: Oxford University Press. www.oed .com.

Parkes, M.B. "The Literacy of the Laity." In *Scribes, Scripts and Readers: Studies in the Communication, Presentation, and Dissemination of Medieval Texts*, 275–97. 1973. Reprint, London: Hambledon Press, 1991.

Patt, William D. "The Early 'ars dictaminis' as Response to a Changing Society." *Viator* 9 (1978): 133–55.

Peters, John Durham. "Mass Media." In *Critical Terms for Media Studies*. Edited by W.J.T. Mitchell and Mark B.N. Hansen, 266–79. Chicago: University of Chicago Press, 2010.

Pettit, Edward, ed. and trans. *Anglo-Saxon Remedies, Charms, and Prayers from British Library MS Harley 585*. 2 vols. Lewiston, NY: Edwin Mellen Press, 2001.

Pollington, Stephen. *Leechcraft: Early English Charms, Plant Lore, and Healing.* Norfolk: Anglo-Saxon Books, 2000.

Pope, John C., ed. *Homilies of Ælfric: A Supplementary Collection.* EETS o.s. 259, 260. Oxford: Oxford University Press, 1967–8.

Poppe, Erich, and Bianca Ross, eds. *The Legend of Mary of Egypt in Medieval Insular Hagiography.* Dublin: Four Courts Press, 1996.

Priebsch, Robert. "The Chief Sources of Some Anglo-Saxon Homilies." *Otia Merseiana* 1 (1899): 129–47.

– "John Audelay's Poem on the Observance of Sunday and Its Source." In *An English Miscellany Presented to Dr. Furnivall in Honour of his Seventy-Fifth Birthday*, 397–407. 1901. Reprint, New York: AMS Press, 1973.

– *Letter from Heaven on the Observance of the Lord's Day.* Oxford: Blackwell, 1936.

– "Quelle und Abfassungszeit der Sonntagsepistel in der irischen 'Cáin Domnaig.' Ein Beitrag zur Entwicklungs- und Verbreitungsgeschichte des vom Himmel Gefallenen Briefes Christi." *MLR* 2 (1907): 138–54.

Remley, Paul G. *Old English Biblical Verse: Studies in "Genesis," "Exodus" and "Daniel."* Cambridge: Cambridge University Press, 1996.

Richardson, Malcolm. "The *Ars dictaminis,* the Formulary, and Medieval Epistolary Practice." In *Letter-Writing Manuals and Instruction from Antiquity to the Present.* Edited by Carol Poster and Linda C. Mitchell, 52–66. Columbia: University of South Carolina Press, 2007.

– "The Fading Influence of the Medieval *Ars Dictaminis* in England after 1400." *Rhetorica: A Journal of the History of Rhetoric* 19.2 (2001): 225–47.

Riddy, Felicity. "'Publication' before Print: The Case of Julian of Norwich." In *The Uses of Script and Print, 1300–1700.* Edited by Julia Crick and Alexandra Walsham, 29–49. Cambridge: Cambridge University Press, 2004.

Riedinger, Anita R. "The Englishing of Arcestrate: Woman in *Apollonius of Tyre.*" In *New Readings on Women in Old English Literature.* Edited by Helen Damico and Alexandra Hennessey Olsen, 292–306. Bloomington: Indiana University Press, 1990.

Roberts, Jane. "The Rich Woman and Her Sealed Letter." *ANQ* 17.2 (2004): 3–6.

– "What Did Anglo-Saxon Seals Seal When?" In *The Power of Words: Essays in Lexicography, Lexicology and Semantics In Honour of Christian J. Kay.* Edited by Graham D. Caie, Carole Hough, and Irené Wotherspoon, 131–57. Amsterdam and New York: Rodopi, 2006.

Roberts, Jane, and Christian Kay, eds, with Lynne Grundy. *A Thesaurus of Old English in Two Volumes.* Amsterdam and Atlanta: Rodopi, 2000.

Roberts, Phyliss B. "The *Ars Praedicandi* and the Medieval Sermon." In *Preacher, Sermon and Audience in the Middle Ages*. Edited by Carolyn Muessig, 41–62. Leiden, NL: Brill, 2002.

Rollason, David. *Saints and Relics in Anglo-Saxon England*. Oxford: Basil Blackwell, 1989.

Rouse, Richard H., and Mary A. Rouse. "The Vocabulary of Wax Tablets." In *Vocabulaire du livre et de l'écriture au moyen âge*. Edited by Olga Weijers, 220–30. Turnhout, BE: Brepols, 1989.

Rowley, Sharon M. *The Old English Version of Bede's "Historia Ecclesiastica."* Cambridge, UK: D.S. Brewer, 2011.

Rusche, Philip Guthrie. "The Cleopatra Glossaries: An Edition with Commentary on the Glosses and Their Sources." PhD. diss, Yale University, 1996.

Ryan, W.F. *The Bathhouse at Midnight: An Historical Survey of Magic and Divination in Russia*. University Park: Pennsylvania State University Press, 1999.

Scheil, Andrew P. "Bodies and Boundaries in the Old English *Life of St. Mary of Egypt.*" *Neophililogus* 84 (2000): 137–56.

Schottenloher, Karl, ed. *Der Müncher Buchdrucker Hans Schobser, 1500–1530*. Nieuwkoop, NL: B. de Graaf, 1967.

Schröer, Arnold, ed. *Die Angelsächsischen Prosabearbeitungen der Benediktinerregel*. Darmstadt, DE: Wissenschaftliche Buchgesellschaft, 1964.

Schulenburg, Jane Tibbetts. *Forgetful of Their Sex: Female Sanctity and Society, ca. 500–1100*. Chicago: University of Chicago Press, 1998.

Scragg, Donald G. "Cotton Tiberius A.III Scribe 3 and Canterbury Libraries." In *Anglo-Saxon Books and Their Readers: Essays in Celebration of Helmut Gneuss's "Handlist of Anglo-Saxon Manuscripts."* Edited by Thomas N. Hall and Donald Scragg, 22–30. Kalamazoo, MI: Medieval Institute Publications, 2008.

– ed. *The Old English Life of Mary of Egypt*. Kalamazoo, MI: Western Michigan University, 2005.

Sharpe, Richard. "The Use of Writs in the Eleventh Century." *ASE* 32 (2003): 247–91.

Sisam, K. *Studies in the History of Old English Literature*. 1953. Reprint, Oxford: Oxford University Press, 1962.

Skeat, Walter W., ed. *Ælfric's Lives of Saints*. EETS o.s. 76, 82, 94, 114. Oxford: Oxford University Press, 1881–1900; reprinted in two volumes, 1966.

Skemer, Don C. *Binding Words: Textual Amulets in the Middle Ages*. University Park: Pennsylvania State University Press, 2006.

Snook, Ben. *The Anglo-Saxon Chancery: The History, Language and Production of Anglo-Saxon Charters from Alfred to Edgar*. Woodbridge, UK: Boydell Press, 2015.

Spalding, Mary Caroline. *The Middle English Charters of Christ*. Bryn Mawr, PA: J.H. Furst, 1914.

Stallybrass, Peter, Roger Chartier, John Franklin Mowery, and Heather Wolfe. "Hamlet's Tables and the Technologies of Writing in Renaissance England." *Shakespeare Quarterly* 55.4 (2004): 379–419.

Steiner, Emily. *Documentary Culture and the Making of Medieval English Literature*. Cambridge: Cambridge University Press, 2003.

Stenton, Frank M. *Anglo-Saxon England*. 2nd ed. Oxford: Oxford University Press, 1947.

– "The Road System of Medieval England." In *Preparatory to Anglo-Saxon England: Being the Collected Papers of Frank Merry Stanton*. Edited by Doris Mary Stenton, 234–52. Oxford: Oxford University Press, 1970.

Stevenson, Jane. "Brothers and Sisters: Women and Monastic Life in Eighth-Century England and Frankia." *Nederlands archief voor kerkgeschiedenis/Dutch Review of Church History* 82.1 (2002): 1–34.

– "The Holy Sinner: The Life of Mary of Egypt." In Poppe and Ross, *The Legend of Mary of Egypt*, 19–50.

Stewart, Susan. *On Longing: Narratives of the Miniature, the Gigantic, the Souvenir, the Collection*. Durham, NC: Duke University Press, 1993.

Stock, Brian. *The Implications of Literacy: Written Language and Models of Interpretation in the Eleventh and Twelfth Centuries*. Princeton, NJ: Princeton University Press, 1983.

– *Listening for the Text: On the Uses of the Past*. Philadelphia: University of Pennsylvania Press, 1990.

Storms, G. *Anglo-Saxon Magic*. 1948. Reprint, New York: Gordon Press, 1974.

Swan, Mary. "Remembering Veronica in Anglo-Saxon England." In *Writing Gender and Genre in Medieval Literature: Approaches to Old and Middle English Texts*. Edited by Elaine Treharne, 19–39. Cambridge, UK: D.S. Brewer, 2002.

Szarmach, Paul. E. "More Genre Trouble: The Life of Mary of Egypt." In *Writing Women Saints in Anglo-Saxon England*. Edited by Paul E. Szarmach, 140–64. Toronto: University of Toronto Press, 2013.

Talbot, C.H., ed. and trans. *The Life of Christina of Markyate: A Twelfth-Century Recluse*. Oxford: Oxford University Press, 1959.

Tangl, Michael, ed. *Die Briefe des Heiligen Bonifatius und Lullus*. MGH, *Epistolae Selectae* 1. Berlin: Weidmannsche Buchhandlung, 1916.

Taylor, Beryl R. "Continuity and Change: Anglo-Saxon and Norman Methods of Tithe-payment before and after the Conquest." *Bulletin of the John Rylands University Library of Manchester* 83.3 (2004): 27–50.

Taylor, John. "Letters and Letter Collections in England, 1300–1420." *Nottingham Medieval Studies* 24 (1980): 57–70.

Tinti, Francesca. "Introduction." In *Pastoral Care in Late Anglo-Saxon England*. Edited by Francesca Tinti, 1–16. Woodbridge, UK: Boydell Press, 2005.

– *Sustaining Belief: The Church of Worcester from c.870 to c.1100.* Farnham, UK: Ashgate, 2010.

Tollerton, Linda. *Wills and Will-Making in Anglo-Saxon England.* Woodbridge, UK: York Medieval Press, 2011.

Townsend, David. "The Naked Truth of the King's Affection in the Old English *Apollonius of Tyre.*" *Journal of Medieval and Early Modern Studies* 34.1 (2004): 173–95.

Treharne, Elaine. "Bishops and Their Texts in the Later Eleventh Century: Worcester and Exeter." In *Essays in Manuscript Geography: Vernacular Manuscripts of the English West Midlands from the Conquest to the Sixteenth Century.* Edited by Wendy Scase, 13–28. Turnhout, BE: Brepols, 2007.

– *The Old English Life of St Nicholas with the Old English Life of St Giles.* Leeds: Leeds Studies in English, 1997.

– "Producing a Library in Late Anglo-Saxon England: Exeter, 1050–1072." *Review of English Studies* n.s. 54 (2003): 155–72.

Trilling, Renée R. "Heavenly Bodies: Paradoxes of Female Martyrdom in Ælfric's *Lives of Saints.*" In *Writing Women Saints in Anglo-Saxon England.* Edited by Paul E. Szarmach, 249–73. Toronto: University of Toronto Press, 2013.

van Engen, John. "Letters, Schools, and Written Culture in the Eleventh and Twelfth Centuries." In *Dialektik und Rhetorik im früheren und hohen Mittelalter.* Edited by Johannes Fried, 97–132. Munich: R. Oldenbourg Verlag, 1997.

Vikan, Gary, and John Nesbitt. *Security in Byzantium: Locking, Sealing and Weighing.* Washington, DC: Dumbarton Oaks Center for Byzantine Studies, 1980.

Vindolanda Tablets Online. http://vindolanda.csad.ox.ac.uk/.

Watt, Diane, and Clare A. Lees. "Age and Desire in the Old English *Life of St Mary of Egypt*: A Queerer Time and Place?" In *Middle-Aged Women in the Middle Ages.* Edited by Sue Niebrzydowski, 53–67. Cambridge, UK: D.S. Brewer, 2011.

Whitelock, Dorothy. "Bishop Ecgred, Pehtred and Niall." In *Ireland in Early Mediaeval Europe: Studies in Memory of Kathleen Hughes.* Edited by D. Whitelock, R. McKitterick, and D. Dumville, 47–68. Cambridge: Cambridge University Press, 1982.

– ed. and trans. *English Historical Documents, c. 500–1042.* 2nd ed. London: Eyre Methuen, 1979.

– "The Numismatic Interest of an Old English Version of the Legend of the Seven Sleepers." In *Anglo-Saxon Coins: Studies Presented to F.M. Stenton on the Occasion of His 80th Birthday, 17 May 1960*. Edited by R.H.M. Dolley, 188–94. London: Methuen, 1961.

Whitman, Walt. *Leaves of Grass*. Edited by Jerome Loving. Oxford: Oxford University Press, 1990.

Wilcox, Jonathan. "Ælfric in Dorset and the Landscape of Pastoral Care." In *Pastoral Care in Late Anglo-Saxon England*. Edited by Francesca Tinti, 52–62. Woodbridge, UK: Boydell Press, 2005.

– *Ælfric's Prefaces*. Durham, UK: Durham Medieval Texts, 1994.

– "The Dissemination of Wulfstan's Homilies: The Wulfstan Tradition in Eleventh-Century Vernacular Preaching." In *England in the Eleventh Century*. Edited by Carola Hicks, 199–217. Stamford, UK: Paul Watkins, 1992.

– "A Voice of the Irish in Anglo-Saxon England: Deacon Niall and Embodied Validation in the Old English Sunday Letter Homilies." In *Insular Cultures*. Edited by Mary Clayton, Alice Jorgensen, and Juliet Mullins. ISAS Essays in Anglo-Saxon England 7. Tempe: Arizona Center for Medieval and Renaissance Studies, forthcoming.

Wiley, Dan M. "The Maledictory Psalms." *Peritia* 15 (2001): 261–79.

Willard, Rudolph. "The Address of the Soul to the Body." *PMLA* 50 (1935): 957–83.

– "The Blickling-Junius Tithing Homily and Caesarius of Arles." In *Philologica: The Malone Anniversary Studies*. Edited by Thomas A. Kirby and Henry Bosley Woolf, 65–78. Baltimore: Johns Hopkins University Press, 1949.

Wormald, Patrick. "Charters, Law and the Settlement of Disputes in Anglo-Saxon England." In *The Settlement of Disputes in Early Medieval Europe*. Edited by Wendy Davies and Paul Fouracre, 149–68. Cambridge: Cambridge University Press, 1986.

– *The Making of English Law: King Alfred to the Twelfth Century*. Oxford: Blackwell, 1999.

Wright, Stephen K. "Historical Inscription and Confessional Erasure in the *Parlement of the Thre Ages*." *Fifteenth-Century Studies* 23 (1996): 1–12.

Yoder, Don. *The Pennsylvania German Broadside: A History and Guide*. University Park: Pennsylvania State University Press, 2005.

Zacher, Samantha. *Rewriting the Old Testament in Anglo-Saxon Verse: Becoming the Chosen People*. London: Bloomsbury, 2013.

Zayarnyuk, Andriy. "Letters from Heaven: An Encounter between the 'National Movement' and 'Popular Culture.'" In *Letters from Heaven: Popular Religion in Russia and Ukraine*. Edited by John-Paul Himka and Andriy Zayarnyuk, 165–200. Toronto: University of Toronto Press, 2006.

Zeitlyn, David. "Anthropology in and of the Archives: Possible Futures and Contingent Pasts. Archives as Anthropological Surrogates." *Annual Review of Anthropology* 41 (2012): 461–80.

Index

absence, epistolary. *See* distance, epistolary
accessibility of records, 13, 29, 88–95, 121, 149–53, 169, 177. *See also* archives; cartularies; storage
Adalberto Samaritano, 30n21
Adelbert, 70
Ælfgifu, 28n11, 36, 124
Ælfric of Eynsham, 8, 36, 37, 46–7, 50, 74n40, 81, 104, 121, 122, 123n35, 140n73; *Catholic Homilies*, 101, 112, 129–30, 163–4, 178, 180; *Colloquy*, 91n89; *De Falsis Diis*, 36–7; "The Healing of the King's Son," 129–30; *Letter of Abgar*, 3, 10, 22, 66, 97, 107, 120–32, 144, 145, 167, 191; *Letter to the Monks of Eynsham*, 8n9; *Life of St Basil*, 3, 10, 13, 23, 134, 139, 149, 153–68, 170, 171, 183–4, 192; *Life of St Martin*, 122, 123n35; *Lives of Saints*, 28n11, 66n5, 121, 126, 127, 131, 133n53, 134, 149, 160, 168; *Old English Letter to Sigeweard*, 8n8, 35; *On Auguries*, 50, 157n30; *Preface to Genesis*, 32, 35, 124

Ælfsige, Bishop of Winchester, 36
ærendboc, 47, 49, 51–61
ærende, 33, 49, 50, 51, 93, 138n66, 139
ærend(ge)writ, 5, 48, 49, 50, 50n74, 53n79, 55, 93, 100n102, 123n35, 124, 128, 150, 154n22, 155n23, 157n30, 170, 173n71
ærendraca, 49, 50n74, 112n8, 139
Æthelmær, 121
Æthelred II, King, 110, 111n6, 121n27
Æthelweard, 28n11, 35, 121, 127
Alberic of Monte Cassino, 30n21, 185
Alcuin, 27, 29n15, 30n21, 31, 32, 36n46, 44–5, 51n75, 109n3, 131n52, 139
Aldhelm, 27, 32, 35, 36n46, 131n52; *De Virginitate*, 28, 54–5, 59n97, 131n52, 157n27; *Enigmata*, 59n97; *Epistola ad Acircium*, 27–8
Alfred, King, 8, 27n4, 32, 50n72, 173n71, 179
Altman, Janet Gurkin, 18, 117
Anderson, Earl R., 57n90
Anglo-Saxon Chronicle, 110–11, 188
Anselm of Bec and Canterbury, 27n6

Toronto Anglo-Saxon Series